PSYCHOPATH?

WHY WE ARE CHARMED
BY THE ANTI-HERO

STEPHEN McWILLIAMS

MERCIER PRESS

MERCIER PRESS
Cork
www.mercierpress.ie

© Stephen McWilliams, 2020

ISBN: 978 1 78117 590 3

A CIP record for this title is available from the British Library.

Printed and bound in the EU.

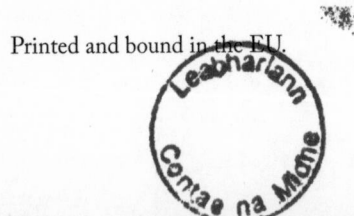

PERMISSIONS

CONTENTS

I

INTRODUCTION

1

DISSECTING THE PSYCHOPATH

'The man without moral feeling is the kind who will take an oath with no sense of responsibility ... a base kind of person, lacking in the most elementary sense of decency and capable of absolutely nothing.'

— *Theophrastus*

Ian McEwan's novel *Nutshell* tells a tale of murder from a rather unique viewpoint. In the days before his impending birth, an eavesdropping but powerless foetus bears unlikely witness to his father's demise at the hands of his mother and her illicit lover. Amid the drama, the unborn narrator makes reference to the sympathy we sometimes feel for a villain. 'We can't help siding with the perpetrators and their schemes,' he observes, 'we wave from the quayside as their little ship of bad intent departs. Bon voyage!'[1] How right he is. There are countless literary and cinematic examples of anti-heroes whose nefarious deeds do little to dissuade us from cheering them on. In the end, everyone loves a fictional psychopath.

And, by this, we don't mean the ordinary villains in almost every novel, action film or television drama. Few of us care when Goldfinger gets his comeuppance in Ian Fleming's classic novel. But there are key anti-heroes for whom we seem quite happy to shelve our own moral compasses as we root for them to prevail. We are seduced by the protagonists in Tarantino and Hitchcock films. We empathise with the talented Mr Ripley. We are so fascinated by Kevin Khatchadourian that we feel the relentless need to talk about him. And we positively tremble with glee at Hannibal Lecter's culinary assertion (with regard to a census taker who once tried to test him) that he 'ate his liver with some fava beans and a nice Chianti'.[2] He inhales sharply through his teeth and sends a shiver up the spine. And yet, deep within ourselves, we find him compelling.

Our fascination is not confined to fiction. In 2014, millions of viewers in Ireland and the UK tuned into Channel 4's *Psychopath Night* to experience the chill of interviews with real-life serial killers. Curious about their own levels of psychopathy, over two million people subsequently took an online psychopath test devised by the British experimental psychologist Kevin Dutton.[3] Netflix seems to carry several series about serial killers at any given point in time. Peruse the shelves of any bookshop and witness the health of the non-fiction crime genre. The real criminal trials of psychopathic killers and fraudsters (especially if they happen to be middle class) are guaranteed to fuel months of media scrutiny and speculation. Of course, as the details of their heinous crimes emerge, these individuals rarely transpire to be likeable, notwithstanding their notoriety and the assumption that they were once very charming in the eyes of their victims. But fictional psychopaths are different. Many of them maintain their appeal even as we witness their dirty deeds in excruciating detail.

But what *is* a psychopath? One of the purposes of this book is to explain exactly that, illustrated by the often-charming anti-heroes we encounter in well-known novels, films and television series. Broadly speaking – and we will return to this in more detail later – the psychopath is a manipulative person who fundamentally lacks a conscience and has a lifelong history of engaging in a wide range of irresponsible, unethical or criminal activities for personal gain. He (for it is most often a *he*) lacks empathy or any sense of remorse and if confronted tends to blame others for his unscrupulous activities. He is often overtly likeable (at least, initially) because of the attention he pays to making a good impression upon those he thinks will be of use to him in his pursuits. This superficial charm may revert to glibness, but with narcissistic or even grandiose overtones. Promiscuous sexual behaviour, many short-term marriages or relationships, adultery and so forth are common. The psychopath lies pathologically (creating what some experts have termed a 'psychopathic fiction') to cover up his actions, or more often for the sheer hell of it, even when lying is totally unnecessary. The psychopath gets bored easily, is impulsive and has a constant need for excitement. He lacks any realistic long-term goals.

When we think of psychopaths, we are naturally reminded of the prison population. But a mere fifteen to thirty per cent of inmates are psychopaths. Still, they commit a greater variety of crimes and are often more violent and aggressive than other prisoners. They tend to be more predatory in nature and are less likely to feel any kind of remorse or guilt for the suffering they have inflicted on other people. They are also far more likely to reoffend. So, even though psychopaths make up less than one per cent of the population, they inflict a much higher proportion of the physical, psychological and socioeconomic damage suffered by society.

But not all psychopaths are serial killers. Indeed, not all are prisoners, even if this is a more likely outcome for them than for the average person. Conservative estimates suggest there are around thirty million psychopaths in the world – at least one in 200 of us, possibly more.[4] Many of these people function perfectly well – to a degree – in everyday life, even if some of the people around them soon learn to dislike them. Many psychopaths use their manipulative skills to carve out impressive careers as CEOs, lawyers, police officers, politicians, advertising executives, estate agents, soldiers, surgeons, and – yes – even the occasional psychiatrist. Serial killers, on the other hand, typically have more than mere psychopathy. They might, for example, have what is termed *paraphilia* (an unusual or extreme sexual fetish that may involve some sort of violence).[5] Combine psychopathy with paraphilia and we have a dangerous individual indeed.

THE PSYCHOPATH THROUGH HISTORY

The psychopath is nothing new to society. Around 300 BC, Theophrastus – a student of Aristotle – wrote about psychopathic traits in a certain type of individual he named 'The Unscrupulous Man'.[6] Such an individual, according to Theophrastus, 'will go and borrow money from a creditor he has never paid ... When marketing, he reminds the butcher of some service he has rendered him and, standing near the scales, throws in some meat, if he can, and a soup-bone. If he succeeds, so much the better; if not, he will snatch a piece of tripe and go off laughing.'

He also remarks that 'The man without moral feeling is the kind who will take an oath with no sense of responsibility ... By nature, he is a base kind of person, lacking in the most elementary sense of decency and capable of absolutely nothing. He leaves his mother without support in her old age ... He knows the inside of the town jail better than his own house ... In court he is capable of playing any role: defendant, plaintiff, or witness. He knows a good many rascals.' In short, popular lore – from Greek and Roman mythology to the Bible and plays of Shakespeare – is filled with stories of individuals with psychopathic traits.

So, what about psychopathy from a more scientific viewpoint? Around 200 years ago, the French psychiatrist Philippe Pinel (1745–1826) described the phenomenon of *manie sans délire* (insanity without delirium), which he regarded as profound immorality and antisocial behaviour in individuals who are often highly intelligent and have no overt signs of mental illness. The British physician James Prichard (1786–1848) later described a similar (albeit broader) phenomenon as *moral insanity*.

The concept of psychopathy as a *personality disorder* rather than a treatable mental illness has been hotly debated for centuries. The British psychiatrist Henry Maudsley (1835–1918) was among the first to assert that the inability to tell right from wrong was innate in some people like, for example, colour blindness. In parallel, the German psychiatrist Emil Kraepelin (1856–1926) set out the criteria for what we now call psychopathy, while his Austrian counterpart Sigmund Freud (1856–1939) described the phenomenon as the 'underdevelopment of the superego'. In Freud's view, therapeutic intervention required the 'patient' to want to get better, which was by definition almost never the case. Much debate ensued, with some psychiatrists arguing that psychopathy was an illness and the law strongly refuting this claim and citing the inappropriate medicalisation of criminal behaviour.[7]

The actual term *psychopastiche* (psychopath) was first coined in 1888 by the German psychiatrist J. L. A. Koch (1841–1908). By the early part of the twentieth century, the label had become rather unwieldy and seemed to include anyone vaguely abnormal. The comparatively imprecise concept of *sociopathy* was first suggested in 1930 by the American psychologist George Everett Partridge (1870–1953) to describe the superficially charming criminal. To this day, there is some confusion between the terms *psychopath* and *sociopath* leading to their sometimes-interchangeable use.

PSYCHOPATHY VERSUS SOCIOPATHY

So, what are the differences between the psychopath and the sociopath? Our modern view of pure psychopathy really began with the American psychiatrist Hervey Cleckley (1903–84) who, in his book *The Mask of Sanity* (1941), was the first clinician to narrow the definition of psychopathy to sixteen characteristics.[8] Based on Cleckley's work, the Canadian psychologist Robert D. Hare refined the concept to produce the *Psychopathy Checklist* (1980), which he revised further in 1991 (the PCL-R).[9] This semi-structured inventory has become the essential modern tool for clinical psychologists around the world to determine whether or not an individual is a psychopath. It is outlined in more detail in Chapter 2 and we will refer to it frequently in this book.

But to summarise briefly, the *Psychopathy Checklist* contains twenty key items divided into four domains (*interpersonal*, *affective*, *lifestyle* and *antisocial*). For each item, the individual may score zero (meaning the item is absent in their normal behaviour), one (meaning it is present to some degree) or two (meaning it is definitely present). For example, 'lack of remorse or guilt' is one of the affective traits. A person with a consistently healthy sense of appropriate guilt (you or me, for example) would score zero for this item. A person who never feels guilt about anything (regardless of what heinous crimes they might have committed) would score two. A person who feels only occasional guilt in specific circumstances, or who feels guilt less than would ordinarily be expected for things they have done, might score one.

The checklist must be based on the individual's life generally and not just on a specific event or offence they may have committed. A score of thirty or more indicates a high level of psychopathy, although a score of twenty-five is often accepted for research purposes (as we will do in this book). However, some researchers (including Kevin Dutton, professor of experimental psychology at the University of Oxford) assert that such a cut-off score is rather arbitrary and that people have varying degrees of psychopathy that are useful for their own success and essential for a functioning society. Either way, the average man on the street will score only four on the *Psychopathy Checklist*. The average woman will score even less.

Psychopathy, as we can see, is a well-defined personality disorder. Sociopathy, on the other hand, is not really defined at all; it is a more informal (and arguably somewhat obsolete) term that describes an individual with a persistent pattern of behaviours and attitudes that are at odds with what society considers socially acceptable and lawful. Usually, however, sociopathic behaviours are said to be appropriate within the sociopath's subculture or social milieu – such as in a criminal gang. For example, the Mafia boss Tony Soprano (see Chapter 12 of this book) should be regarded as a sociopath rather than a psychopath.

Some commentators regard a sociopath as having a more defined moral code with a greater capacity for guilt, empathy, loyalty and caring relationships. The sociopath may even have a conscience, albeit in a narrower context than is normal. Moreover, a sociopath may go to greater lengths to hide their distress and unacceptable behaviour from certain people, where a psychopath may not bother. Finally, some researchers suggest that sociopaths are essentially the result of adverse or neglectful childhood environments. Of course, this is often true of psychopaths too, but (unlike sociopaths) they also tend to be temperamentally abnormal from birth. It could be said, therefore, that psychopaths are partly 'born' of genetics and biology, while sociopaths are exclusively 'made' by adverse early experiences.

THE ANTISOCIAL PERSONALITY DISORDER

To complicate matters slightly, there is a third entity with similar features – the *antisocial personality disorder*. This is broader than psychopathy and perhaps three to four times more common. While such individuals are deceitful, impulsive, aggressive, reckless, irresponsible and remorseless, with behaviour that is ultimately unacceptable to society (including, for example, a lot of petty and opportunistic crimes), they may have empathy, humility and depth of emotion like the rest of us. Essentially, they behave badly but they can have feelings.

It's worth pausing to explain the term 'personality disorder'. We all have personalities, right? Some more than others indeed, but where does the word 'disorder' come into it? Well, because psychiatric illnesses and conditions might otherwise dissolve into mere fragmented opinion, modern psychiatry likes to have specific criteria for diagnosis. Two similar classification systems exist today: the World Health Organisation's *Classification of Mental and Behavioural Disorders* (currently in its tenth edition: ICD-10); and the American Psychiatric Association's *Diagnostic and Statistical Manual of Mental Disorders* (currently in its fifth edition: DSM-5). The DSM-I first appeared in 1952 and contained the term *sociopathic personality*, while its updated sequel in 1968 (the DSM-II) replaced this with the more modern term *antisocial personality disorder*. With each update, definitions have generally become more refined.

According to both the DSM-5 and the ICD-10, '[specific] personality disorders' require evidence of enduring patterns of behaviour that deviate markedly from the cultural norm and affect how a person thinks, feels, controls impulses and relates to others. Any deviation must be long-standing (usually present since late childhood or adolescence), inflexible and poorly adjusted ('maladaptive') to a broad range of personal and social situations – such as at home, at work, while out with friends and so forth. The result must be distressing for the individual or those people close to them. Finally, a personality disorder cannot be attributable to illness per se (either psychiatric or physical). Illnesses are episodic; personalities are permanent.

It is estimated that up to fifteen per cent of the population has a diagnosable personality disorder. Various different types exist. A common one in psychiatric settings is the *emotionally unstable* (or *borderline*) personality disorder (more about that with Tom Ripley in Chapter 6). We have just mentioned the *antisocial* (also known as *dissocial*) personality disorder and will discuss the *schizoid* personality disorder in Chapter 10 (in relation to Dexter Morgan). Other examples include the *paranoid* (think of your angry, suspicious uncle who constantly spouts conspiracy theories and is quick to take offence), *histrionic* (your shallow, seductive, theatrical friend who loves to gossip endlessly between cosmetic surgery appointments) and *schizotypal* (the aloof and eccentric woman down the road who believes in ghosts and holds séances) personality disorders. In addition, there are *anankastic* ('OCD-like'), *anxious/avoidant* ('super-shy'), *dependent* ('super-clingy') and *narcissistic* ('super-self-important') varieties. Just as many of us have a few psychopathic characteristics without being full-blown psychopaths, most of us have some of the above personality traits without having personality disorders. By definition, most people are just normal.

PSYCHOPATHY VERSUS PSYCHOSIS

It is important to reiterate that psychopathy is not mental illness. More specifically, psychopathy has nothing to do with *psychosis* – even though the two words share a first syllable and are phonetically quite similar. Unlike psychopathy, psychosis (the commonest form of which is schizophrenia) involves *hallucinations* (hearing or seeing things that aren't there), *delusions* (fervently believing things that aren't true), *thought disorder* (mixed-up thinking that makes communication very difficult) and *negative symptoms* (social withdrawal, speaking less and dropping out of work or education). However, people with psychosis are no more likely to be psychopaths than you or I.

In this regard, there are certain prominent fictional characters that have no place in this book beyond the next few paragraphs. A fascinating case in point is the 2003 film *Donnie Darko*, the directorial debut of screenplay-writer Richard Kelly. Set in October 1988 in the small American town of Middlesex, the film enjoys a backdrop that is unashamedly 'eighties' in style: stonewash jeans and mullet hairstyles abound, while the principal characters discuss the relative merits of George Bush and Michael Dukakis for president. The genre, meanwhile, is a skilful and rather unique hybrid of horror, science fiction, suspense and teen comedy.

Jake Gyllenhaal plays the eponymous character, a troubled teenager with paranoid schizophrenia (but *not* psychopathy) who sometimes forgets to take his medication. Donnie experiences vivid auditory and visual hallucinations of a human-sized rabbit named Frank, who commands him to perform heinous acts of vandalism and arson. Donnie willingly undertakes these tasks while on nightly somnambulant walks; on one occasion, for example, he damages a bulldog-shaped school statue, planting an axe in its head and writing, in large letters on the ground beneath, 'They made me do it.'

To complicate matters, Donnie narrowly escapes death early in the film. He is out sleepwalking when a large jet engine falls from the sky (stay with me here; there's a point to this) and crash-lands directly on his bedroom. He is not hurt because he is not there (Frank, the human-sized rabbit, has arguably saved his life), but, more curiously, the aviation authorities cannot identify any plane that has crashed in the vicinity or any airline willing to claim ownership of the engine. This inexplicable event becomes a foreshadow of Frank's reappearance to announce to Donnie that the world will end in precisely twenty-eight days, six hours, forty-two minutes and twelve seconds. Faced with this rather pessimistic prophecy, Donnie undertakes the formidable task of trying to understand what is real and what is not.

Any objective viewer can see that Donnie is experiencing a psychotic episode. Not only does he endure hallucinations, paranoid delusions and a variety of other symptoms synonymous with schizophrenia, but his symptoms last the minimum one-month period required by the ICD-10. He even has a few negative symptoms thrown in for good measure, with little dialogue and a penchant for truancy. Yes, Donnie is also a rather chilling character with an expression that can be simultaneously blunted, mocking and menacing. One need only look at the famous scene where he strides portentously with an axe over his shoulder, his head bowed slightly and his eyes staring angrily ahead. But Donnie is not superficial or grandiose. He does not lack remorse or empathy, nor does he seek stimulation. And there is no versatility to his antisocial behaviour.

On the contrary, Donnie displays depth, sensitivity, intelligence and – above all – a conscience. This is in stark contrast to many of the other characters in the film, who often provide comic relief in the form of an absurdly shallow and easily led community. Most notable is local schoolteacher Kitty Farmer, who obsequiously worships a sleazy self-help guru (who may well be a psychopath). Meanwhile, Donnie's consistent anchor to the real world is his girlfriend, Gretchen Ross, to whom he forms a clear emotional attachment. She, in turn, accepts his eccentricities without question. Donnie Darko is simply not a psychopath.

The same is true of various other leading characters in literature and film. Despite the title in Alfred Hitchcock's 1960 film *Psycho*, the motel owner Norman Bates is not a psychopath. As the story unfolds, it becomes evident that Norman believes to a delusional extent that he is, in fact, his own mother (whom, it transpires, he killed many years earlier). Like Donnie Darko, Norman most likely has psychosis. A less plausible but nevertheless possible diagnosis is a condition known as *dissociative identity disorder*. This is a rare neurotic illness in which more than one separate personality exists in the same individual, usually as the result of a deep-rooted trauma. For the record, the 'split personality' of dissociative identity disorder has nothing whatever to do with schizophrenia, which is described above. They are two entirely separate illnesses. Either way, Norman is not a psychopath.

This brings us neatly to *The Strange Tale of Dr Jekyll and*

Mr Hyde. If the main protagonist of Robert Louis Stevenson's classic horror story has any psychiatric diagnosis at all, it is once again dissociative identity disorder. It is certainly not schizophrenia. Indeed, we might argue that Dr Henry Jekyll requires some psychopathic traits to explain the self-indulgent unleashing onto the world of his evil creation. Grandiosity, deceitfulness and irresponsibility spring to mind, although it is unlikely Dr Jekyll would tick enough boxes to earn the label of psychopath.

And finally Walter White, the anti-hero of the much-hyped television series *Breaking Bad*, is not a psychopath. Indeed, the very premise of the story is that an apparently weak, sick and unlucky man ventures into the underworld of illegal narcotics and must survive despite the fact that he is clearly a novice. Initially naïve but determined, he gradually evolves into a hardened criminal as the story develops. In many ways, he is just a family man who thinks he has nothing left to lose. In Walter (played by Bryan Cranston), there is ample evidence of humility, empathy, remorse, self-control and the acceptance of responsibility. His motives (to earn money for his family who will outlive him) are wholesome and admirable to a degree, even if his methods are not. Perhaps the series challenges the viewer to consider whether they would act the same way in similar circumstances.

SEED OR SOIL?

So, are psychopaths born or are they made? This is the theme of

Lionel Shriver's novel *We Need to Talk About Kevin*, in which a mother examines her conscience in the aftermath of her teenage son's Columbine-style massacre at his American high school.

Since the early 1990s, tests that examine the electrical activity in certain parts of the brain (*electroencephalograms* – or EEGs) have shown that such activity is different in psychopaths relative to the general population. These brainwaves (which relate to attention to stimuli and contextual memory) affect the way we evaluate and profit from experience – essentially so we can avoid repeatedly making the same mistakes. It seems emotional memory (remembering how one once felt) is different for psychopaths, meaning they are less likely to experience fear or anxiety in relation to bad things that may have happened to them previously.

Subsequent to this, functional magnetic resonance imaging (fMRI) studies have also compared the brains of psychopaths and non-psychopaths.[10] The fact that oxygen-rich blood and oxygen-poor blood each send out differing MRI signals allows for a technique known as *blood oxygen level dependent* (BOLD) imaging. Because active parts of the brain need more oxygen, fMRI scans can thus determine which parts are active during certain observable tasks. As with EEGs, the fMRI research has highlighted differences between the psychopathic and the non-psychopathic brain. Specifically, the affected areas include: the *limbic system* (the part of the brain that deals with emotion), especially the *hippocampus* (the part that helps us process and store emotional memory) and the *amygdala* (the part that helps us profit from experience); the *temporal pole* (the region of the brain that helps us integrate what we see and hear for subsequent higher processing); and the *orbital frontal cortex* (the part of the brain behind the forehead, just above the eyes, that regulates the input of emotions into our decision-making). This is not an exhaustive list but you get the picture. Scientists have identified a lack of integration between the language and emotional components of thought which causes psychopaths to have difficulty understanding the emotional content of words. This can lead to the rather chilling experience of a serial killer describing their heinous crimes in the calm way they might recount what they had for breakfast.

Some scientists hypothesise that these differences in brain activity may be present from an early developmental age, possibly even from before birth. Twin studies support the idea that genetics accounts for at least half of an individual's likelihood of becoming a psychopath. What remains is likely nurture. Certainly, an adverse childhood will increase the risk of psychopathy, but can psychopaths emerge from idyllic family environments too?

In *We Need to Talk About Kevin*, the protagonist, Eva, is the reluctant mother of a child to whom she cannot relate. From birth, he shows little interest in her, cries incessantly, fails to develop his milestones normally and shows a reluctance to play. Over time, he develops into a manipulative and violent individual. In research (when real psychopaths are interviewed and their childhood histories are examined) it often transpires that they formed an abnormal attachment to their parents, argued with siblings (this sometimes resulting in assault) and consistently had few friends. They also wet the bed long beyond what might be considered normal, set fire to things and were cruel to animals; these last three items are sometimes referred to as the *MacDonald triad*. Punishment throughout childhood typically proved ineffective and these individuals eventually engaged in a teenage life of petty crime, drug and alcohol use, and precocious sex.

Although psychopaths often come from unstable family environments with disinterested parents, this is not always the case. Some have affluent and well-adjusted parents (like the fictional Kevin). Equally, most children reared in adverse circumstances do not grow up to become psychopaths. Researchers have found that evolving psychopaths are often callous and unemotional as children and score differently on certain psychometric tests that relate to the amygdala and the orbital frontal cortex. They are worse at grasping abstract concepts such as metaphors. Moreover, evolving psychopaths are not deterred by the prospect of punishment and – as any parent will testify – this makes child rearing a real challenge. Overall, the emerging consensus is that certain individuals are born with a deficit in emotional intelligence but otherwise have a normal IQ. Negative childhood experiences can exacerbate this emotional deficit and ultimately produce a psychopath.

So, can it be treated? Bear in mind that psychopathy is a personality disorder and not a psychiatric illness. A handful of studies have shown that treating psychopathy with positive reinforcement (rewarding positive behaviour – when you can find it – rather than simply punishing negative behaviour) can be effective in the short term. Such studies are few and far between, however, and their results are hotly contested. Psychopaths are expert manipulators and many will give researchers whatever answers they think necessary to gain early parole. The prevailing belief is that the best way to limit a dangerous psychopath's effect on society is simply to keep him or her away from it.

***

Psychopaths in real life can often appear quite likeable, especially if we have something they want, such as access to our money, power or influence. In such cases, the psychopath will go to considerable lengths to convince us that they are the type of person we should trust. Once they have exploited us and we cease to be of use to them, they will abandon us and we will be left wondering what on earth happened. In some instances, we may not even realise we have been conned, especially if nobody points it out to us. Either way, it is a myth that a real psychopath can never be likeable; sometimes it will just take the benefit of hindsight to work out their true character.

2

THE FICTIONAL PSYCHOPATH

'Everybody lies.'

– Gregory House MD[1]

Psychopaths are essential in fiction. From a writer's perspective, they tend to exist within the plot to present a challenge for the hero, who, of course, we usually admire. Most fictional psychopaths are deliberately unlikeable, even if the overall effect is sometimes absurdly comical. Think of all those James Bond villains parodied by Mike Myers in his *Austin Powers* films. Others are simply repulsive without the humour. But often enough it is the protagonist himself who is psychopathic. Such an anti-hero needs to be charismatic if we as readers (or viewers) are to remain interested in his overcoming whatever challenge the plot throws at him. The likeable fictional psychopath is what this book is all about: the despicable anti-hero whom we admire despite ourselves.

This list has been carefully chosen. Novels are the best source, especially where they are part of a series that allows for the gradual development of a character over time. This gives us plenty of backstory, telling us a great deal about the fictional psychopath's biographical misadventures. Television shows that run for several seasons do likewise, as they often incorporate flashbacks or other techniques that provide background information on the anti-hero. Films are a little more difficult, given that they are rarely more than two hours in length. As they usually contain insufficient detail in their own right for our purposes, they have only been included where they represent adaptations of existing novels.

The term 'psychopath' should not be used lightly. Many fictional anti-heroes are not psychopaths. Some are sociopaths, some have antisocial personality disorders and others are not on the spectrum at all. Most importantly, opinions may differ and thus we need an objective method of deciding whether or not our fictional anti-heroes are true psychopaths before we bother discussing them any further. The *Psychopathy Checklist*, devised by Canadian psychologist Robert D. Hare and referred to in Chapter 1, is considered the gold standard in deciphering psychopathy, provided it is used properly by an expert who thoroughly interviews and investigates the individual.[2]

In real life, an *index event* (the crime that led to the forensic assessment) is not enough evidence upon which to base an opinion. Indeed, a competent assessor will often exclude the index event and instead focus on the individual's case history. In this book, we do not always have that luxury. As a good plot is often driven by a series of index events, the latter may comprise much of the information we have about the anti-hero. Where backstories are provided, key gaps may exist, and obviously we are not in a position to interview fictional characters to fill in these gaps. As a result, some artistic licence is necessary when applying the *Psychopathy Checklist* to a fictional character, which hopefully the reader will forgive. To compensate for missing information, we will generally allow ourselves the research cut-off score of twenty-five.

The traits in the *Psychopathy Checklist* are divided into four domains.[3] *Interpersonal* traits govern how the psychopath makes himself appear to others; *affective* traits relate to how the psychopath feels (or rather does *not* feel) on an emotional level; *lifestyle* traits pertain to the manner in which the psychopath interacts with society (see endnote 5, p. 271, on the two *sexual* traits); and *antisocial* traits are those that lead to behaviours that society deems to be unacceptable (those traits that will get you arrested). The specifics of the traits are as follows:

Interpersonal Traits

1. Glibness/Superficial charm
2. Grandiose sense of self-worth
3. Pathological lying (lying relentlessly, even when it is not necessary)
4. Manipulation for personal gain (this often involves 'impression management')[4]

Affective Traits

5. Shallow affect (an impaired ability to feel emotion even if one can mimic how it looks to feel it)

6.   Callousness or lack of empathy
7.   Lack of remorse or guilt
8.   Failure to accept responsibility for one's own actions (a tendency to blame others instead)

Lifestyle Traits

9.   Parasitic lifestyle (taking advantage of the kindness or vulnerability of others)
10. Impulsivity (acting suddenly without weighing up the risks and benefits)
11. Lack of realistic long-term goals (making plans far beyond one's obvious capabilities)
12. Need for stimulation or excitement
13. Irresponsibility (failing to live up to one's obligations or commitments)
14. Promiscuous sexual behaviour[5]
15. Many short-term (marital) relationships (or unstable interpersonal relationships in the youth version of the *Psychopathy Checklist*)

Antisocial Traits

16. Poor behavioural controls
17. Early behavioural problems
18. Juvenile delinquency
19. Criminal versatility (engaging in a variety of crimes instead of specialising in one)
20. Revocation of conditional release, such as parole violation

To complicate matters, there may be more than one subtype of psychopath. Some experts assert that there are really three, namely the *classic* psychopath, the *manipulative* psychopath and the *macho* psychopath.[6] All three subtypes score highly in the affective traits listed above, while the classic psychopath scores highly in all four categories of traits. The manipulative psychopath scores highly in the affective and interpersonal traits but scores relatively less in the lifestyle and antisocial traits. In essence, such an individual is more likely to be a charming confidence trickster than a demonstrative risk-taker or menacing bully. The macho psychopath scores highly in the affective, lifestyle and antisocial traits but scores relatively less in the interpersonal traits. Such an individual is more likely to be a demonstrative risk-taker or menacing bully than a charming confidence trickster. While the manipulative psychopath will charm you out of your life savings, the macho psychopath will put you in hospital. The classic psychopath could possibly do both.[7]

The above is all very well in real life, but in fiction the reader (or viewer) usually possesses a level of omniscience that bestows some immunity to the impression management of a psychopath. Surely, we readers can see past their games? Therefore, how could a fictional psychopath possibly be likeable? Before we embark on the actual reasons, it is important to remember that the average reader and viewer will usually only finish a book or film if they have some affinity for (or at least fascination with) one of the main protagonists. When the latter happens to be a psychopath, it is especially important to the author or director that we like the protagonist sufficiently to persist with the story. So, perhaps the most fundamental reason the fictional psychopath is likeable is that he simply *must* be so for his very survival as a fictional entity.

The real question we should be asking, however, is how the author or director achieves the anti-hero's likeability notwithstanding their nefarious deeds. There are at least ten possible reasons outlined below. Of course, these reasons might be applied to anyone and not just fictional psychopaths, but they are particularly necessary for the latter, given that we also have a host of reasons not to like them.

The first reason we like a fictional psychopath (or a real one, for that matter) is their calmness and courage under fire. Surgeons and firefighters save lives. CEOs and politicians lead the masses. Kevin Dutton, professor of experimental psychology at Oxford University, holds that society needs its psychopaths precisely because these individuals do not scare easily; instead they relish the challenge of the seemingly impossible and embark upon it while scarcely raising their heartbeat.[8] Virtually all of our chosen fictional psychopaths fall into this category.

The appearance of vulnerability is the second reason. Psychopaths are predators. Lock yourself unarmed in the tiger enclosure of your local zoo and wait to see who comes out on top. My money is on the tiger. Yet tigers are on the endangered species list as their habitat and food supply dwindle. Predators can be vulnerable. Vulnerability is complicated. Even when fictional psychopaths (like their real-life counterparts) are not remotely vulnerable, they can still appear so in the eyes of an empathic reader who wants to afford them the benefit of the doubt. Examples include Patricia Highsmith's infamous anti-hero Tom Ripley, who plays the role of the triumphant under-dog when we first meet him in *The Talented Mr Ripley*. They also include Ben Lovatt, the minor in question in Doris Lessing's novel *The Fifth Child*. Ben is both threatening and vulnerable, like a fierce but endangered animal, and humans have long sought to hunt or tame ferocious creatures – sometimes simply for sport. On a more concrete level, it is difficult for any reader not to feel empathy for a child, no matter how naughty they may be.

So, what's the third reason? It is our societal fascination with secrecy. We simply love it. Virtually every sensational media scoop is based on a scandal, some sort of heretofore secret unmasked. Psychopaths, meanwhile, are chameleons. They live among us and look like us and act like us. Their success lies in their ability to blend in, to keep their true nature secret. And it is this very idea that seems to capture the public imagination.

Given this secrecy, it is all the more thrilling when a fictional psychopath takes us into their confidence. This is the fourth reason we like them. Examples include Patrick Bateman in Bret Easton Ellis' novel *American Psycho* and Alex DeLarge in Anthony Burgess' novel *A Clockwork Orange*. Perhaps most notably, they include Francis Urquhart (or Frank Underwood) 'breaking the Fourth Wall' to reveal the inner workings of his devious mind in the television series *House of Cards*.[9] Or does he simply apply his impression management to the viewer in the same way he does to his fellow characters? Either way, it is a very effective tool for winning over an audience. Reveal your own perspective from the outset and you will get us on your side. In hearing the anti-hero's confession (albeit often a fake one), we feel strangely privileged to be part of their inner circle. We also feel a sense of security (ignoring the fact that it may be misplaced), safe in the assumption that our anti-hero would never turn on us. After all, why would they tell us their innermost secrets if they did not like us?

Occasionally, when a fictional psychopath will not confide in us, we like them just the same if they open up to another character, especially if that character is likeable or vulnerable in their own right. For example, Hannibal Lecter confides in Clarice Starling as he assumes the *de facto* role of her psychotherapist while helping her to catch a serial killer. Similarly, in *The Fifth Child* the reader sympathises with Ben's loyal and long-suffering mother Harriet – perhaps the real hero of the story. The sympathy we have for her reflects well on her son. Indeed, if she has made the decision to tolerate his destructive behaviour, who are we to question her judgement?

The fifth reason we like a fictional psychopath is that we are seduced by their charm. Even in real life, most psychopaths are very, very skilled at creating a good impression. Their charm, although superficial, can fool almost anyone in the wrong place at the wrong time. Once a good initial impression has been made, many who encounter the psychopath will dismiss subsequent information that contradicts their established opinion. It is no different in fiction. Indeed, it may be worse because the reader or viewer is constantly 'in the wrong place at the wrong time'. We see exactly what the author or director wants us to see. If we are meant to be charmed we will be charmed. And most of the fictional psychopaths for our purposes are very charming indeed.

The sixth reason we like a fictional psychopath is that we never find them boring. They are charismatic whirlwinds of energy. Again, almost all of the psychopaths in this book exemplify this. Especially noteworthy is Dexter Morgan from his eponymous television series. It is important to note that not being boring is quite different from being charming. While Dexter can switch on the superficial charm when he wants to, he is not always especially beguiling; yet, he is an interesting character who constantly keeps us entertained. Conversely, think of all the dull people with integrity you know in real life. Fiction has little room for gloomy characters, especially if they are meant to be anti-heroes. Psychopaths can spice things up with ease as they fearlessly and without conscience do the things ordinary people would never dare to. It is hard not to find this compelling.

Enter the seventh reason: we like fictional psychopaths who have looks, talents or skills we admire. In real life, psychopaths have a particular set of skills conducive to being a psychopath. This includes the innate ability to analyse their victim's desires, expectations and regrets and then give the impression they can fill that void, that they can empathise with their victims. Joshua Greene, a psychologist at Harvard University, describes two types of empathy: 'hot' and 'cold' varieties. 'Hot' empathy is what you or I might consider empathy, namely the ability to truly feel what others feel by observing their reactions. 'Cold' empathy is the ability to work out dispassionately other people's feelings, thoughts and motivations without actually feeling them yourself. The lack of empathy experienced by psychopaths is really a lack of 'hot' empathy. To compensate, they often excel at 'cold' empathy and know instinctively what buttons to press to elicit the reaction they want for their own personal gain. No doubt fictional psychopaths can do this too, but they also tend to have an exaggerated range of other 'non-psychopathic' skills that truly leave us in awe. Examples include Tom Ripley (a talented mimic, skilled musician and connoisseur of fine art) and James Bond (yes, some incarnations of Bond are psychopathic, yet he is a resourceful and exceptionally lucky spy who is also good-looking and a charming seducer of women). At the very least, they gain some of our respect.

The eighth reason is a little deeper, perhaps more psycho-dynamic than the others.[10] It is that the fictional psychopath appeals to an innate part of us that longs to be bad. Fiction is all about escapism, after all, the opportunity to explore a parallel existence with none of the consequences. Do we unconsciously use fiction to fantasise about how we might exact revenge on those who have offended us in real life? Or conversely do we project our own conscience onto the fictional psychopath to make them seem more acceptable than they actually are? Either way, as we begin to identify with the fictional psychopath, we are more likely to develop an affinity for them.

Fictional psychopaths become more likeable when their victims make them look good. This is the ninth reason on the list. Examples include James Bond, Tom Ripley, Hannibal Lecter and Dexter Morgan who, despite their lack of conscience, never kill innocent women or children. Indeed, they don't really seem to kill at all without good reason, however perverse their reasoning might be. Instead, they kill when they are threatened or bullied by some short-sighted adversary who has underestimated their ruthlessness. The fictional psychopath's victims are often depicted as greedy, superficial or irritating. In other instances, they are simply more evil than the psychopathic protagonist we admire. Think of all those eccentric Bond villains, or the serial killers Hannibal Lecter helps the FBI to apprehend. So, regardless of the fictional psychopath's self-serving primary motivation, they can still make themselves look good in our eyes by killing off characters we truly abhor.

Finally, the tenth reason we like a fictional psychopath is that the backdrop to their story makes them look good. This is similar to the ninth reason, except that it is the environment or circumstances rather than another character that cause us to forgive their nefarious deeds. Think of James Bond in the context of the Cold War. He is the better of two evils.

The box below summarises the ten reasons why some fictional psychopaths are likeable. Frankly, it lists the reasons anyone might be likeable. Still, let's call it the *Psychopath Likeability Scale* so that we can refer to it easily in later chapters. We will score each reason with 0, 2 or 4 to allow for a potential grand score of 40. This will be given equal weight to the *Psychopathy Checklist* when we compare our anti-heroes in the final chapter.

Psychopath Likeability Scale

1. They are calm and courageous in the face of danger.
2. They seem vulnerable.
3. They appeal to our fascination with secrecy.
4. They take us into their confidence.
5. We are seduced by their charm.
6. We never find them boring.
7. They have looks, talents or skills we admire.
8. They appeal to a part deep within us that longs to be bad.
9. Their victims make them look good.
10. The backdrop makes them look good.

This book makes no claim to be the definitive list of likeable fictional psychopaths. Indeed, there are many such anti-heroes who might have been included but for various reasons are not. For example, fans of the television drama *House MD* will be familiar with the eponymous character played by the British actor Hugh Laurie. Given Gregory House's tendency to lie and manipulate, his apparent lack of empathy at times, his need for stimulation and excitement, his promiscuity, and his clear defiance of rules and regulations, couldn't we make a reasonable argument for 'corporate' psychopathy? Possibly so, but his character over eight seasons could be said to lack internal consistency, in that there are also plentiful examples of feelings and behaviours that defy the label of psychopathy. He is certainly likeable.

From a literary perspective, another case in point is *Lolita's* Humbert Humbert, a thirty-eight-year-old European literary scholar whose absent-minded professorial demeanour perhaps makes him vaguely likeable, particularly to those characters who do not realise what he is capable of. As readers, we are armed with much of the shocking truth because he takes us into his confidence, albeit as an unreliable narrator. Perhaps he comes across as somewhat vulnerable – though this may simply be the upshot of his impression management.

In essence, Humbert is a serial paedophile who becomes obsessed with the twelve-year-old daughter of his landlady. When the child – Dolores 'Lolita' Haze – loses her mother in a car accident, Humbert (by now her stepfather) fetches her from camp and then proceeds to travel around the United States repeatedly sexually assaulting her until she finally manages to escape his clutches. *Lolita* was written by the Russian author Vladimir Nabokov and published in 1955. The novel, which was included in *TIME* magazine's 100 best English-language novels published between 1923 and 2005, was adapted for the silver screen by Stanley Kubrick in 1962 and again by Adrian Lyne in 1997. We might have included *Lolita* as a chapter in this book, but frankly Humbert's behaviour is abhorrent.

In keeping with Kubrick, we have Alex DeLarge in Anthony Burgess' 1962 novel *A Clockwork Orange* and Kubrick's 1971 cinematic adaptation. A dystopian social and political commentary set in the not-too-distant future, the novel opens with the fifteen-year-old protagonist and his 'droogs' as they set off on a violent rampage purely for the purpose of entertainment. DeLarge could be a psychopath, a sociopath or a juvenile delinquent. Perhaps more interesting is the novel's theme of whether or not he can be treated. In the book, DeLarge is apprehended, whereupon his forensic psychiatrists prescribe him the fictional 'Ludovico technique', which involves forcibly exposing him to violent images while giving him medication to induce nausea in an effort to stop his violent behaviour.[11]

DeLarge is likeable not merely because of the vulnerability inherent in his being a minor exposed to barbaric treatment while incarcerated. As narrator, he takes us into his confidence from the outset, and he is certainly anything but boring. But what places a little doubt on his psychopathy is his appreciation of Beethoven, a composer renowned for evoking considerable depth of emotion in listeners. DeLarge seems to feel a connection with the classical composer's suffering. Kubrick's adaptation was nominated for the 1971 Academy Award for Best Picture but sadly lost to *The French Connection*. Still, Alex DeLarge is a probable psychopath with a likeable streak whom we might easily have included in this book.

Of course, there are other noteworthy anti-heroes of the silver screen. Two obvious film directors each have a long list of potential psychopaths for inclusion on account of their likeability. The first is Quentin Tarantino, the king of violent black comedy. Perhaps his most famous film is the postmodern *Pulp Fiction*, with its eclectic use of dialogue, intersecting storylines, references to popular culture and relentless violence as a comedic tool. It was nominated for seven Academy Awards and Tarantino (along with co-writer Roger Avary) won an Oscar for Best Original Screenplay.

Virtually all of the anti-heroes in Tarantino films are likeable on account of their charm, but two clear examples are Vincent Vega and Jules Winnfield played respectively by John Travolta and Samuel L. Jackson. As they cruise along the highway to retrieve a briefcase from a low-level gangster who has been disloyal to their collective boss (Wallace), Vega and Winnfield joust like an old married couple about anything from what the French call a Big Mac quarter-pounder (a 'Royale with cheese', as it happens) to the explicit nature of a foot massage. Eventually they arrive at their destination, where Winnfield says, 'Come on, let's get into character' and they brutally shoot the gangster dead. Their only casual concern is how to cover their tracks. Whether technically sociopaths or psychopaths, they are nevertheless likeable for their seductive charm, their vulnerability to their boss, Winnfield's intellect and Vega's stylish dancing (clearly one of the reasons Travolta was cast). But as Tarantino typically films mere snapshots in the lives of his characters (rather than taking the longitudinal view), we do not know enough about their backstories to assert psychopathy and include them meaningfully in this book.

Equally, Alfred Hitchcock is a connoisseur of the psychopath. With over sixty films to his credit, where indeed do we start? *Rope* (1948) might be a good example, in which two friends strangle a classmate simply for the intellectual thrill of it and then proceed to throw a party for the victim's family and friends while the victim lies in a trunk that they use as a buffet table. The killers regale their guests (who include their former teacher played by James Stewart) with their intellectual views on the essence of the perfect murder. They are vulnerable mostly on account of their youth. They are talented, skilful and certainly not boring. We assume they are psychopaths but, as with Tarantino's characters, we have insufficient biographical detail to back up this assumption. Hitchcock's films are replete with likely psychopaths, but there is one notable exception who has already been mentioned: Norman Bates, who clearly has psychosis rather than psychopathy.

So, with this in mind, the following are the clear front-runners when it comes to the likeable fictional psychopath:

1.   **Amy Elliott Dunne** in *Gone Girl* by Gillian Flynn.

2. **James Bond** in Ian Fleming's novels.

3. **Francis Urquhart** (or Frank Underwood) in the television series *House of Cards*.

4. **Tom Ripley** in *The Talented Mr Ripley* by Patricia Highsmith.

5. **Kevin Khatchadourian** in *We Need to Talk About Kevin* by Lionel Shriver.

6. **Ben Lovatt** in Doris Lessing's novel *The Fifth Child*.

7. **Hannibal Lecter** in *The Silence of the Lambs* by Thomas Harris.

8. **Montressor** in Edgar Allan Poe's *The Cask of Amontillado*.

9. **Dexter Morgan** in the television series *Dexter*.

10. **Patrick Bateman** in Bret Easton Ellis' novel *American Psycho.*

11. **Tony Soprano** in the television series *The Sopranos.*

On this list are some of the most famous fictional psychopaths ever created. At least three of the contenders on our list are the anti-heroes of highly successful television series, while all but one of the remainder are the principal protagonists of novels sufficient in number or detail to provide the biographical detail needed. Most of the novels have been made into films. Perhaps *The Cask of Amontillado* is an indulgence. Either way, it goes to show how readers, cinema-goers and television aficionados are ever hungry for the archetypal psychopath. Provided, of course, they are likeable.

II

CONTENDERS

3

THE AMAZING PSYCHOPATH

'The way some people change fashion regularly, I change personalities.'

– Amy Elliott Dunne[1]

Although most psychopaths in real life – the lion's share, if you like – are probably men, spare a thought for the archetypal often-psychopathic *femme fatales* in fiction. Think of all those suggestively named Bond girls who are happy to sleep with 007 before betraying him to the enemy. Similarly Demi Moore's portrayal of Meredith Johnson in Barry Levinson's film adaptation of Michael Crichton's *Disclosure* is the epitome of corporate psychopathy. But perhaps the finest example of a female psychopath in fiction is Amy Elliott Dunne, the protagonist in Gillian Flynn's tense psychological thriller *Gone Girl*.

Published in June 2012, the novel was nothing short of a sensation, climbing to the top of the *New York Times* bestseller list. A 2014 film adaptation, written by the author and directed by David Fincher, starred Ben Affleck and Rosamund Pike in the leading roles. It was very successful, both commercially and critically; indeed, it led to a plethora of award nominations that included an Oscar nomination for Pike.

The plot centres on the disappearance of the beautiful and accomplished Amy Elliott Dunne on the date of her fifth wedding anniversary. Amy is the only child of children's authors Marybeth and Rand Elliott, whose once-successful series of *Amazing Amy* books is based on a fictionalised version of their daughter. Early in the tale, we learn of how Amy met her future husband, Nick, when they were both up-and-coming writers in New York. Together, they attended glamorous parties and hinted at a life of endless possibilities: they were a golden couple. Alas, their good fortune was short-lived as the recession inevitably took its toll. Ultimately, unemployment, financial worries and Nick's ailing parents meant he and Amy were forced to leave New York for his hometown of North Carthage, Missouri.

In the novel, Amy mostly recounts the past in diary format, while Nick narrates the present. From the outset, we are not so sure about Nick. He is depicted as a rather absent-minded and smug young man with loose morals. But is he a murderer? With Amy now missing, the police suspect an altercation in the household and are immediately suspicious of him. He copes poorly with media scrutiny and, as public mistrust in him grows, he becomes a social pariah, first locally and then nationally. It seems obvious to everyone that Amy's husband has something to hide.

Then the police find Amy's diary, unmasking a marriage

that is not as blissful as initially perceived. Amy appears naïve and earnest, and is clearly unhappy living in North Carthage. Both their house and Nick's business venture (a liquor emporium simply named 'The Bar') are funded by Amy's trust fund, which implies that she is being taken advantage of. They have little income, yet Nick seems to charge numerous extravagant purchases to his credit card. He has recently taken out a life assurance policy on Amy. It transpires that he has been having an affair with a young student attending a local college where he teaches media studies. Amy's diary goes on to reveal that she has become gradually more afraid of her angry and unpredictable husband. Indeed, she describes taking steps to buy a gun in order to protect herself from him. So, when she disappears, it seems to the police that Nick has motive, means and opportunity; his only defence rests in the absence of something crucial to prove a murder – the body.

Of course, there is a very good reason for this. Amy is not dead. When she is ready, she confides in the reader that she has plotted her exit in order to frame her husband for homicide. Having bought an old car, she leaves evidence of a domestic disturbance at their house and then drives to a motel where she resides undercover. All does not go according to her plan, however. Before long (indeed, the moment she lets down her guard), her money is stolen by her motel neighbours and she is forced to sleep in her car. Ever resourceful, she seeks refuge in the high-walled country retreat of her former boyfriend and creepy admirer Desi Collins. Ironically, she finds herself trapped in the manner she has already fictionalised in her diary. Her *de facto* imprisonment begs the question: has she bitten off more than she can chew? While there, she sees Nick on national television, publicly apologising and begging her to return home. Ultimately, she frames Desi by faking a sexual assault in front of his ubiquitous CCTV cameras and then proceeds to murder him in his bed. Finally, she returns home, tearful and covered in blood for the benefit of the television press.

Unsurprisingly, it transpires that Amy left her diary deliberately for the police to find, untrustworthy as it was. Her description of Nick as an aggressive man is inconsistent with what the reader can clearly see. Her portrayal of herself as a victim does not seem to add up either. And in a triumph of impression management, Amy's fictitious depiction of their marriage allows her to slowly punish her disappointing husband for the wasted years he has cost her and his audacity to have an affair with a younger woman right under her very nose. Amy's motive is revenge – to see Nick publicly humiliated, most likely prosecuted for murder and possibly even executed. It seems the sympathetic 'Amazing Amy' of the diary (and of the early part of the marriage) is a manufactured persona.

Amy's extreme impression management is only one of her many psychopathic traits. In terms of the interpersonal domain, there are numerous examples of *glibness and superficial charm*. Amy is charm itself; men and women alike hang on her every word, dazzled by her wit, cleverness and charisma. A string of former boyfriends have never quite gotten over their obsession with her. She easily charms a less-glamorous neighbour into a perceived friendship. When Amy goes missing, nobody in the community has an unkind word to say about her – at least not at first. Indeed, a whole nation of young readers that grew up with Amazing Amy seems to adore our anti-hero as they confuse her with her fictional counterpart. Only those close to Amy can see what she is really like. Nick's father is suspicious of her. Nick's twin sister, Go, dislikes her intensely. Even Nick himself tires of his wife after a year or two of marriage as reality begins to creep in. Her allure is just a façade.

As for a *grandiose sense of self-worth*, Amy throws what must be one of the greatest narcissistic tantrums in literary history. Obviously, it is reasonable for any spouse to be upset when learning about their partner's adultery, but not to the point where they publicly frame said partner for murder in an effort to regain absolute control of the relationship. And Amy has a strong track record of taking offence when key people do not worship her. She dishes out punishment equally well; her past is strewn with teenage school peers and old boyfriends who have inadvertently scorned her only to find themselves with reputations as stalkers or rapists. Nick is simply the latest to offend, being the man she accuses of having 'single-handedly de-amazed Amazing Amy'.[2] It is only by pleading for mercy publicly on network television that Nick persuades Amy to come home, an act of contrition that appeals to the extreme narcissism that might have originated in her upbringing. She is, after all, the only child of shallow, emotionally neglectful parents who have carefully walked the tightrope of constantly telling her how brilliant she is while simultaneously holding her up to public scrutiny against a perfect fictionalised version.

So, what about *pathological lying*? This is not the usual type of lying – the kind we all do to spare the feelings of others or cover up minor peccadilloes. Instead the pathological liar falsifies constantly out of habit, sometimes without even realising they are doing it. If found out, the psychopath will simply shrug it off without any sense of embarrassment or they will rework the facts to iron out any inconsistencies. Apart from the fact that Amy admits to lying about her whole personality during the first few years of her relationship with Nick, her narrative in the first half of the novel is entirely comprised of an elaborate series of lies aimed at carefully framing her husband for murder. In the past, she lied about being stalked by a school friend, about being date-raped by a former boyfriend, and about Desi Collins once attempting suicide over her:

> *I'd always liked that lie about Desi trying to kill himself over me. He had truly been devastated by our breakup, and he'd been really annoying, creepy, hanging around campus, hoping I'd take him back. So he might as well have attempted suicide.*[3]

Amy is a chronic pathological liar. She seems to lie for the sheer hell of it. Equally, she *manipulates* those around her *for personal gain*, being the expert at impression management that she is. She cons Nick into marrying her, then frames him, then manipulates her way into the arms (and the bed) of the former boyfriend she once lied about, and finally cons her way safely home again.

Score for interpersonal traits = 8/8

Amy also ticks all the boxes in the affective domain. Her *shallow affect* is such that it is difficult to discern any real emotion in her other than jealousy and rage. Any sense of fear in her is very limited indeed. She may display other emotions but she does not seem to truly feel them. That is not to say she isn't perceptive; in her diary, she dissects the personalities of others with relative ease. Like many psychopaths, she is highly adept at identifying the weak points of others in order to trick them into doing what she wants them to do. But this is a skill (based on 'cold' empathy) rather than an emotional response. Nick's Achilles' heel, for example, is his laid-back nature and his poor attention to detail. Sometimes his only ambition appears to be the avoidance of conflict and Amy initially provides this with ease to snare her man. As she remarks, 'For someone like me, who likes to win, it's tempting to want to be the girl every guy wants.'[4] And as she assumes the role of Cool Girl, she adds that, 'I could feel myself getting shallower and dumber.' Nick 'loved a girl who doesn't exist'.[5]

Paradoxically, Amy seems acutely aware of her own

shallowness. In her own eyes, her identity is who she appears to be rather than who she really is. On one occasion, she blames social media for this, noting that, 'It's a very difficult era in which to be a person, just a real, actual person, instead of a collection of personality traits selected from an endless automat of characters.'[6] Her feelings of emptiness are amplified by her constant comparison to her parents' other creation, Amazing Amy, who is smarter, funnier, more accomplished, more adventurous and more successful than the real Amy will ever be. This is something the hordes of journalists and reviewers at book launches seem quite happy to point out.

And with this paucity of real emotion comes a remarkable *callousness and lack of empathy*. Lack of 'hot' empathy, that is. Amy cares about nobody but Amy. Nick is the target of her rage, but the fallout of her actions on others is of no concern to her. She casually uses a sincere neighbour as a friend to back up her fake story of spousal abuse. She spares no thought for those she has framed in the past, while the effect on her parents of her deliberate disappearance doesn't seem to bother her. 'My parents are worried, of course,' she says, 'but how can I feel sorry for them, since they made me this way and then deserted me?'[7]

It is likely that Amy finds it hard to imagine the subtle feelings of others because she has so few of them herself, and there are symbolic as well as literal examples of this. If you believe her diary, Nick fails to turn up for an anniversary dinner she has cooked and she remarks ominously that, 'I'm killing two lobsters I won't even eat.'[8] In the end, of course, she ruthlessly kills Desi Collins with an utter *lack of* any sense of *guilt or remorse*. His death ensures his silence and allows her to frame him for kidnapping.

And for all of the above, Amy *accepts no responsibility*. She is truly convinced that those who trifle with her are to blame for their own downfall – Desi should have gotten over his teenage crush; her parents, Marybeth and Rand, should not have been so self-absorbed; Nick should have been a better husband. So, unburdened by conscience, Amy returns home safe in the knowledge she now has the upper hand in her marriage. Permanently.

Score for affective traits = 8/8

So, what about the lifestyle domain? On the face of it, Amy appears conscientious and hardworking. She has forged a career as a human-interest writer (playfully penning light-hearted, agony-aunt-style multiple-choice quizzes for a magazine) and seems to want to work for a living. On the other hand, her earning capacity appears quite limited, with much of her wealth derived from a parental trust fund, which she deeply resents. Her inheritance has bankrolled The Bar, but we presume she has never pulled a pint in her life. And, of course, we suspect she will ultimately sell the rights to her kidnapping story for millions, allowing her to profit at the expense of everyone around her. So, while Amy likes to be seen as independent, her *lifestyle* could be described as *parasitic* to a degree.

Although Amy shows some capacity for self-control and plans meticulously much of what happens during the course of the book, she does show some signs of *impulsivity* on occasion. For example, when Greta (Amy's neighbour at the motel in which she hides out while purporting to be missing) inadvertently insults her, Amy describes her petty revenge thus: 'I tiptoe into her kitchen, go into her fridge, and spit in her milk, her orange juice, and a container of potato salad ...'[9] There are few other such examples of impulsivity, but Amy is undoubtedly reckless and *irresponsible* in all that she does to drive the plot.

Notwithstanding Amy's meticulous planning, she *lacks realistic long-term goals*. From the outset, her entire deception is so short-sighted that it should really have ended in disaster. To begin with, her disappearance is clearly unsustainable. Although she tells us her plan is to kill herself as soon as she is certain that Nick has been arrested, humiliated and convicted, it is the view of experts such as the American psychiatrist Hervey Cleckley that psychopaths rarely die from suicide. Moreover, with around $12,000 in her purse, Amy has dramatically underestimated the amount of money she will need to survive unsupported for more than a few months. And what will happen after that? Either she has to return to her family with her tail between her legs or really disappear forever with an entirely different identity. And if she returns, does she expect that things will ever be the same again? In the end, Amy's outcome relies more on sheer luck and the survival instinct of a psychopath than it does on realistic goal-setting. Still, this is fiction so perhaps we should make allowances.

The first time we meet Amy in the story, she strikes us as a highly intelligent individual who is bored very easily. According to Nick, 'Amy was once a woman who did a little of everything, all the time.'[10] The inventive birthday presents, the anniversary treasure hunts, the ability to mingle effortlessly at social engagements are seemingly typical. She can 'cook French cuisine and speak fluent Spanish and garden and knit and run marathons and day-trade stocks and fly a plane and look like a runway model doing it'. Amy's need to be busy is one of the things Nick finds so attractive. Of course, this broad but shallow repertoire could just be her impression management, while there is no evidence that she feels compelled to involve herself in skydiving, high-stakes gambling or illicit drug taking. But Amy still demonstrates a strong *need for excitement* and we get a real sense of the thrill of subterfuge when she orchestrates her disappearance at considerable risk to herself and her reputation.

Does Amy show signs of *promiscuous sexual behaviour*? Early in her diary she makes reference to how many sexual partners she has had by the age of thirty-one:

> … *I sound quite slutty, don't I? Pause while I count how many … eleven. Not bad. I've always thought twelve was a solid, reasonable number to end at.*[11]

Of course, we don't quite know whether or not to believe Amy, especially as her diary is by her own admission a work of fiction. Still, she uses highly sexualised and often coarse language at times during the book, while she is quite willing to act as a seductress to advance her own cause – not least when she wants to implicate Desi Collins for her month-long absence. There is no solid evidence of pervasive promiscuity, but the narrative implies it strongly. Meanwhile Amy has *many short-term relationships*, but they are not *marital* relationships. Indeed, she is so invested in the institution of marriage that she is willing to take drastic steps when she discovers her husband's adultery.

Score for lifestyle traits = 8/14

In terms of the antisocial domain, Amy shows mixed evidence of *poor behavioural controls*. On the one hand, anyone who dares cross her risks being publicly labelled a stalker, rapist or murderer. Her past is strewn with such apparently impulsive lies to the authorities about people who once trusted and admired her. On the other hand, Amy shows us that she is quite capable of making a socially unacceptable plan and sticking ruthlessly to it with scant allowance for the distraction of emotion.

There is little in the plot to suggest *early behavioural problems* in Amy. In the film, we see a photograph of her posing with a cello next to a drawing of Amazing Amy doing the same. The scene suggests a model child. The story gives little account of any *juvenile delinquency* (although that is not to say that it definitely didn't happen), while *revocation of conditional release* does not apply as Amy has never been to prison. Indeed, the only definitive antisocial trait in Amy (except for some *poor behavioural controls*) is *criminal versatility*. From deception to fraud, to attempting to purchase an unlicensed firearm, to perverting the course of justice, to murder, Amy shows us that she is a very versatile criminal indeed.

Score for antisocial traits = 3/8 (one item not applicable)

Amy's overall score is 27 out of 38, which suggests that she is a psychopath. Her strong scores in the interpersonal and affective domains, coupled with her weak score in the antisocial domain, indicate that she leans more towards *manipulative* psychopathy than *macho* psychopathy. She is more a 'talker' than a 'doer'.

There are one or two inconsistencies, however. For example, any expert will tell you that real psychopaths do not tend to have obsessive-compulsive traits. Recall that their amygdala is underactive. They do not ruminate over whether or not they left the oven on or forgot to lock the front door. Psychopaths characteristically fail to profit from experience precisely because they do not dwell upon such benign problems. They simply do not care. But in Nick's narrative, he remarks that:

> *Amy could spend an entire evening out fretting that she left the stove on, even though we didn't cook that day. Or was the door locked? Was I sure? She was a worst-case scenarist on a grand scale.*[12]

These words do not describe a psychopath, although we do have to ask ourselves whether Nick has simply failed to observe the real Amy, as he succumbs to her highly skilled impression management. Either way, if we ignore the occasional inconsistency and accept that Amy scores strongly for psychopathy, this leaves us with the fundamental question as to why we spend most of the book and film wishing for her to succeed.

It is first worth noting that decline is one of the major themes in *Gone Girl*. Both protagonists are writers who lament the decline of paper journalism in favour of the Internet. Indeed, it leads to their unemployment. The *Amazing Amy* series is also in decline, with each new book selling fewer copies than its predecessor until, at last, Marybeth and Rand are dropped by their publisher. Amy and Nick, meanwhile, move to North Carthage, a town whose economic decline is written all over the walls of the derelict local shopping mall; the motive for their migration is to care for Nick's ailing parents, one of whom is terminally ill while the other has dementia. But, most importantly, we are witnesses to the decline of Amy and Nick's marriage.

In this regard, Nick doesn't do himself any favours. In the opening chapters, he seems nice enough, although not nearly as charismatic as his clever wife. Frankly, she appears somewhat out of his league. As Amy's disappearance ensues, Nick alludes to the numerous lies he has told the police. He exudes a sense of guilt and, when we realise that he is harbouring a secret, we automatically wonder if he is Amy's killer after all. The secret transpires to be his affair, but the press and public alike misinterpret his doleful demeanour to be the result of his guilty belief that any search for Amy is futile. This contrasts sharply with the earnest public appeals of Marybeth and Rand. Alas, their 'Amazing Amy' tag is initially quaint, but it quickly grows tired and clichéd. At times, we get a sense that Marybeth and Rand mourn the loss of their tarnished brand more than their actual daughter. Such oddness in Amy's first-degree relatives sets her up nicely to appear like the victim she plots to portray.

In a sense, we might say that Amy has simply had enough. She knows she deserves better. In a modern world where goodness is inherently dull and badness sexy, her attraction lies in her façade of sassiness, flamboyance and mischief. She gives the impression (however false) that she has a strong sense of herself and that there are limits to what she will put up with. So, surrounded by decline, she decides to rebel against what she perceives to be the final straw – the prospect of divorce. Nick's affair is the trigger and thus it is hard not to approve of her rage (notwithstanding the violence). She and Nick make a good-looking couple and readers want their marriage to succeed. Strangely, it seems we can identify better with a dysfunctional marriage than with a divorce.

It is easy to admire the slick and covert nature of Amy's *modus operandi*. The reader loves a well-kept secret. Equally, her fearlessness and courage under fire add to her allure. She is a strong female lead. Still, her likeability lies also in her vulnerability (or, at least, in our perception of her vulnerability).

Initially, she clearly has the upper hand as she relaxes by the pool and watches her husband squirm in endless public scrutiny. She smugly lets the reader in on her ruse but perhaps a little too soon, in that things inevitably begin to fall apart when her money is stolen and she is forced to sleep in her car. She then seeks refuge with Desi Collins, only to find herself trapped in the manner she has ironically fictionalised in her diary. As previously noted, her *de facto* imprisonment begs the question: has she underestimated the situation? In the end, her desperate effort to escape is something to which the reader can relate. It gives the impression of vulnerability.

More fundamentally perhaps, she is vulnerable to herself. She is her own worst enemy. So great is her narcissism that it makes her susceptible to carefully planned manipulation, such as the rather transparent trap laid by Nick when he gives an interview on network television. He lies through his teeth to Amy and a million other viewers hungry for a very public act of contrition. Hiding his anger and resentment, he expresses humble regret for his adultery and begs Amy to come home so they can rekindle their relationship. So grandiose is Amy that she falls for it hook, line and sinker. Her vanity is her Achilles' heel.

But there are other reasons we root for her to succeed. Through her narration of every second chapter in the novel, Amy takes us into her confidence. Although the first half of her account is largely false by her own admission, the remainder is refreshingly honest. Or at least it appears to be, notwithstanding the impression management presumably at play. Certainly, she gives us the details of what she did, how she did it and why she did it. As readers, perhaps we feel privileged at appearing to garner her trust.

However superficial Amy's charm might be, it is difficult not to be seduced by it. Nick succumbs to it and so does virtually everyone else in the novel. Amy has looks, talents and skills we admire, being beautiful, intelligent, perceptive and accomplished. She is a voracious reader, a quick study and a brilliant planner when she sets her mind to it. And bored as Amy might feel (like many psychopaths), she is not boring to the reader. She contrasts dramatically with her alter ego (Amazing Amy is so perfect, so benign and so dull) and with her pedestrian husband. Even at a time of crisis, Nick's heroism is lacklustre; he is not a man of action. Yet Amy has the refreshing temerity to do the things ordinary people never do and it is hard not to admire her for that.

As is often the case with the fictional psychopath, Amy's victims make her look good. These include her lugubrious, lazy, adulterous husband; her self-obsessed, neglectful parents; and a weak, rather weird ex-boyfriend who stalks her and preys on her vulnerability at the first real opportunity. There are exceptions among the minor characters, but in general it is hard to identify with Amy's victims over and above the anti-hero herself. But then, this might simply be Gillian Flynn's genius as she skilfully presents the narrative of a psychopath who has a tendency to blame others for her own misfortunes.

Finally, does Amy's backdrop make her look good? Well, yes, if we take the abstract viewpoint and see her backdrop as that of decline. So, as she rises up to fight against the demise of everything she needs in life for survival – her economic security, her marriage and her dignity – the reader cannot help but cheer her on a bit. Perhaps psychopathy is better than complacency.

4

THE SECRET PSYCHOPATH

'In poker, you never play your hand; you play the man across from you.'

– James Bond[1]

Some readers might not automatically associate James Bond with psychopathy. Others would, however – not least Kevin Dutton (whom I have mentioned previously) and Peter Jonason, a social-personality psychologist currently based at Western Sydney University.[2] Jonason and colleagues, for example, refer to 'James Bond psychology' in describing 'The Dark Triad' of Machiavellianism, narcissism and psychopathy.[3] The authors suggest that such individuals tend to manipulate others by possessing high levels of extroversion, self-esteem, individualism and competitiveness, and low levels of conscientiousness and anxiety. In many ways, James Bond may be the perfect example of a non-criminal psychopath – one who is charming, daring, persuasive and ruthless.

But not everyone agrees. David Cox, professor of psychology at Simon Fraser University, British Columbia, studied British bomb-disposal experts during the Northern Ireland 'Troubles' some decades ago.[4] At the outset, the researchers anticipated that psychopaths would possess both a need for excitement and the requisite fearlessness in the face of adversity that would combine to make them ideal for the job. Instead, they found that most soldiers viewed their psychopathic colleagues as unreliable and impulsive, with insufficient attention to detail to allow them to practise safely. The few who made it through training did not last much longer thereafter. So, we are left wondering whether a psychopath would really make a good spy, given his lack of allegiance to comrades or causes, his unreliability, his impulsivity and his carelessness.

In any case, James Bond (or at least most versions of him) ought to make a dreadful spy. Dashingly handsome, he is anything but inconspicuous, while he destroys almost every location he visits, he drinks so much that he must be constantly inebriated or hungover, and – let's face it – he relies mostly on pure luck for his triumphs. The traits that make him exciting and likeable as a fictional character are the very reasons he would never last long in the real world of espionage. Or is this really true? Who should we believe?

Perhaps some confusion arises because Bond is not simply one character; he is an entire genre that has evolved over decades and seems to undergo a fresh revival every couple of years. At the time of writing, the most recently released cinematic instalment is 2015's *Spectre*, Daniel Craig's fourth sojourn as 007 in the second of the franchise to be directed by Sam Mendes. To date there have been twenty-four 'official' films made by Eon Productions (with number twenty-five, entitled *No Time To Die*, now at post-production stage), in addition to a spoof adaptation of *Casino Royale* (1967) and Sean Connery's reprise of the role in *Never Say Never Again* (1983). More about the films later.

From a literary perspective, Ian Fleming wrote twelve original novels and two collections of short stories. Various subsequent books have been commissioned by the Ian Fleming Estate, the first of which appeared just a few years after Fleming's death in 1964. Entitled *Colonel Sun*, it was penned in 1968 by Robert Markham – better known as Kingsley Amis, the Booker-Prize winning author of *Lucky Jim*. Written in Fleming's style, *Colonel Sun* followed the timeline of the original novels, more or less beginning where *The Man with the Golden Gun* ended. From the early 1980s, a series of commissioned novels by John Gardner described a modernised, more contemporary James Bond. Gardner wrote some sixteen books until his retirement in 1997, whereupon Raymond Benson took the helm and penned another twelve or so. In 2011, the American writer Jeffery Deaver was invited to write a novel entitled *Carte Blanche,* which similarly depicted Bond in contemporary times.

But in the eyes of many readers, Bond belongs in the fifties and sixties – an era in which his chain smoking, vodka martini savouring while on the job, and unapologetic misogyny are lent a vague air of acceptability in the eyes of the 'now we know better' brigade. Or perhaps it is only possible to convey the true loneliness of Cold War espionage in an era predating the Internet and mass communication. With this in mind, Sebastian Faulks – author of *Birdsong* and *Human Traces* – was approached by the Ian Fleming Estate in 2006 to write a new novel in celebration of the late Bond-creator's centenary. Representing an unusual departure from the more literary style for which the author is better known, *Devil May Care* (2008) sold over 44,000 hardback copies for Penguin UK in its first four days. It was only the second Bond sequel to be set in the timeline of the original Fleming novels, the first being *Colonel Sun*, as we have noted. In the eyes of many readers who had endured the run of modern-day Bond adventures penned by Gardner and Benson, the iconic hero had finally returned to what remains the most iconic decade – the 1960s.

So, what's it all about? It's all run-of-the-mill Fleming stuff really, where Bond is pitted against Dr Julius Gorner, a villain with a simian hand who hates all things British. Dr Gorner is consumed by a desire to flood dear old England with enough narcotics to outdo nineteenth-century China but, becoming impatient, he settles for the far simpler plan of attacking the Soviet Union with nuclear warheads housed aboard a marine craft that is, in fact, a modified aeroplane. The idea is to provoke a counter attack against London. Assigned to the case, Bond is first introduced to Dr Gorner at a tennis match, whereupon he succeeds in wounding the villain's narcissism by beating him at his own game. The scene is strongly evocative of one in Fleming's 1959 novel *Goldfinger* in which the eponymous villain is beaten in a round of golf at his own club. Still, there's something reassuring in the regurgitation of a tried-and-tested plot-line that allows the MI6 super-spy to save the world once again.

Unsurprisingly, Bond also gets the girl. Her name is Scarlett Papava and it is she who initially introduces him to Dr Gorner, from whom she wants Bond to help her rescue her twin sister Poppy. In the process, Bond learns about Dr Gorner's factory in the Middle East. Thus ensues a burglary, a daring escape and a visit to Mother Russia in order to sabotage a heinous plan that seeks to change the face of the world as we know it. If it all sounds a bit Austin Powers (the popular James Bond spoof), that's probably because it is. But the novel still has everything we would hope for in a Fleming thriller: an absurd villain with an even more absurd plan; an eccentric henchman called Chagrin; a racy female sidekick; Felix Leiter; and, of course, M. Seamlessly, Faulks took up exactly where the master himself left off.

William Boyd did something similar in 2013 with his novel *Solo*. In choosing Boyd, the Ian Fleming Estate clearly wanted a more literary author once again – in this instance one whose distinguished career includes a Whitbread First Novel Prize and a James Tait Black Memorial Prize, among other accolades. Boyd was even awarded a CBE in 2005. His novels include the historical spy thriller *Restless* (which won the Costa Novel of the Year) and *Any Human Heart* (which features Ian Fleming as a character), and he undoubtedly seemed a perfect fit. Boyd was born in Ghana in 1952 and spent much of his childhood in West Africa, so perhaps it is fitting that he chose to base a significant portion of his Bond adventure in the land of his youth. *Solo* is set in 1969 – a time at which Boyd must have been around seventeen years old. It is easy to see how such a young man might gaze at the jungles and villages of Biafra during the Nigerian Civil War and picture James Bond tackling villains.

The novel is set in the fictional country of Zanzarim, which is clearly meant to represent Biafra. Bond is sent there to investigate some underhand dealings with the able assistance of a local MI6 contact, a young woman who goes by the tag of Eufa Blessing Ogilvy-Grant. (Not as suggestively named as some Bond girls, or has it just gone over my head?) Either way, civil war looms and our heroes find they have no choice but to flee the country along with all the other expatriates. Alas, they are captured by a Rhodesian mercenary named Kobus Breed who, in true Bond-villain style, has a disfigured face and a permanently weeping eye. Bond escapes into the jungle but is eventually recaptured and – in a curious twist – shot by both Breed and Ogilvy-Grant. Left for dead, Bond (being the amazing MI6 agent that he is) recovers sufficiently to track his would-be murderers to Washington in search of revenge. In the process, he uncovers an illicit operation that uses injured refugee children to smuggle heroin from Africa into the United States. With the help of the CIA, Bond manages to foil the operation, restore order once again and arrive home in time for early evening cocktails.

As with *Devil May Care*, *Solo* is written in the style of Ian

Fleming, moreover with close attention to the character's historical detail and the events of previous books. Boyd is said to have scrutinised all of Fleming's novels in chronological order prior to putting pen to paper. The end result is grittier than *Devil May Care*, with a simpler but entirely more believable plot. But then, perhaps believability has never been what the Bond genre is about. Some of the most entertaining novels and films have been every bit as far-fetched as the protagonist himself. Either way, Boyd's offering sold well and appeared as a top-ten bestseller in the UK.

This brings us to the most recent additions to the Bond book list, namely Anthony Horowitz's *Trigger Mortis* and *Forever and a Day*. Once again, the Ian Fleming Estate chose an author of some pedigree to write a historical novel for the series. In addition to writing for the television series *Midsomer Murders* and the BAFTA-winning *Foyle's War*, Horowitz has written several bestselling novels including *House of Silk*, *Moriarty* and *Magpie Murders*. Moreover, he is the author of the Alex Rider series of children's books that have sold in excess of twenty million copies worldwide. In 2014, he was awarded an OBE.

Trigger Mortis goes back in time further than its commissioned predecessors, being set in 1957 amid the space race. It begins just two weeks after the events of *Goldfinger* and we observe Bond still entertaining Pussy Galore at his flat in Chelsea. Unsurprisingly, this relationship is short-lived – although it lasts long enough for us to witness Auric Goldfinger's former Mafioso contacts attempting to suffocate Pussy by covering her in gold paint. Bond is sent on a mission to the Nuremburg racing track to prevent his old adversaries in SMERSH from murdering a famous British racing driver in the name of Russian sporting supremacy.[5] In doing so, Bond stumbles upon a complex plan to sabotage a United States rocket that would endanger the lives of thousands of New York citizens.

The novel has all the usual ingredients and a little extra to boot – guns, rockets, fast women and fast cars (a Maserati 250, on this occasion). Even the plot moves quickly, if still characteristically unbelievable as per the genre. Perhaps Horowitz's Bond is a little kinder (less psychopathic, if you like) than Boyd's. The prose itself contains original Fleming passages salvaged from the attic by the Fleming family, thus ensuring that the style of the novel as a whole is close to that of Fleming's. The usual characters appear – M, Bill Tanner the chief of staff, the ever-flirtatious Miss Moneypenny, and so forth. Bond girls are in plentiful supply as usual, although it comes as some surprise to Bond to find that his attempts to woo the beautiful young expert racing instructor Logan Fairfax are outdone by Pussy Galore herself. Completing the book's trio of strong female characters is Jeopardy Lane, a resourceful CIA agent from New York who saves Bond's bacon on more than one occasion. Finally, the villain of the story is Sin Jai-Seong (better remembered as Jason Sin), a bitter South Korean exile bent on revenge.

Forever and a Day, meanwhile, goes right back to Bond's first fictional outing. As a prequel to *Casino Royale*, it is set in the early 1950s and sees our anti-hero replacing the old 007 who has been murdered in Marseilles. As such, Bond's debut mission is to travel to the Riviera and resume his predecessor's secret investigation. In terms of plotting, characterisation and authentic Fleming style, it is almost certainly the best of the recent Bond novels.

If these recent Bond novels have tended to go back in time, the offerings for the silver screen have leaned heavily on reinventing Bond for the modern age. The 2006 film *Casino Royale* starred a reincarnated hero in the form of Daniel Craig as a rookie who has just earned his double-0 status. Reverting to the grittier and less-humorous style of the Connery years (and, indeed, the Fleming novels themselves), the revival has been followed to date by three subsequent films (*Quantum of Solace*, *Skyfall* and *Spectre*) whose storylines ultimately tie together quite nicely. All in all, the genre has certainly stood the test of time.

But perhaps more enigmatic than Bond was Fleming himself. The second of four brothers, he was born in London on 28 May 1908. He was educated at Eton (and later in Austria and Germany) and tried many careers before eventually settling on novel-writing at the ripe old age of forty-four. His original plan was enrolment in the armed forces and, as such, he spent a brief period training at the Royal Military College at Sandhurst. Faced with expulsion for alleged womanising, he quickly left his army days behind in favour of other pursuits. Next, he tried his hand at diplomacy and sat the exams for the Foreign Office. He reputedly did quite well at these, but he did not gain enough marks to be accepted for a diplomatic career. In the 1930s, he spent some time working for Reuter's news agency, a job he was said to have enjoyed immensely. More importantly, he acquired the skills necessary to produce snippets of newsworthy information with speed and accuracy. Alas, the job did not pay very well and Fleming left to become a stockbroker, albeit not a particularly successful one.

It was not until the outbreak of the Second World War that Fleming really began to shine. Recruited to Room 39, the headquarters of the British Admiralty's Naval Intelligence Division, as personal assistant to the director, he remained there throughout the war. During his time at the Admiralty, he accumulated many of the ideas, characters, incidents and anecdotes that were eventually to find their way into the subsequent James Bond books. After the war, Fleming joined Kemsley Newspapers as foreign manager, supplying headlines primarily for use in *The Sunday Times*. It was through his travels that he stumbled upon the small piece of land in Jamaica where he built his holiday home 'Goldeneye'. From 1952 until his death in 1964, Fleming wintered annually there, taking just two months each year to draft the latest Bond adventure.

Fleming married his long-time mistress Ann Rothermere in 1952. Although it was the writer's first and only marriage, it was by then her third. A son, Caspar, soon followed and it was for him that Fleming wrote his only children's story, *Chitty Chitty Bang Bang*, later filmed as a musical starring Dick Van Dyke and Sally Ann Howes. Fiction was not the only string to

Fleming's bow. In the late 1950s, he produced a series of articles for *The Sunday Times* about the diamond industry, published later as *The Diamond Smugglers*. Then, in the early 1960s, he took a trip around the world and wrote another collection of cosmopolitan pieces entitled *Thrilling Cities*.

Many commentators have suggested that James Bond was primarily based upon Fleming himself, the novels being a kind of fantasy autobiography – or at least a narrative of how Fleming would have liked to have lived his life. In truth, his time at Naval Intelligence was far less exciting than one might perceive through the novels, although the fictional spy did share his creator's expensive tastes, love of sport and reputation for womanising. As a strong athlete in his younger years, Fleming's interests included golf and snorkelling. He also enjoyed motoring and book collecting. A committed bibliophile, he built up an impressive collection that included volumes varying from the first book on golf to Einstein's *Theory of Relativity*. The collection now apparently resides at the University of Indiana.

But Bond is obviously Fleming's legacy. By the time he died, his novels had become so enormously successful that his fans included President John F. Kennedy. Alas, Fleming survived only long enough to see Connery in the first two Bond films, *Dr No* and *From Russia with Love*. Each of Fleming's twelve Bond novels followed the last to build a chronology (and essentially a fictional biography), with later novels occasionally referring to the events of earlier ones. We are given some biographical detail of the character's childhood at the end of the novel *You Only*

Live Twice. In his fictional obituary of Bond, who is 'missing, believed killed', M describes our anti-hero's origins as follows:

> *James Bond was born of a Scottish father, Andrew Bond of Glencoe, and a Swiss mother, Monique Delacroix, from Canton de Vaud. His father being a foreign representative of the Vickers armaments firm, his early education, from which he inherited a first-class command of French and German, was entirely abroad. When he was eleven years of age, both his parents were killed in a climbing accident in the Aiguilles Rouges above Chamonix, and the youth came under the guardianship of an aunt, since deceased, Miss Charmian Bond, and went to live with her at the quaintly named hamlet of Pett Bottom near Canterbury in Kent.*[6]

M goes on to explain that the young Bond attended public school and thereafter, around the age of twelve, 'passed satisfactorily into Eton, for which College he had been entered at birth by his father'. Alas, it seems 'his career at Eton was brief and undistinguished and, after only two halves, as a result ... of some alleged trouble with one of the boys' maids, his aunt was requested to remove him'. Bond then attended his father's *alma mater* of Fettes, where, 'though inclined to be solitary by nature, he established some firm friendships among the traditionally famous athletic circles at the school'. While there, he fought twice as a lightweight and 'founded the first serious judo class at a British Public School'. Bond turned seventeen in 1941 and, by lying about his age and seeking the help of an old colleague of his father, he 'entered a branch of what was subsequently to become the Ministry of Defence'.[7] Initially a lieutenant, he ended the war as a commander.

Bear in mind that this is an account of Bond's life from M's perspective, presumably sanitised for *The Times'* obituary page. Either way, before considering whether or not Bond qualifies as a fictional psychopath, it is worth recapping (in the table below) the basic premises and characters of each of these twelve novels. Other principal characters are highlighted in bold.

Novel	Basic Plot
Casino Royale (1953)	Bond is dispatched to a casino in Royale-les-Eaux to ruin the Soviet agent **Le Chiffre** by beating him in a high-stakes game of baccarat. Bond wins with the help of CIA agent Felix Leiter. Bond forms a relationship with double agent **Vesper Lynd**, who later kills herself rather than betray him.
Live and Let Die (1954)	Bond is sent to Harlem, New York to bring down **Mr Big**, a voodoo cult leader suspected of selling seventeenth-century gold coins to finance SMERSH spy operations in the United States. Bond tracks Mr Big to the Caribbean and runs off with his fortune-telling girlfriend **Solitaire** while Felix Leiter is fed to the sharks and gravely injured.

Novel	Basic Plot
Moonraker (1955)	Bond plays bridge at an exclusive London club with self-made millionaire **Sir Hugo Drax** (who cheats at cards). Assisted by **Gala Brand**, Bond later discovers that Drax is an ex-Nazi working for the Soviets and foils a plan to use the nuclear missile defence project 'Moonraker' to destroy London.
Diamonds Are Forever (1956)	Bond is sent to infiltrate a diamond-smuggling ring in the United States. Aided by **Tiffany Case**, Bond follows the trail to Las Vegas where he comes up against the Spangled Mob and its henchmen **Wint** and **Kidd**. The mob's leader, **Seraffimo Spang,** is killed in a train crash, whereupon Bond follows his brother **Jack Spang** to Sierra Leone to finish the job.
From Russia with Love (1957)	Bond is targeted by SMERSH for elimination on the Orient Express. Lured to Istanbul by the beautiful **Tatiana Romanova** in a trap laid by **Colonel Rosa Klebb,** Bond travels ostensibly to acquire a Spektor decoding device. On the train, he encounters Russian operative **Red Grant** and a fight to the death ensues. Klebb later tries to kill Bond and almost succeeds.

Novel	Basic Plot
Dr No (1958)	Bond is dispatched to Jamaica to investigate the disappearance of MI6 operative Commander John Strangways and his secretary. Bond discovers Strangways had been investigating **Dr Julius No,** a Chinese-German who lives in Crab Key and runs a guano mine. With the aid of his old friend **Quarrel** and a local woman named **Honeychile Ryder**, Bond visits Crab Key and stops Dr No sabotaging American missile tests at Cape Canaveral.
Goldfinger (1959)	Bond is sent to Miami to investigate how **Auric Goldfinger** is managing to cheat at canasta. It transpires that Goldfinger is smuggling gold to finance the western activities of SMERSH. Captured by Goldfinger, Bond uncovers 'Operation Grand Slam' in which the villain plans to steal the United States' gold reserves from Fort Knox. Bond naturally foils the plot, assisted by Felix Leiter and **Pussy Galore** (who defects from Goldfinger's gang).

Novel	Basic Plot
Thunderball (1961)	Bond travels to the Bahamas to investigate SPECTRE, a non-aligned international terrorist organisation that has hijacked a plane and seized two nuclear bombs, which it threatens to detonate in a major western city if an exorbitant ransom is not paid.[8] Again working with Felix Leiter, Bond meets **Dominetta 'Domino' Vitali**, sister of the doomed plane's pilot and girlfriend of **Emilio Largo**, the SPECTRE operative running the blackmail operation. Largo is tracked using a nuclear submarine and the bombs are recovered. Domino kills Largo in an act of revenge for her brother's death.
The Spy Who Loved Me (1962)	**Vivienne Michel** is working at an American motel (the Dreamy Pines Motor Court) when a couple of thugs turn up to burn it to the ground. They have been hired by the owner, who wants to make a fraudulent insurance claim. On the verge of sexually assaulting Michel, the thugs are interrupted by the chance arrival of James Bond, who saves Michel and kills the thugs.

Novel	Basic Plot
On Her Majesty's Secret Service (1963)	Bond forms a relationship with the reckless **Contessa Teresa 'Tracy' di Vicenzo**. Through her, he learns that **Ernst Stavro Blofeld** (the leader of SPECTRE) is now based in Switzerland with his sidekick **Irma Bunt**. Bond uses a contact at the College of Arms in London to gain access to Blofeld's mountaintop lair and thwarts his plans to unleash biological warfare. Blofeld escapes, however, and kills Tracy just a few hours after she and Bond marry.
You Only Live Twice (1964)	Bond enters a difficult period after the murder of his wife. M gives him one last shot at redemption with a near-impossible mission to Japan aimed at acquiring Soviet radio-transmission recordings. The Japanese agree to offer these in return for Bond's commitment to kill **Dr Guntram Shatterhand**, a recluse who operates the 'Castle of Death'. Following training in the arts of the ninja warriors, Bond arrives at the castle only to discover that Shatterhand and his wife are in fact **Blofeld** and **Bunt**. He kills Blofeld but acquires a head injury as the castle is destroyed. He ends up lost in Russia.

Novel	Basic Plot
The Man with the Golden Gun (1965)	Bond returns to London brainwashed by the Russians into killing M. The assassination fails and Bond (after 'de-programming') is given a new assignment to kill the Cuban assassin **Francisco 'Pistols' Scaramanga**. Based in Jamaica, Scaramanga is believed to be the killer of several British agents. Bond uncovers a KGB plot to destabilise the region and foils it by killing a number of gangsters, including Scaramanga himself.

One of the reasons it is difficult to determine whether or not Bond is a psychopath is that there are so many different incarnations of him. Even if we confine ourselves to the better-known of these, we are left with Fleming's original literary character in the novels outlined above, the variations in the novels of Markham, Faulks, Boyd and Horowitz, and the very visible on-screen portrayals in twenty-four Eon Productions films by six different actors. The first and, in my opinion, best of these was Sean Connery, who established the role for cinema and succeeded in combining the ruthlessness of Fleming's literary character with the casual charm required for the silver screen. He starred in six 'official' films, namely *Dr No* (1962), *From Russia with Love* (1963), *Goldfinger* (1964), *Thunderball* (1965), *You Only Live Twice* (1967) and *Diamonds Are Forever*

(1971). In 1983, he reprised the role in an 'unofficial' remake of *Thunderball* entitled *Never Say Never Again*.

The Australian model-turned-actor George Lazenby starred in *On Her Majesty's Secret Service* (1969). As he played Bond only once and therefore had no real opportunity to define his version of the character, his rather stilted performance could be forgiven. Next was Roger Moore, who made seven Bond films over a twelve-year period. His portrayal departed considerably from both Connery's archetype and Fleming's literary character. Moore's 007 oozed charm and humour and was even rather camp at times, but lacked the sense of isolation, fear and ruthlessness one might expect from a Cold War spy. Still, after Lazenby, the producers were clearly keen to re-establish a charismatic actor in the role and with Moore they succeeded. It took *Live and Let Die* (1973) and *The Man with the Golden Gun* (1974) for him to settle into the role, but *The Spy Who Loved Me* (1977), *Moonraker* (1979), *For Your Eyes Only* (1981) and *Octopussy* (1983) were all strong performances. Alas, by the time he made the lacklustre *A View to a Kill* (1985) at the ripe old age of fifty-seven, he was clearly too over the hill to play Bond.

Timothy Dalton marked a return to the tougher, grittier and more serious Bond depicted in the novels. However, in an interview with the BBC in 1987, Dalton observed that Fleming's creation is 'a man who often is extremely vulnerable; I mean passage after passage after passage throughout the books are where you see signs [he is] taut and wrenching with nerves, where you know he'd have to have a drink or a pill just to stay calm in order to do the job he had to do'.[9] Perhaps so (although I am not convinced), but Dalton's portrayal of Bond is less charming and, in many ways, less easy to watch from the cinema-goer's perspective. Still, Dalton is a classically trained actor, who was probably the most faithful of all the Bond actors to Fleming's original concept. Moreover, Dalton was nearly twenty years younger than Moore, and so allowed for more believable action in *The Living Daylights* (1987) and *Licence to Kill* (1989), even if the latter is arguably rather too violent in parts.

Following a six-year Bond hiatus, Pierce Brosnan took up the role in *Goldeneye* (1995). His portrayal was similar to Moore's, in that it was charming and humorous, but with less grit and ruthlessness evident. Moreover, *Tomorrow Never Dies* (1997), *The World Is Not Enough* (1999) and *Die Another Day* (2002) allowed for little development of the character. As with Moore's portrayal, Brosnan's Bond could be accused of lacking depth.

Then, in 2006, the genre was re-launched with Daniel Craig cast in the leading role of *Casino Royale*. The pendulum had swung once again, such that Craig's Bond was based closely on Fleming's original character, but with an earnest acknowledgement of modern themes and norms. With a nod to the Jason Bourne films, Bond became a plausible action man once again, while also transcending technology to retain the sense of sheer isolation depicted in the novels.

Being a good spy in real life may or may not be compatible

with psychopathy. But who is to say that, if Bond were real, he wouldn't enjoy a fruitful career in the world of espionage? And might psychopathy be one of the reasons for his success? Beginning with the interpersonal traits of the *Psychopathy Checklist*, we arrive first at *glibness and superficial charm*. This is an easy one, regardless of which on-screen Bond we base our opinion on. Virtually every film is replete with glib one-liners. In *Goldfinger*, Bond electrocutes a would-be assassin by pushing him into a bath full of water and then tossing an electric fan in to finish the job. In Connery's Scottish brogue, he then casually remarks that the scene is 'shocking, positively shocking'. In *Diamonds Are Forever*, Bond girl Plenty O'Toole introduces herself at a Las Vegas casino and Bond enquires if she was, 'Named after your father, perhaps?' Bond is less glib in the literary format (with the possible exception of the novel *You Only Live Twice*, which was written after the premiere of *Dr No*), but his charm pervades book and film alike. And, without a doubt, this charm is superficial.

So, what about a *grandiose sense of self-worth*? Bond certainly has a big ego. He is confident with clever, beautiful women. He believes he deserves the finer things in life such as well-tailored suits, Bollinger champagne and Beluga caviar, hand-rolled cigarettes, high-stakes gambling and first-class foreign travel. There is an air of aristocracy in his depiction, although we learn very little about his background until his obituary in the penultimate novel *You Only Live Twice*. On the other hand, he earns a modest salary doing a difficult and dangerous job largely for Queen and country. He seeks no fame or recognition, and knows he will probably die alone and without any gratitude for his sacrifices. Given the self-destructiveness inherent in his hedonistic lifestyle, it might be more accurate to say his pattern of existence reflects chronic self-loathing rather than grandiosity, notwithstanding the smugness evident in most of the cinematic portrayals. But this is not necessarily inconsistent with psychopathy.

In terms of *pathological lying*, lest we forget, Bond is in the business of espionage. His entire currency is information (and misinformation) in the context of the Cold War. In this regard, the line between truth and myth is ethically blurred and it is doubtful that Bond really cares about anything other than the mission. He is a 'blunt instrument' (as M refers to him in the film *Casino Royale*), albeit one who is bound to the Official Secrets Act. As such, Bond lies constantly, often to innocent people who do not even suspect they are being manipulated. He is brilliant at impression management and supremely persuasive. In some cases, those who naïvely believe his untruths pay the ultimate price. But is this lying pathological? Importantly, it is often done in a professional capacity and less frequently on a whim or for personal gain. Equally, his talent at manipulation is mostly exercised on behalf of Her Majesty's Secret Service. As such, *manipulation for personal gain* is not something he could be accused of – at least not to a greater degree than anyone else.

Score for interpersonal traits = 4/8

Turning our attention to the affective traits, and specifically *shallow affect*, Bond shows limited evidence of any emotional depth in either the novels or the films. In the former, his trivial musings are usually about food, casual sexual encounters or what brand of car he should buy next. He rarely deals in emotions, or even acknowledges them. But he is a good study who knows what emotions should look like. Like the amateur psychologist that many psychopaths are, he reads people and senses their 'tell' with an eye to manipulation. In the film version of *Casino Royale*, he explains to Vesper Lynd that, 'in poker, you never play your hand; you play the man in front of you'. Elsewhere (at dinner on a train in Montenegro, en route to the casino), he sums up Vesper exceptionally well almost at first glance:

> *Well, your beauty's a problem. You worry you won't be taken seriously … this one overcompensates by wearing slightly masculine clothing, being more aggressive than her female colleagues which gives her a somewhat prickly demeanour and, ironically enough, makes it less likely for her to be accepted and promoted by her male superiors who mistake her insecurities for arrogance. Now, I'd have normally gone with only child but, you see, by the way you ignored the quip about your parents, I'm gonna have to go with orphan.*[10]

Bond appears to fall in love with Vesper in *Casino Royale*, yet the fact of her demise draws no more sympathy from him than the remark, 'The bitch is dead.' Equally, our anti-hero marries

Contessa Teresa 'Tracy' di Vicenzo during *On Her Majesty's Secret Service*. Tracy is murdered hours later by Blofeld, but perhaps our main response is to wonder how long in any case their marriage would have lasted; how long it would have taken her to realise that Bond is a vessel of pure emptiness?

So, what about *callousness and lack of empathy*? Bond has plenty of the 'cold' empathy we alluded to in earlier chapters, but what about the so-called 'hot' empathy? He appears unmoved by others' bereavement; in *Spectre*, when the recently widowed Lucia Sciarra asks Bond, 'Can't you tell I'm grieving?' he simply replies, 'No.' Bond barely mentions that it is he who killed her husband, but then his actions often lead directly to the deaths of many people, not all of whom are villains. Bond girls are shot, mauled by animals, fatally gilded or drowned in oil, while mere bystanders are at equal risk of premature demise during action sequences. Our anti-hero loses little sleep over their fates. According to Vesper Lynd in *Casino Royale*, he sees women as 'disposable pleasures, rather than meaningful pursuits' and she is mostly correct in her assertion. Bond doesn't really care what happens to his girls once he has gone to bed with them. He doesn't really care about other people at all.

Bond's hardness of demeanour is alluded to in his physical appearance. In the novel *Moonraker*, Gala Brand remarks that he is:

> ... *certainly good-looking* ... *Rather like Hoagy Carmichael in a way. That black hair falling down over the right*

*eyebrow. Much the same bones. But there was something a
bit cruel in the mouth, and the eyes were cold.*[11]

The concept of the psychopathic stare is nothing new; psychopaths, indeed, tend to blink a little less than the rest of us – likely a marker of lower baseline anxiety. The coldness in Bond's eyes is a reflection of his character throughout the Ian Fleming novels, but there is an occasional compromise in subsequent offerings. For example, Anthony Horowitz briefly touches on the ethics of killing in *Trigger Mortis* when a slightly more sympathetic Bond questions the need to kill a young henchman who appeals to his better nature. A hint of empathy becomes evident here, but this is a rare occurrence. For the most part, Bond cares little for those whose deaths he has caused. He *lacks any sense of remorse or guilt* and feels utterly justified in his actions on behalf of Queen and country. In this sense, he *fails to take responsibility for his own actions*. He is simply following orders, a justification that no doubt helps him sleep at night.

Score for affective traits = 8/8

Bond's lifestyle traits begin with his being *parasitic*. He is certainly very wasteful. It is a running joke in the films that Q routinely admonishes him to 'please return all the equipment in one piece'. Instead, Bond inevitably destroys the expensive car, plane, watch or pen entrusted to him without any regard for the expense incurred. Moreover, despite earning what is presumably a meagre government salary, he acquires expensive champagne, cigarettes, jewellery and tailored suits. We can only presume that these items are funded by the spoils of gambling or the misplaced goodwill of others. Some of what he consumes is not paid for at all. Either way, Bond certainly likes his creature comforts and never settles for anything but the best, regardless of need.

Bond has an unquenchable *need for excitement*. His daily job involves combat with henchmen, hanging off tall buildings, jumping out of planes without a parachute and breaking into enemy lairs, risking capture and torture. He needs the adrenaline rush. And when not incurring the dangers inherent in a mission, he likes to drink heavily and take pills, gamble for high stakes, drive fast cars (often recklessly) and sleep with beautiful women, many of whom are married to powerful crime lords. Whenever we see him engaged in the humdrum of ordinary existence (usually at the beginning of any given novel), he seems thoroughly bored. Ordinary life is not enough to stimulate Bond.

Some of this risk taking requires *impulsivity*. Psychopaths do not typically spend time weighing up the pros and cons of their actions. Instead, they act first and think later – or sometimes not at all. In several of the films (for example, *Licence to Kill*, *Quantum of Solace* and *Spectre*) he 'goes rogue' on some personal vendetta. Although we like to think Bond's impulses are guided by well-honed instinct, he frequently causes millions of dollars of damage and endangers countless lives. In truth, he is often *irresponsible.* Any successes rely on luck as much as anything else and, in real life, an impulsive spy is a reckless one of little use to anyone for reasons already outlined. But on the silver screen an action hero who is not impulsive or irresponsible is unlikely to be entertaining, so these are necessary traits for him to carry the film. Still, this doesn't make him any less psychopathic.

Does Bond *lack realistic long-term goals*? Admittedly, he makes no reference to any grandiose or unrealistic ambitions. He knows he may not live long enough to achieve them. In the film *Casino Royale*, Bond remarks to M that, 'I understand double-0s have a very short life expectancy so your mistake will be short-lived'; with this acknowledged brevity in his choice of career, it would be understandable if he did not over-invest in his pension. Instead, like most psychopaths, he lives for the moment, spending or gambling what money he has rather than saving it, preferring casual sexual liaisons to mature relationships. His short-term goals are usually clearly evident, but long-term ones are in short supply, realistic or otherwise.

And speaking of relationships, Bond displays ample evidence of *promiscuous sexual behaviour*. Women are 'disposable pleasures rather than meaningful pursuits', as Vesper Lynd remarks. Recall his expulsion from Eton over 'some alleged trouble with one of the boys' maids'. To be fair, the original Fleming novels suggest that he engages in a new relationship roughly once per year. This might reasonably make him a seasoned bachelor rather than a womaniser. His sex life is far more casual in the films, with two or three Bond girls per outing the norm. He was at his most promiscuous in *On Her Majesty's Secret Service*, perhaps as a nod to the 'free love' movement of the late 1960s. This improved a little in the 1980s, with Timothy Dalton's more conservative Bond likely reflecting public concern about the spread of HIV. Either way, Bond has *many short-term relationships*, although he gets married only once.

Score for lifestyle traits = 13/14

Bond is not antisocial, however. To assert *poor behavioural controls* in him is a step too far. He may act impulsively but he never does so pointlessly. Similarly, there is little in any of the plots to suggest *early behavioural problems*. Until the publication of *You Only Live Twice* in 1964, we knew little about Bond's background at all. The novels and films give us no evidence of any *juvenile delinquency*, although we cannot confirm that it is not the case. More specifically, revocation of conditional release does not apply, as Bond has never been to prison (unless we count capture by the enemy). Finally, *criminal versatility* is not applicable either, as Bond has a licence to kill. His acts may be immoral but they are not illegal and therefore criminal versatility is difficult to determine.

Score for antisocial traits = 0/6 (two items not applicable)

James Bond's total score of 25 out of 36 suggests he is a fictional psychopath. He scores well in terms of affective and lifestyle traits but not interpersonal or antisocial traits. He does not neatly fit into any subtype, although he perhaps leans more towards *macho* psychopathy. Either way, he is one of the best-loved literary and cinematic characters on earth. So, can these two ideas be compatible? Secrecy is partly the key. As happens with many fictional psychopaths, we are fascinated by Bond's singular ability to hide his psychopathy from his fellow characters until it is too late. Equally, we admire his calm courage under fire.

So, how does vulnerability fit into this? Recall Timothy Dalton's remark to the BBC that Fleming's creation must constantly self-medicate with alcohol, pills, gambling and promiscuous sex in order to cope with the inherent stress of espionage. Again, this point is debatable, but Bond does show his vulnerable side from time to time, giving us the impression of an underdog who must be cheered on. At the end of the novel *From Russia with Love*, for example, Rosa Klebb stabs him with a poisoned dart, almost killing him and ensuring the need for months of convalescence. In the novel *You Only Live Twice*, a head injury leads to amnesia and several months spent as a fisherman in remotest Japan before the Russians capture and brainwash him. Yes, the essential premise is that Bond is a resourceful, persuasive and ruthless character who usually wins. Perhaps some vulnerability humanises him, like Superman with his kryptonite.

Although the films and especially the novels are seen from Bond's viewpoint, he is never the narrator. This serves to stir within us some sympathy for his cause, while still allowing us to reserve judgement if we choose. But he falls short of taking us into his confidence. Much of what we know about him amounts to his *modus operandi* on missions, some daily habits and lists of preferences. Think of his trademark vodka martini 'shaken not stirred', his Bentley (in the novels) or Aston Martin (in the films), scrambled eggs and bacon for breakfast, and the habit of setting his morning shower first as hot and then as cold as he can tolerate. Beyond this, he can be quite elusive both to readers and other characters. Indeed, there are parts of the early novels in which it is unclear whether Fleming himself understands Bond fully. Perhaps it is the spy's armour that fascinates us, but it doesn't necessarily win us over.

However, Bond has many redeeming features. Superficial as he is, his charm is nonetheless seductive. He is ready with a quip in the face of danger, while his image is that of a stoic gentleman, chivalrous (albeit misogynistic), well-spoken, well-educated and well-connected. Equally, he is never boring. His constant need for stimulation provides excitement for the reader and viewer alike. Of course, the irony is that when Fleming wrote *Casino Royale*, he wanted the story rather than the character to be the centrepiece. He remarked in *The New Yorker* (April 1962) that, 'When I wrote the first one, in 1953, I wanted Bond to be an extremely dull, uninteresting man to whom things happened; I wanted him to be the blunt instrument ... when I was casting about for a name for my protagonist I thought, My God, that's the dullest name I've ever heard.'[12] Alas, Fleming clearly failed in that regard.

Portrayed as handsome in a cruel sort of way, Bond also has many admirable talents and skills. While these are modest enough in the early books, every instalment seems to introduce something new in his repertoire. In the film of *You Only Live Twice*, we learn that he took a First in oriental languages at Cambridge (although his background is cited differently in the book). He is a naval commander, a competent deep-sea diver, a daring parachutist, an accurate marksman, a lethal combat fighter, a whizz at high-speed car chases, a better golfer than Goldfinger, a smooth skier, an even smoother dancer, and a better poker player than almost anyone. M constantly mutters his irritation at yet another subject on which Bond proffers expertise, from lepidopterology (study of moths and butterflies) to distilling sherry. Perhaps we ought to be equally irritated (it is probably just impression management, after all), yet we like him all the more for it.

James Bond even has his own long-running cliché, namely that, 'Women want to be *with* him and men want to *be* him.' While the latter may be far more common than the former, the spy certainly appeals to a part of his audience that longs to be bad. True to the lyrics of the title track 'You Only Live Twice', composed by John Barry and Leslie Bricusse and sung by Nancy Sinatra, you have 'one life for yourself and one for your dreams'. What teenage boy destined to become an accountant or supermarket manager doesn't yearn to be plucked from obscurity to the even greater obscurity of MI6?

Do Bond's victims make him look good? Somehow our

attention is skilfully steered from the Bond girls and innocent bystanders to focus on the megalomaniacs bent on world destruction. Often, they are physically unattractive, many with some sort of disfigurement – missing limbs (Dr No), weeping tear ducts (Le Chiffre), facial scarring (Alec Trevelyan) and third nipples (Francisco Scaramanga). All are psychopaths in their own right, with no redeeming features, and it is easy to forgive Bond for his own shortcomings as he rids the world of far worse offenders. Equally, in the original Fleming novels, the follow-up books by Markham, Faulks, Boyd and Horowitz, and most of the early films, the setting is the Cold War. One expects a level of ruthlessness during times of war and we accept that the end sometimes justifies the means, especially if it ensures we can all sleep safer in our beds. Bond builds up quite the body count during his missions, but those who die might reasonably be deemed casualties of war and not casualties of the spy himself. As such, the backdrop adds to his appeal.

So, as we can see, Ian Fleming created a fictional psychopath who is likeable nonetheless. Although only vulnerable to a degree and disinclined to take us into his confidence, his courage, charm, looks, talent and skills win us over. He appeals to the 'baddie' within us all, while his victims and the backdrop both make him look good. He has been a popular icon for over half a century, revived every couple of years with great success. Fleming's masterpiece is a cultural genre in its own right, showcasing perhaps the ultimate fictional anti-hero – the psychopath we cannot help but admire.

5

THE POLITICAL PSYCHOPATH

*'All members of a Cabinet are referred to as Right Hon-
ourable Gentlemen. There are only three things wrong
with such a title ...'*

– Francis Urquhart[1]

It is hard to conceive of a more dangerous psychopath than
one with absolute power. The obvious case in point is Frank
Underwood, played by Kevin Spacey in the Netflix television
series *House of Cards*. Underwood is a senior Democratic politician who hails from South Carolina and at the outset has
already spent half a lifetime successfully convincing voters that
he is a committed, competent and honest leader with their best
interests at heart. But we sense that many colleagues within
the party do not agree. Underwood's superficially charming
Southern drawl barely masks a ruthless Machiavellianism that
ultimately allows him to snake his way up the greasy political
pole to the highest office in the land. Underwood lies, cheats,
exploits and steals with alacrity. Those who cross his path
usually live to regret it. Occasionally, they do not live at all.

Spacey garnered much praise for his portrayal of Underwood, and was nominated five times for the Primetime Emmy Award for Outstanding Lead Actor in a Drama Series, along with Golden Globe and Screen Actors Guild Awards. But Underwood is not as new a character as some might assume. He was conceived as the Right Honourable Francis Ewan Urquhart MP, CBE, by the British novelist Michael Dobbs in the late 1980s. The original novel was also entitled *House of Cards*, and its subsequent BBC television adaptation attracted much critical acclaim. It starred Ian Richardson (who won a BAFTA for his portrayal of Urquhart) and presented a similar *dramatis personae* as the later American version. The British and American plots are virtually identical in their respective first series, with both featuring a scorned protagonist bent on revenge. When we first meet Urquhart, he is the government chief whip and a hard-right-wing politician with designs on the top job. Like Underwood, he is an exceptionally smooth operator. A master at impression management, when questioned directly on a sensitive issue by a member of the opposition or the press, he invariably replies, 'You might think that but I couldn't possibly comment', allowing for plausible deniability while communicating exactly what he wants to say.[2]

Urquhart was born in 1936. As the youngest son of the Earl of Bruichladdich, he hails from old money and has the attitude to go with it.[3] He says himself that 'The Urquharts were a proud warrior family from the Highlands of Scotland.'[4] His older brother William is the current Earl who runs the family estate and sits ('occasionally') in the House of Lords. His eldest brother

Alistair died in the Second World War, sowing the seeds of a difficult childhood. Indeed, Urquhart's 'mother had crumbled, never recovered, lived in memory of her lost son and neglect of Francis ...'[5] Our anti-hero was not academically brilliant, notwithstanding his Fettes education, but was noted at school for his diligence and single-mindedness. He subsequently took a commission in the British Army (national service still existed at the time) and spent three years in Cyprus, whereupon he was commended for his bravery in the line of duty (although we later learn that he murdered two insurgents and set fire to their bodies). After resigning his commission, he enrolled in Oxford University, where he later embarked upon an academic career teaching Italian Renaissance history. He retains an enthusiasm for poetry and Shakespeare, especially *Macbeth*, but other than game-shooting he never developed any real interests outside politics. He eventually left academia altogether in favour of the Conservative Party and his real *raison d'être* – power.

Urquhart is first presented to us in the political vacuum that exists in the aftermath of Margaret Thatcher. The Conservative Party has just won a general election, albeit with a slimmer majority than before, while the prime minister, the Right Honourable Henry Collingridge MP, is viewed as weak and politically indecisive. Seeking to take advantage of the inevitable cabinet reshuffle, Urquhart forwards the prime minister a proposal for a new cabinet with a marked swing to the right. Unsurprisingly, the proposal includes a prominent ministerial position for Urquhart himself. Alas, the politically moderate Collingridge is not impressed and passes Urquhart over entirely, consoling him with the observation that he is far too valuable keeping the backbenchers in line as chief whip.

Enraged, Urquhart decides to retaliate. First, he sees to it that the prime minister is embarrassed in front of the press by a series of carefully planned political blunders. To seal the deal, Urquhart then orchestrates a fake insider-trading scam in the name of the prime minister's alcoholic brother, Charles. As Charles is so chaotic that he cannot recall whether or not he actually bought the shares in question, it appears as though the prime minister supplied confidential information to his brother in an effort to get rich. Urquhart leaks the story to the press and, in doing so, befriends Mattie Storin, an enthusiastic young reporter for the tabloid newspaper *The Daily Chronicle*. The two soon develop an Oedipal-style (or technically speaking, given their respective genders, an 'Electra-style') sexual relationship in which Mattie refers to Urquhart as 'Daddy'. The affair is a calculated one, conducted entirely with the knowledge and consent of Urquhart's wife, Elizabeth (the equally psychopathic daughter of a whiskey magnate).[6]

With the prime minister disgraced into resignation, Urquhart then sets about eliminating his own political rivals one by one. He choreographs a clash between the health secretary Peter McKenzie and a demonstration rally at what was meant to be a routine photo opportunity. To make matters worse, McKenzie accidentally causes his chauffeur to knock down someone with a disability. Next, Urquhart acquires photographs of the education secretary, Harold Earle, with his arms around a rent boy and threatens to leak the photographs to the press. Urquhart further arranges for the press to allege that the environment secretary, Michael Samuels, harboured far-left-wing political leanings as a student. Finally, he blackmails the foreign secretary, Patrick Woolton, with a tape recording of a one-night stand that Urquhart had the audacity to arrange for him in the first place. The fruits of the chief whip's labour are that he now finds himself on the brink of becoming prime minister.

But some loose ends remain. Not least of these is Roger O'Neill, the party's public relations consultant whom Urquhart blackmailed into helping him to bring about Collingridge's downfall. O'Neill's cocaine addiction leads to worsening psychological instability that Urquhart recognises as a threat. To ameliorate this, he invites O'Neill to his country house near Southampton, plies him with alcohol, mixes rat poison into his stash of cocaine and then sends him on his merry way. O'Neill, finding it hard to remain awake behind the wheel, pulls over at a service station and snorts his final, fatal dose. The authorities do not know what to make of the death, but Mattie puts two and two together with fatal consequences for herself. She makes the mistake of confronting Urquhart in the deserted roof garden of the Houses of Parliament and the soon-to-be prime minister responds by pushing her off the roof to her death. Urquhart, of course, claims it was suicide.

Indeed, so absurd is the idea that the new prime minister

might be a cold-blooded murderer, that nobody questions whether Urquhart might in fact be lying. But what Urquhart doesn't know is that Mattie took the precaution of recording their conversations and, worse still, someone has found the recording of her murder. This twist provides much of the dramatic tension in the two subsequent novels and their respective television adaptations, *To Play the King* and *The Final Cut*.

In the former, Urquhart has been prime minister for some years and is now in his second term of office. But he is growing bored and seeks a new challenge, one that presently emerges in the guise of a new king, one with an inconveniently strong sense of social justice and the tendency to make impromptu speeches on this topic to the public. Sensing a threat to his own absolute power, Urquhart discredits the king, first by leaking scandalous secrets regarding the royal family, and second by renewing his own mandate in a general election. As the king now finds himself colluding with the opposition, a constitutional crisis emerges that ultimately calls for his abdication.

But Urquhart's celebration of victory does not last long. He has underestimated his protégé, the party chief whip Tim Stamper MP. Embittered by Urquhart's failure to recognise and reward his loyalty, Stamper (who, it transpires, is the possessor of Mattie Storin's tape) attempts first to blackmail and then to discredit the prime minister. Urquhart's retaliation is characteristically ruthless; he has Stamper killed in a car bomb that is made to look like an IRA terrorist attack. Also killed in the explosion is Sarah Harding, Urquhart's young political advisor, whose relationship with the prime minister is remarkably like that of Mattie Storin. It seems Urquhart likes to stick to a winning formula.

The third instalment is *The Final Cut*, which revisits the wayward prime minister in the final months of his eleven-year term of office. On this occasion, Urquhart attempts to secure his legacy by brokering a peace deal in Cyprus that secretly involves amassing a personal fortune in the form of exploitation rights for offshore oil. Alas, his past is catching up with him, not least as a determined Cypriot woman pursues him for proof that he murdered her two uncles (the two insurgents referred to earlier) while he was a young army officer posted in Cyprus. To divert attention from this (and desperate to outdo Margaret Thatcher, to whom he refers as 'that bloody woman'), Urquhart orders military action in Cyprus. But 'our Falklands War', as he calls it, goes badly wrong when three schoolgirls are killed by British Army officers at a road block demonstration. Urquhart's hard-line insistence on 'the rule of law' does not prevent him from losing party support. Finally – on the verge of arrest for murder – he is himself assassinated, thus preserving his legacy. He is honoured in a state funeral.

Michael Dobbs was in a unique position to conceive of Francis Urquhart, being closely involved with the Conservative Party in the 1970s, 1980s and 1990s. Indeed, he created Urquhart after a particularly nasty argument with the Iron Lady herself.[7] Dobbs was born on 14 November 1948 (the same date as Prince Charles, as it happens) in Hertfordshire. He was educated at Cheshunt Grammar School and Christ Church College, Oxford, where he graduated in 1971. He then moved to the USA to attend the Fletcher School of Law and Diplomacy at Tufts University, Massachusetts, where he graduated in 1977 with an array of higher degrees that included a doctorate. During his period at the Fletcher School, he worked as an editorial assistant and political feature writer for *The Boston Globe*.

In 1977, Dobbs returned to London to work with the Conservative Party. He was an advisor to Margaret Thatcher from 1977 to 1979 (before she became prime minister), a party speechwriter from 1979 to 1981, a government special advisor from 1981 to 1986, and party chief of staff from 1986 to 1987. In the mid-1990s, he was deputy chairman under John Major. Throughout all of this, he wrote prolifically. He was a columnist with *The Mail on Sunday* from 1991 to 1998 and hosted *Despatch Box* (a BBC Two current affairs programme) from 1998 to 2001. *House of Cards* (1989) was his debut novel, followed shortly after by *To Play the King* (1992) and *The Final Cut* (1994). He also penned numerous other novels, including a series about Winston Churchill (2002–05). With a life peerage in 2010, he became Baron Dobbs of Wylye, Wiltshire.

Francis Urquhart endures as Dobbs' masterpiece, but is he a true fictional psychopath? To determine this definitively, we need to refer once again to the *Psychopathy Checklist*.

Beginning with the interpersonal traits, Urquhart's

superficial charm is evident throughout the plot. He ingratiates himself with everyone around him, from his cabinet colleagues to the prime minister and his brother Charles, to the media (especially Mattie) and the public at large, who see him as the humble and grateful recipient of their support. He is brilliant at impression management and his charm is part of the reason for this. In the age of media, how else could a man like Urquhart make it to the top? Notwithstanding his outward displays of humility, however, he clearly possesses a *grandiose sense of self-worth*. Hailing from aristocratic beginnings, he sees the prime ministerial position as his birthright and is consumed with jealousy of Margaret Thatcher for her longevity in the position. Anyone else who threatens to keep him from the top job is dealt with harshly.

So, what about *pathological lying*? In Episode Two of the first series, as Urquhart sets Woolton up with his fateful one-night stand, he remarks to his cabinet colleague that, 'I think you know I prefer plain speaking and plain dealing, Patrick, as do you ...'[8] The sheer audacity of this remark! It is so blatantly untrue, as evident in virtually all of Urquhart's actions. He lies constantly, sometimes pathologically, in that it isn't always overtly necessary for him to lie. Perhaps he does it as a precaution or simply out of habit. Either way, he engages in frequent *manipulation for personal gain*, most notably when it comes to his political ambitions.

Score for interpersonal traits = 8/8

Turning to the affective traits, does Urquhart have a *shallow affect*? Certainly, he is prone to short-lived, dramatic displays of feeling. The original novel makes occasional reference to anxiety; for example, at the outset, when (in a rare display of clumsiness) he attempts to persuade Collingridge to reshuffle the cabinet: 'Urquhart's face refused to betray the turmoil that was growing within. He had been too anxious about the reshuffle and cursed himself for his folly.'[9] But Urquhart is mostly fearless, his feelings confined essentially to jealousy or rage. Beyond this, he appears to have little depth; it is doubtful he could label most of his emotions were he asked to do so by some fictional psychotherapist. Mostly, he greets those around him (including the viewer) with a demeanour of cheerful smugness. Indeed, it is remarkable (and perhaps more than a little implausible) that an intelligent woman like Mattie cannot see through Urquhart's wafer-thin façade much sooner as he patronises her into believing every word he utters. Like many psychopaths, his ability to mimic the emotion he sees in others results in his being credited with feelings he does not truly possess. Even his relationship with his wife seems superficial.

In a similar manner, Urquhart displays an obvious *lack of empathy*. He is devoid of 'hot' empathy anyway. In line with his emotional shallowness, he is utterly incapable of putting himself in anyone else's shoes from an emotional perspective. For example, in *The Final Cut*, when his orders result in British troops gunning down three innocent schoolgirls in Cyprus, Urquhart stands alone in parliament justifying his actions with some rhetoric about the 'rule of law'. The obvious loss suffered by the families of these three children does not seem to cross his mind even for a moment. Urquhart *rarely takes responsibility for his own actions*; instead he holds others to account for the disasters he calculatedly thrusts upon them. Most notably, having just ruined Collingridge's political career, Urquhart nonchalantly explains his actions to the viewer thus:

Not feeling guilty, I hope? If you have pangs of pity, crush them now. Grind them under your heel like old cigar butts. I've done the country a favour. He didn't have the brain or the heart or the stomach to run a country like Great Britain. A nice enough man but there was no bottom to him. His deepest need was that people should like him. An admirable trait, that, in a spaniel or a whore; not, I think, in a prime minister. Mmm? And we've done him a favour too, if he did but know it. He was in the trap and screaming from the moment he took office; we simply put the poor bastard out of his agony. After life's fitful fever, he sleeps well. So, let's not indulge ourselves in any squeamishness. All right? Because this is just the start.[10]

But Urquhart's *lack of remorse or guilt* is not absolute; there are one or two exceptions. Throughout *To Play the King*, he is haunted by flashbacks of Mattie falling to her death. The fact that she shrieks 'Daddy!' as she plummets makes his betrayal all the harder for him to stomach. Equally, Urquhart seems to show some remorse in *The Final Cut* as he remembers the two young men he murdered in Cyprus. But these are rare examples; virtually every other dirty deed that Urquhart does is entirely without feelings of guilt. He murders Roger O'Neill without a second thought, while his own path to power is littered with the shattered careers of colleagues whom he once duped into considering him a friend. Through all this, Urquhart is not one bit bothered.

Score for affective traits = 7/8

So, what about lifestyle traits? Urquhart is hardworking enough, but his success is hardly based on honest toil. Instead, he was born into old money, sent to public school, commissioned to the army and then further educated at Oxford University. His subsequent political success is built entirely on the demise of others. Like a plague of ravenous insects, he descends, devours and then departs. As such, there is certainly a *parasitic* element to his lifestyle, although it is not absolute. Meanwhile, he is good at weighing up the pros and cons of his actions. Like a chess player, brilliant at manipulation, he thinks a few steps ahead at all times. In this regard, he is not especially *impulsive*, although the incident in which he pushes Mattie off a roof is an exception. Otherwise, he covers his tracks with precision. Similarly, Urquhart's *long-term goals are realistic*. He knows his strengths and weaknesses and plays to the former. Ultimately, he achieves his goal of becoming prime minister, which vindicates him as realistic in his ambitions.

But Urquhart displays a clear *need for excitement*. At the outset of *To Play the King*, having been prime minister for several years, he confesses to his wife that he feels a sense of anti-climax. Elizabeth agrees that he needs a new challenge and of course she is correct. Conveniently, an idealistic and naïve new king provides easy prey for the cannibalistic prime minister. In engaging in such a joust, jeopardising the British monarchy itself for his own amusement, Urquhart shows that he is *irresponsible*. Note also his attempts in *The Final Cut* to turn a peace deal in Cyprus into 'our Falkland's War', as he and his wife refer to it. So, even if we discount his more obvious crimes (such as murder), Urquhart is irresponsible without a shadow of a doubt.

Although Urquhart is married only once, he engages in *many short-term relationships*, not least with young admirers that include the reporter Mattie Storin and the political advisor Sarah Harding. But these relationships are not motivated by lust. As Frank Underwood remarks elsewhere, 'Everything in the world is about sex, except sex; sex is about power.'[11] His English counterpart certainly sees it this way and, as such, his extramarital relationships should not be prized above his enduring loyalty to his wife. Instead, it would be fairer to say that Urquhart engages in *promiscuous sexual behaviour* albeit with his wife's consent. Indeed, when some young admirer calls to the door and her utility is instantly spotted, Elizabeth announces not so subtly to her husband that she proposes to take a trip down to the country for a few days. Such casual relationships typically have a political goal in mind, although it is clear that Urquhart also enjoys himself.

Score for lifestyle traits = 7/14

Finally, we come to the antisocial traits, beginning with *poor behavioural controls*. Urquhart can lose his temper easily – indeed, the very premise of *House of Cards* is his extreme reaction to a perceived insult from the prime minister. Because our anti-hero is not impulsive, he can wait for his revenge, which, as we know, is a dish best served cold. And such revenge is inevitable because Urquhart simply cannot help himself. However, some attention is paid to his childhood during the course of the novels and there is no real evidence of any *early behavioural problems*. Similarly, his backstory contains no *juvenile delinquency* of note. As with many of our fictional psychopaths, *revocation of conditional release* does not apply as he has never been in prison. But Urquhart shows *criminal versatility* in everything he does. Throughout the stories, he commits fraud, deception, bribery, blackmail and murder with alacrity to further his political aims. His criminal repertoire is a large one. He just never gets caught.

Score for antisocial traits = 4/8 (one item not applicable)

With a total *Psychopathy Checklist* score of 26 out of 38, Francis Urquhart falls firmly into the category of a fictional psychopath. Moreover, despite his penchant for murder, his relatively higher score in the interpersonal and affective domains makes him a *manipulative* psychopath rather than a *classic* or a *macho* one. He is a 'talker' rather than a 'doer', although there are some obvious exceptions. Either way, the question remains as to why we – as readers and viewers – are utterly mesmerised by his every calculating move. Certainly, it's hard not to be fascinated by his ability to hide his psychopathy from fellow characters until it's too late. Equally, we admire his calm courage under fire. But are there any other reasons?

Could it be vulnerability, for example? It is difficult to see this in Urquhart. Yes, he is passed over for promotion in the beginning of the story; indeed, he acknowledges a degree of vulnerability in the lengths to which he goes in order to protect his political career. And yes, on a more personal level, he shows some psychological vulnerability in his flashbacks to the traumatic killings in his past. But, for the most part, Urquhart is quite capable of taking care of himself – often at the expense of others.

Instead, Urquhart wins us over by taking us into his confidence. It is the hallmark of the BBC and Netflix series alike. By 'breaking the Fourth Wall', as it is termed, Urquhart looks us squarely in the eye, smiles mischievously and outlines his nefarious schemes in full. He might proffer a conspiratorial remark such as, 'Someone's in trouble; someone's going to get it in the neck – but not us, eh?'[12] In doing so, he makes us silently complicit. And he enjoys every minute of the attention we give him so willingly. We may not like what he does, but we feel privileged to have earned his trust and perhaps even a little reassured. Surely he would never make victims of *us*, having so obviously befriended us?

In the same manner as many of the characters in the story, we are utterly seduced by Urquhart's charm. His charisma lends itself to public office, while his paper-thin smile is perfect for the shallowness of the media age in which he reigns. His manufactured warmth flicks on and off to order, allowing his friends to bask while his enemies are left out in the cold. Such dexterity with his admittedly limited emotional range is nevertheless a remarkable talent. He is brilliant at impression management, as we have said. But he has many other talents and skills we admire. Urquhart is an intelligent and well-educated man, a decisive leader and an articulate public speaker.

It is partly because of these talents that Urquhart never bores us. He certainly never allows himself to become bored, such is his constant need for excitement. Instead of wasting his time dancing to the dull tune that entertains so many of his political peers, Urquhart writes his own score. And as the plot thickens, we hang on his every word, scrutinise his every misdeed and admire the sheer badness in him. To some degree, Urquhart appeals to a part deep within us all that longs to *be* bad. Not that we condone his worst crimes, but it is only fiction after all. And it is hard not to admire his audacity as he goes straight for the jugular and gets the job done.

As we have seen in previous chapters, another item conferring likeability on a fictional psychopath is that their victims somehow make them look good. Typically, the victim is a worse psychopath than the protagonist, with no moral compass whatsoever. In some cases, the victim might have underestimated the anti-hero and tried to bully them into submission. In others, the victim is depicted as weak, irritating or yet more superficial than the anti-hero. Thus, the fictional psychopath can make themselves look good by killing off characters we really do not like.

Crucially, this involves the psychopath never killing women and children. Indeed, they never kill at all without good reason. Here, Urquhart falls down in terms of likeability. He often kills women and children. Mattie, despite her role as a streetwise ace reporter in search of a scoop, has many childlike qualities. She even refers to Urquhart as 'Daddy', pledging loyalty to him moments before he murders her. Sarah Harding occupies a similar role as Urquhart's political advisor in *To Play the King*, and displays surprising vulnerability in assuming she can trust a man simply because of his high-status position. In his youth, Urquhart murders two Cypriot soldiers in what appears to be a war crime. Later, as prime minister, his direct instructions to the army at a road block demonstration result in the deaths of three innocent schoolgirls. Alas, Urquhart's victims make him look bad.

But there are, of course, exceptions. Roger O'Neill, the brash and cocaine-addicted press secretary of the Conservative Party, is a case in point. Such is the paucity of his own moral compass that he is easily blackmailed into carrying out some of

Urquhart's dirty deeds. Similarly, Tim Stamper – Urquhart's scorned chief whip – has such a track record of unscrupulous behaviour in his own right that he garners little of our sympathy. In the end, he has the temerity to blackmail Urquhart. Strangely, we find ourselves protective of our anti-hero and are glad to see Stamper get his comeuppance. But, for the most part, Urquhart's victims are far more likeable than he.

Finally, does the backdrop make our psychopathic protagonist look good? Unfortunately not, in this case. Although, as a society, we may not be especially fond of politicians, none of Urquhart's colleagues are as psychopathic as he. Equally, neither the political nor the economic contexts call for the behaviour he so fervently displays. His *raison d'être* is power for its own sake and all in the name of his own legacy. In the end, his backdrop offers him no mitigating circumstances whatsoever. Still, when we consider our *Psychopath Likeability Scale* in its totality, Francis Urquhart scores quite highly. Yes, certain factors tarnish his image, but he is vulnerable to a small degree, while his courage, charm, talents and skills ensure that we never find him boring. He takes us into his confidence and appeals to that part within us that longs to be bad. He also appeals to our love of secrecy. We want him to succeed, but can the same be said for his more recent American cousin, Frank Underwood?

***

Underwood is closely based on Urquhart. They even share the same initials. As fans of the Netflix series will know, the outset sees Underwood as the Democratic Party majority whip in the House of Representatives. Like Urquhart, there is initially an element of the underdog about Underwood. He hails from Gaffney, South Carolina and is a graduate of The Sentinel Military College (presumably a fictional version of The Citadel) and thereafter Harvard Law School. His smooth Southern accent drips like treacle off the tongue as he charms us with his wit and powers of observation. Like Urquhart, he breaks the Fourth Wall by confiding directly in the viewer and, like most psychopaths, he is a skilled amateur psychologist. We think we know him well because he is a creature of habit. He smokes cigarettes clandestinely with his wife Claire; he plays violent video games in his basement; his favourite lunch is grilled ribs at a backstreet steakhouse, gorged upon cannibalistically in much the same manner as he devours his political prey.

Underwood's rise to the premier position mirrors that of Urquhart. Both ascensions are achieved with a cunning mix of fraud, deception, bribery, blackmail and murder. Many of the other main characters are also twinned with those in the opposing series. In the Underwood story, Zoe Barnes is a young and ambitious (and perhaps less naïve and less likeable) reporter in lieu of Mattie Storin; Underwood's sidekick, Doug Stamper, is virtually identical to Urquhart's sidekick, Tim Stamper; Claire Underwood – like Elizabeth Urquhart – is a strong spousal conspirator who lends to the story an element of *folie à deux*.[13] The weak presidential predecessors to Underwood and Urquhart are remarkably similar. And there are many other examples.

But are there any key differences? Beau Willimon, the producer of the Netflix series, once remarked that the surname 'Urquhart' was changed principally to displace the Dickensian image it evoked. Underwood, in his view, sounded more all-American. Of course, Urquhart is an aristocrat by birth, as we have seen, while Underwood is a self-made man and the son of an alcoholic who died of a heart attack in his early forties. In one episode, Underwood evokes a vivid childhood memory of walking in on his father to find the barrel of a shotgun in the older man's mouth. Seemingly Underwood Sr asked the young Francis to pull the trigger and the boy refused. With characteristic callousness, Underwood candidly remarks that he could have spared the family several more years of alcohol-fuelled problems had he simply finished the job there and then.

But background is not the only difference between Underwood and Urquhart. The American protagonist's political leanings are far more manoeuvrable than those of the far-right Scottish aristocrat. Although Underwood is a member of the more liberal Democratic Party, his politics are essentially pragmatic. Perhaps another contrast with Urquhart is Underwood's sexual ambiguity. While Urquhart is staunchly traditional and heterosexual to the core, Underwood's backstory alludes to a homosexual relationship at military college. Elsewhere in the story, there is a strongly implied *ménage à trois* between Frank and Claire Underwood and their Secret Service agent.

There are few real differences in their psychopathy, but what about their likeability?

In a sense, Underwood is less likeable than Urquhart; any vulnerability we might see in the latter is virtually absent in the former. While Underwood's political ambitions are sometimes under threat, we never really lose confidence in his ability to deal with them. Unlike Urquhart, he is never bothered by moments of guilt or flashbacks to dirty deeds of old. But he is likeable in other aspects. He takes us into his confidence, breaking the Fourth Wall from the outset, just like his Scottish counterpart. As he drip-feeds his tactics to us, we feel privileged and a little reassured. Even in this, Underwood manipulates the viewer quite easily; as tension builds in the episode in which he murders Zoe Barnes, he waits until the final scene before acknowledging us, as if to highlight that we are little more to him than worthless voyeurs. Similarly, in Series Three, when angered by Claire, he turns his rage on the viewer and demands to know, 'What are you looking at?'

Still, superficial as it is, we are mostly cautiously beguiled by Underwood's charm. Those characters around him are equally seduced by his mellifluous Southern accent until he stings them all one by one. He is certainly never boring, while he is every bit as talented and accomplished as Urquhart. Perhaps even more so than Urquhart, he appeals to that part of us all that longs to be bad. Underwood is indeed worse than Urquhart, yet his victims make him look better. Zoe Barnes is tougher and more streetwise than Mattie Storin. She is a greater threat to our anti-hero's ambitions and, in a sense, really should know better. Most of Underwood's other victims are irritating and small-minded politicians for whom it is difficult to have much sympathy.

Either way, how could we not admire the sheer audacity of both Francis Urquhart and Frank Underwood? Perhaps the former is a little more likeable and the latter a little more psychopathic, but both exemplify the lure of any anti-hero who keeps us coming back for more.

6

THE BORDERLINE PSYCHOPATH

*'I always thought it'd be better to be a fake somebody than
a real nobody.'*

— *Tom Ripley*[1]

Few fictional psychopaths are quite as complex or as appealing
as Tom Ripley. Patricia Highsmith's charming anti-hero first
appeared over sixty years ago in her 1955 crime novel *The
Talented Mr Ripley*. She wrote four further Ripley volumes,
namely *Ripley Under Ground* (1970), *Ripley's Game* (1974),
The Boy Who Followed Ripley (1980) and *Ripley Under Water*
(1991). Together, the five novels are sometimes referred to as
the 'Ripliad', a sort of chronology of one of the most iconic
fictional psychopaths of the twentieth century.

Several noteworthy film adaptations have ensued. The first
was a pre-new-wave French *film noir* piece entitled *Plein Soleil*
(1960), directed by René Clément and starring Alain Delon as
Tom Ripley. Re-titled *Purple Noon* for an American audience,
it was well received and is considered by many to remain the
best adaptation of *The Talented Mr Ripley* to this day. In 1977,
The American Friend appeared as a rather bleaker adaptation of

Ripley's Game, starring Dennis Hopper as Ripley and directed by Wim Wenders. A more faithful version of the same novel was filmed by Liliana Cavani in 2002 and starred John Malkovich in the title role. In 2005, an adaptation of *Ripley Under Ground* was served up by Bond director Roger Spottiswoode (*Tomorrow Never Dies*, since you ask) and starred Barry Pepper as Ripley.

But the most famous adaptation of them all is the late Anthony Minghella's version of *The Talented Mr Ripley*, starring Matt Damon, Jude Law, Gwyneth Paltrow and Cate Blanchett. With breathtaking visual appeal, its vivid portrayal of loneliness, jealousy and psychopathy is matched by its skilful use of music as a subliminal tool to ratchet up the tension. Gabriel Yared wrote the original score for which he won the 2000 Broadcast Film Critics Association Award for Best Composer. He was also nominated for an Academy Award, a BAFTA and a Golden Globe, among other accolades. Indeed, the film's overall critical reaction was very positive indeed, with nominations for five Academy Awards, seven BAFTAs and five Golden Globes. Disappointingly, the only actual win was a BAFTA for Best Actor in a Supporting Role, awarded to Jude Law for his portrayal of Dickie Greenleaf.

Either way, it is the very concept of Tom Ripley that has had generations of readers sublimely intrigued for some six decades. This concept, of course, is down to just one woman. She was born Patricia Plangman in Fort Worth, Texas in 1921, the only daughter of two artists, Jay Plangman and Mary Coates, who divorced shortly before Patricia was born. In 1924,

Mary Coates remarried, and her husband – the artist Stanley Highsmith – became the young Patricia's adoptive father. The family moved to New York in 1927, although Patricia would spend a subsequent year living with her grandmother in Fort Worth at the age of twelve. Her grandmother was to have a strong influence on her literary endeavours, teaching her to write at an early age and giving her access to an extensive library. Highsmith later attended the Julia Richmond High School and thereafter Barnard College, where she studied playwriting, English composition and the art of the short story. She graduated in 1942.

Failing to land a job in one of the mainstream magazines, Highsmith spent much of the 1940s writing for comic-book publishers in New York and Mexico. She soon realised she could make more money as a freelance comic-book writer and earned her living this way while working on her short stories. In 1950, she published her first psychological thriller, entitled *Strangers on a Train*. Containing scenes of graphic violence that would become her trademark, the book was spotted by the director Alfred Hitchcock, who made it into a film shortly afterwards. Although the book experienced only modest success initially, the film naturally shone a spotlight on Highsmith's writing talents and her ability to keep us readers on the edge of our seats.

Her second novel, *The Price of Salt* (1952), was written under the pseudonym Claire Morgan. Highsmith disassociated herself from the book for many years after its publication, partly because of the degree to which she plumbed the depths of her own personal life for its content. Another novel entitled *The Blunderer* was published in 1954, but it was *The Talented Mr Ripley* – published a year later – that was to garner Highsmith the literary attention she truly deserved. It was awarded the Edgar Allan Poe Scroll by the Mystery Writers of America and, more importantly from our perspective, introduced the world to the paradoxical anti-hero Tom Ripley. Highsmith would ultimately write twenty-two novels, eight books of short stories and around 8,000 pages of handwritten diary entries during her career, but Ripley was her masterpiece.

Highsmith never married or had children. Although regarded as bold and funny during her younger years, her life experiences would make her cynical, misanthropic, temperamental and prone to drinking alcohol to excess. Her intimate relationships (she was bisexual) rarely lasted more than a few years. She liked to remain a private person inasmuch as her worldwide success would allow. Indeed, she preferred her own company or that of animals; she kept cats and bred snails at her home in Suffolk, England.

Highsmith lived in Europe from 1963 onwards, mostly in France and Switzerland. But she retained her US citizenship, notwithstanding the high taxation she incurred as a result. Her views were sometimes rather anti-American. She was critical of the twentieth-century culture and foreign policy of her motherland, for example, and this culminated in a collection of short stories entitled *Tales of Natural and Unnatural Catastrophes*

(1987). She was an atheist and moreover vociferously anti-Semitic; while in Switzerland, she wrote over thirty articles and letters opposing the state of Israel and the influence Jewish people had both internationally and within the United States. Paradoxically, many of her friends were Jewish and included the authors Saul Bellow and Arthur Koestler.

Highsmith died of cancer in Locarno, Switzerland in February 1995 at the age of seventy-four. She was cremated in Bellinzona and a memorial service took place in the Catholic church in Tegna, Switzerland. Her last novel, *Small g: a Summer Idyll*, was published around a month after her death, while her fame was posthumously enhanced four years later with Anthony Minghella's adaptation of *The Talented Mr Ripley*. In 2014, Highsmith's 1964 novel *The Two Faces of January* was adapted for film by Hossein Amini and starred Viggo Mortensen and Kirsten Dunst. But then, Highsmith was also honoured in her lifetime. *The Two Faces of January* won the 1964 Gold Dagger Award of the Crime Writers' Association of Great Britain in the category of Best Foreign Novel. Most notably, Highsmith was honoured with the *Chevalier dans l'Ordre des Arts et des Lettres* by the French Ministry of Culture. Her letters and diaries are housed in the Swiss Literary Archives in Bern.

So, as we can see, Mr Ripley was not alone in being talented. But was Highsmith's anti-hero really a psychopath? To determine this, we need to re-examine his fictional biography, including what little detail the novels give us about his past. In this regard, we are told that he was orphaned at the age of five and that he was reared in Boston by his aunt Dottie, an austere woman who mocked him as a 'sissy'. As a teenager, Ripley tried to run away from home to the promise of New York, but ultimately did not succeed until the age of twenty, when he moved to the Big Apple to make a pittance as a con artist. At this point, his story is taken up in Highsmith's first Ripley novel and Anthony Minghella's screen adaptation, which we shall use for the purpose of chronology.

Circumstances see Ripley playing piano at a cocktail party, wearing a blazer borrowed from a friend who attended Princeton University. He is approached by Herbert Greenleaf, a wealthy shipping magnate who assumes that Ripley must know his son Dickie. Dickie, it transpires, went to Princeton, is roughly Ripley's age, but is somewhat wayward in the eyes of his father. Greenleaf offers Ripley $1,000 to travel to Italy in order to persuade his son to return to the United States, and the impecunious Ripley naturally accepts. That he has never met Dickie and never attended Princeton are minor details that Ripley dismisses without a second thought.

He sets off for Italy and, upon arrival, encounters Meredith Logue, the heiress to a textile fortune now on sabbatical in Italy. In their brief interaction, Ripley impulsively pretends to be Dickie; in his own words, it is 'better to be a fake somebody than a real nobody'.[2] Ripley focuses on his mission and orchestrates an accidental meeting on the beach with Dickie and his fiancée, Marge Sherwood. Dickie does not even pretend to recall Ripley, and the ruse is not maintained for much longer.

Ripley subsequently visits Dickie for lunch and admits to him the essential purpose of his visit. Enraged, Dickie insists that Ripley inform his father that he has no intention of ever returning to the United States or to the family business.

From this point onwards, Ripley's talents really begin to kick in. Feigning a love of jazz music, he weasels his way into Dickie's confidence. The two young men devise various ways of extracting more and more money from Herbert Greenleaf under the fake pretext that Ripley is on the verge of persuading Dickie to repatriate. As their warped relationship evolves, Ripley travels to Rome with Dickie and meets his friend Freddie Miles. Miles is instantly suspicious of Ripley, and is openly rude as he mocks a lack of breeding to which Dickie seems oblivious. The plot thickens as a local woman (Dickie's mistress, now pregnant with his child) drowns herself by suicide because Dickie has refused to provide her with any level of commitment. Dickie is affected profoundly by her death, although his pride will not allow him to admit it. Instead, he becomes increasingly irritable, tiring of Ripley and his suffocating presence.

Ripley, however, is rapidly becoming dependent on Dickie to maintain the opulent lifestyle he so voraciously covets. There is even a hint of sexual attraction, with strong references to Ripley's bisexuality throughout the book and film alike. As a final gesture of goodwill, Dickie invites Ripley to San Remo, where he is scouting for somewhere new to live. The two young men take a boating excursion out to sea and Ripley takes the opportunity to suggest he return to Italy the following year so that they might become housemates together. Dickie responds with contempt, telling his companion that he finds him 'quite boring' and that soon he'll finally be relieved to see the back of him. Enraged with pathological jealousy or perhaps simply sensing imminent abandonment, Ripley bludgeons Dickie to death.

> *He looked at Dickie. Was he dead? Tom crouched in the narrowing prow of the boat, watching Dickie for a sign of life. He was afraid to touch him, afraid to touch his chest or his wrist to feel a pulse.*[3]

Ripley scuttles the boat to conceal his crime and then swims ashore. He returns to his hotel where the concierge mistakes him for Dickie and – not for the first time – he realises he can successfully pass himself off as the young playboy to cover up his crime and maintain his adopted lifestyle of opulence. He forges Dickie's signature, modifies his passport and begins to draw down his trust fund. Using Dickie's typewriter, he forwards a letter from Dickie to Marge telling her that he is leaving her and plans to live in Rome. He checks into two separate hotels as himself and as Dickie, and sends letters back and forth between one and the other to create an illusion that Dickie is alive and well. Indeed, it all goes well until a complication re-emerges in the form of Meredith Logue who, of course, believes Ripley to be Dickie. This threatens to be his undoing.

Still, over the months that follow, Ripley rents an opulent Roman apartment in Dickie's name. Freddie Miles tracks him down via the American Express office and immediately senses that something is not quite right. The apartment is filled with neo-classical ornaments and an expensive grand piano, yet Miles knows that Dickie has no taste for either and cannot play. Ripley is now dressed like Dickie, with the same hairstyle and mannerisms. Miles looks him up and down condescendingly and remarks that, 'the only thing around here that looks like Dickie is you'.[4] As he leaves the building, the landlady informs him that Signor Dickie (who, she says, often keeps everyone awake with his piano) is certainly at home. Miles turns on his heel and races back upstairs to the apartment, whereupon Ripley whacks him over the head with a large statue, killing him almost instantly. Ripley carries the body out to Miles' Alfa Romeo and drives to the countryside where he abandons the vehicle and carefully disposes of the body.

The Italian police are naturally suspicious, as is Marge Sherwood. Indeed, her friend, Peter Smith-Kingsley, tries to be conciliatory with Ripley on her behalf. Over the months that follow, Ripley barely manages to remain a step ahead. In due course, he forges a suicide note from Dickie and then moves to Venice to rent an apartment under his own name. Herbert Greenleaf appears to trust Ripley, but nonetheless hires a private detective, Alvin MacCarron, to investigate his son's disappearance. However, Marge is wise to the psychopath in her midst and confronts Ripley directly when she unwittingly discovers Dickie's rings in his bathroom. Now on the verge of exposure, Ripley considers murdering Dickie's fiancée and would do so but for the last-minute arrival at the apartment of Smith-Kingsley to defuse the situation.

In a final twist, MacCarron reveals that Dickie has a history of violence and that he suspects Dickie of murdering Miles. Thus Herbert Greenleaf decides to drop the investigation. Ripley is asked not to cooperate with the Italian police lest any scandal might arise affecting the Greenleaf name and, in return, Herbert rewards him by transferring a large amount of Dickie's trust fund into Ripley's bank account. Marge is shocked by this gesture and openly accuses Ripley of murder before Herbert and MacCarron drag her away.

And thus, it appears Ripley is on the verge of covering up two perfect murders. Alas, one more loose end returns to haunt him. Setting off on a cruise with Smith-Kingsley (it is implied that they are now lovers), Ripley runs into Meredith and her family. Smith-Kingsley knows him as Ripley, while Meredith knows him as Dickie, so he faces a dilemma that can only be resolved by murdering Smith-Kingsley and dumping him overboard. This is something he does with a curious sense of remorse.

In *Plein Soleil* – the original 1960 adaptation of *The Talented Mr Ripley* – Ripley does not get away nearly so lightly. Although the film follows roughly the same storyline as the original novel and has the visual appeal of Minghella's 1999 adaptation, Alain Delon's Ripley is not as overtly vulnerable as Matt Damon's. His murder of Philippe (as Dickie is renamed in the film) is more calculated, boldly alluded to – even planned – in advance. Philippe is stabbed in cold blood by a significantly calmer Ripley than in the 1999 version. No argument precedes the murder, while the disposal of the body is more an act of pragmatism than a desperate attempt to cover up a crime of passion. Delon's Ripley is essentially more psychopathic and in this regard we naturally side with him less than we do with Damon's. Although Patricia Highsmith expressed disapproval at Clément's decision to have Ripley captured at the end of the film, viewers are perhaps more inclined to think this particular version of Ripley got exactly what he deserved.

Ironically enough, Delon's Ripley may have a little more in common with the Ripley of Highsmith's book. Although clearly shocked at first by Dickie's violent death, literary Ripley almost instantly reverts to cool problem-solving mode, albeit with a sense of urgency. Indeed, if literary Ripley is afraid of anything at that moment, it is the risk of drowning at sea rather than the potential consequences of his homicidal deed.

In Highsmith's eyes, of course, *The Talented Mr Ripley* is just the beginning of her anti-hero's spree of villainy. Throughout his career, he commits fraud, forgery, deception and murder with impunity, often resorting to the impersonation of others to evade capture. The second novel, *Ripley Under Ground*, takes place six years later when our anti-hero is in his early thirties and living in France, married to Heloise Plisson – the heiress to a millionaire pharmaceutical manufacturer. He still lives comfortably on Dickie's trust fund, subsidised by various carefully concealed dealings in stolen goods and an elaborate art forgery racket under the legitimate front of Derwatt Ltd. Philip Derwatt was a brilliant painter who died a few years previously and in whom Ripley and a select gathering of aficionados showed some interest. Following Derwatt's death, the incorrigible Ripley becomes a silent partner in a scheme that involves another painter named Bernard Tufts forging Derwatt paintings to pander to an ever-growing market that is convinced Derwatt is alive and well in Mexico. The racket goes well until an American art collector by the name of Thomas Murchison somehow spots the forgery and confronts Ripley about it. Ultimately, Ripley is forced to resort to murder once again to protect his financial security and his reputation.

In 2005, *Ripley Under Ground* was adapted for the silver screen by Roger Spottiswoode. As well as Barry Pepper, it starred Willem Dafoe as Murchison, and featured Alan Cumming and Tom Wilkinson among its cast. Without losing any of the tension we might expect from a Ripley film, this adaptation remains light-hearted and even farcical at times. Certainly, Pepper's Ripley is one of the shallower examples of our anti-hero. It is hard to take him seriously enough to consider him a psychopath. Perhaps this adds to his likeability. Otherwise, Spottiswoode remains relatively faithful to the plot, although he deviates a little with the character of Heloise, who seems to know a lot more about her husband's antics than is evident in the novel. In the film, she turns out to be just as psychopathic as her husband.

In *Ripley's Game* – the third novel of the series – our anti-hero is asked by an unscrupulous associate named Reeves Minot to commit murder on his behalf. Ripley declines on the grounds that 'There's no such thing as a perfect murder', but Minot does not leave their rendezvous empty-handed.[5] Ripley has recently been insulted by a local picture framer in Fontainebleau and sees an opportunity for revenge. The framer in question is Jonathan Trevanny, an impecunious British expatriate with myeloid leukaemia, who naturally fears dying and leaving his wife Simone and their young son without any means of support. Minot offers Trevanny money and the chance to visit some esteemed medical specialists in Berlin in return for the perpetration of a couple of well-planned murders. As we might reasonably expect, Trevanny initially refuses; he is not a psychopath, after all. But he desperately needs the money and doubts he will live much longer, so he ultimately accepts Minot's offer and travels to Berlin to commit the killings. He succeeds clumsily with the first, but the second – that of a Mafia boss on a train – almost goes wrong and requires Ripley (who, it transpires, has been shadowing him) to intervene at the last minute and finish off the job. From this point onwards, the Mafia seek their revenge, placing everyone in danger. Ultimately, Trevanny is shot at his house by an Italian gangster.

The novel, probably the bleakest of the five, certainly gave rise to the two bleakest film adaptations. The first was Wim Wenders' *The American Friend*, which starred Bruno Ganz as Jonathan Zimmermann (Trevanny was renamed for the purpose of the film). The style was very much *film noir*, set amid the dismal Berlin winter. Although Zimmerman (Trevanny) travels from there to Paris to commit the murders (in the novel, as we have seen, it is the other way around), the adaptation otherwise stuck relatively faithfully to the original Highsmith plot. Now on his third outing, Ripley appears much more the hardened criminal, a ruthless man in his mid-forties with little of the naïvety displayed in *The Talented Mr Ripley*. Moreover, Wenders' film offers none of the visual attraction, sunshine or music that abounds in Minghella's later adaptation.

Perhaps in an effort to ameliorate this, Liliana Cavani remade *Ripley's Game* in 2002, with John Malkovich as Ripley, Ray Winstone as Reeves Minot and Dougray Scott as Jonathan Trevanny. This time the tale was set in Italy, with the scene of the murders restored to Berlin. Cavani adhered closely to the original Highsmith plot but, again, Malkovich portrayed a meaner, harder Ripley with far less of the vulnerability inherent in Matt Damon's version. The location, with its classical architecture and the more ubiquitous presence of fine art and music, lent the film a slightly more glamorous feel. Alas, *Ripley's Game* was set in mid-winter and (like *The American Friend*) failed to deliver the feel-good factor of the classic Ripley films by Clément and Minghella.

The final two novels are perhaps less well known because they were never made into films. In *The Boy Who Followed Ripley*, our anti-hero attempts to help sixteen-year-old Frank Pierson, the son of a recently deceased American tycoon. Pierson has fled the United States because (as it transpires) he murdered his father by pushing him off a cliff. Ripley's reputation has led Pierson to seek out our anti-hero's advice, and this ultimately results in the two travelling to West Berlin where Pierson – in a plot twist – is kidnapped. Ripley (likely driven by the need for excitement) rescues the boy and murders his kidnappers, but Pierson remains plagued by guilt and eventually dies from suicide, throwing himself off the same cliff where his father met his demise. Our anti-hero does not seem especially perturbed by this development.

In *Ripley Under Water*, our protagonist is once again visited by problems related to the Derwatt scam. An odious American named David Pritchard threatens to expose Ripley's role in the disappearance of Thomas Murchison. He begins following and photographing Ripley, and dredges local canals in search of the body. He finally finds it and dumps it on Ripley's doorstep before calling the police. Ripley acts swiftly as usual, moving the corpse to a pond outside the Pritchards' rented house. Hearing the commotion, Mr and Mrs Pritchard emerge from the building and fall into the pond while trying to remove the body. Unable to swim, they drown and ultimately the police are left – once again – with no leads.

Throughout his fictional career in crime, Ripley is directly or indirectly responsible for some fourteen deaths, at least nine of which are murders. He is certainly a spree killer, possibly a serial killer, but is he a psychopath? Running through the *Psychopathy Checklist*, let's begin with the interpersonal traits.

There is little doubt that he is both *glib and superficially charming*. His ability to beguile those around him is almost boundless, requiring absurdly exceptional circumstances for them to question his behaviour or his motives. On one occasion during Minghella's adaptation he admires a bespectacled Dickie for resembling Clark Kent; Dickie doffs the glasses and Ripley quips endearingly that he looks like Superman. Elsewhere, Ripley is witty in social settings, using his abilities as a mimic to entertain others. How else would he snake his way into the lives of Herbert Greenleaf, Peter Smith-Kingsley, Bernard Tufts, Jonathan Trevanny and numerous others? While the more mild-mannered of his acquaintances succumb easily to his charm, even those more streetwise are briefly fooled. And when the penny finally drops, Ripley remains chillingly in control of his charm until the point at which he resorts to murder.

What about a *grandiose sense of self-worth*? Ripley's sense of entitlement is evident throughout the five stories. He doesn't just settle for some job in a shipyard or a factory; instead he masquerades as a university graduate in an effort to improve his prospects. He shows no reluctance in accepting a large sum of money from Herbert Greenleaf, nor does his intrusion into the life of the Greenleaf family ever seem to Ripley to be anything other than his due. In later novels, he sets himself up as a country gentleman as though to the manor born. He sees himself as a connoisseur of music and the arts, albeit more legitimately than many wealthy individuals with similar designs in mind. Perhaps more importantly, Ripley is so narcissistic that he reacts with dramatic violence when rejected by Dickie Greenleaf and insulted by Jonathan Trevanny. Despite his sometimes-modest demeanour, Ripley thinks very highly of himself indeed.

There are countless examples of *manipulation for personal gain* in all five novels. Ripley likes to 'take the past and put it in a box in the basement and never go down there', and such a *modus operandi* leaves him free to reinvent himself at will.[6] Indeed, his impression management is relentless, from his initial encounter with Herbert Greenleaf to his attempt to hoodwink David Pritchard. He persuades the naïve Bernard Tufts to forge Derwatt paintings against the artist's better judgement. He even convinces a dying father to become a killer. All of it is with his own interests in mind so, from a psychopathy perspective, Ripley ticks the manipulation box. Similarly, *pathological lying* is almost his trademark. He admits as much to Dickie when asked about his talent, as he cites 'forging signatures, telling lies, impersonating practically anybody'.[7] From his initial dishonesty with Herbert Greenleaf about his pedigree, Ripley's tendency to lie (even when not necessary) is more or less constant. See how easily he introduces himself as Dickie Greenleaf to Meredith Logue before he has even met Dickie or contemplated impersonating him to cover up a murder. Later, he casually invents a fiancée named Frances, whom he claims resides in New York, simply to enhance his fake persona in the eyes of Dickie and Marge. There is little doubt that Ripley is a pathological liar.

Score for interpersonal traits = 8/8

So, what can we say about Ripley and the affective traits of psychopathy? In terms of *shallow affect*, only Matt Damon's portrayal suggests a man pervasively tortured by the confused and changeable emotions of his flawed character. And is there really much evidence of anything other than jealousy and rage? Perhaps he appears anxious at times, but arguably less so than most people would during the events that ultimately unfold. Ripley certainly maintains a cool head in times of real crisis. On one occasion, Damon's Ripley seems terrified that the boat Dickie is carelessly piloting will capsize in the choppy waters off San Remo. Elsewhere, he appears profoundly moved by the murder scene of an opera. But these displays of emotion are short-lived, rarely replicated and somewhat inconsistent. Even his love for Peter Smith-Kingsley seems a little contrived and ultimately ends in murder. And if we accept Ripley's emotional displays at face value, they still only appear in Minghella's adaptation. In the other films and in the novels, Ripley shows limited emotional range. He is brilliant at mimicking the emotional responses of people around him but has very little sense of himself. His skills at impression management do little to feed his own soul.

Throughout the five novels and the various film adaptations, there is little evidence of any *empathy* in Ripley. Little evidence of any 'hot' empathy, in any case. We might be duped into empathising with *him*, but that is a different matter entirely.

What level of callousness would allow a young man to murder a contemporary, having accepted a significant sum of money from the victim's father? How else could the young man then embezzle the victim's money by impersonating him and then (to cover up his crimes) attempt to convince the victim's fiancée that he has left her? Bear in mind that the same young man is later prepared to profit from a father's terminal illness in a transaction with the criminal underworld. With few exceptions, Ripley shows himself to be callous and almost always lacking in the empathy we would anticipate in a normal individual.

Similarly, Ripley's *lack of remorse* is evident throughout the novels. He rarely dwells upon the victims of his past; indeed, when old nemeses return to haunt him (for example, David Pritchard in *Ripley Under Water*), Ripley's absence of any emotional connection with his victims or their relatives lends an almost farcical air to the events that unfold. As we can see, he is quite content to take an exhumed corpse and dump it elsewhere unceremoniously for his own ends. Even in Anthony Minghella's adaptation of *The Talented Mr Ripley*, Dickie's murder is followed by a sense in Ripley of initial panic and then single-mindedness, but certainly not guilt. He is quite capable of living with himself after what he has done.

Ripley therefore *fails to accept any real responsibility for his own actions*. Indeed, there is a sense that anyone who meddles in his affairs only has themselves to blame for the consequences. Thomas Murchison is murdered because of his attempt to expose Derwatt Ltd in *Ripley Under Ground*; Jonathan Trevanny dies prematurely because he insults our anti-hero at a party in *Ripley's Game*; David Pritchard drowns in *Ripley Under Water* as a direct result of his interference. Despite all the people who end up dead because of Ripley, he never owns up to anything, nor does he attempt to learn from experience. Instead, he goes on killing while actively evading justice as he covers up his crimes with alacrity.

Score for affective traits = 8/8

Ripley displays many of the lifestyle traits associated with psychopathy. To begin with, he is *parasitic*; he lives comfortably off his ill-gotten gains and the means of others. Having murdered Dickie, he proceeds to bleed Herbert Greenleaf of his son's trust fund. He feeds off the posthumous reputation of Philip Derwatt and the painstaking work of Bernard Tufts as he profits from a forgery racket. Indeed, given the many references to Ripley being homosexual, we ought to be cynical of his marriage to a French heiress. Ripley rarely seems to do an honest day's work, yet he ends up a very wealthy man.

Many of Ripley's actions, as already discussed, show him to be *reckless and irresponsible*. Yet he displays an enduring sense of obligation to his wife, Heloise, and occasionally to other characters such as Jonathan Trevanny and Frank Pierson (although both end up dead after their brush with Ripley). Moving to the next item, our anti-hero is *impulsive*. He spends little time weighing up the pros and cons of his worst actions; the murder of Dickie – Ripley's first murder, as far as we know – seems to be committed entirely on impulse and in response to uncontrollable rage. Indeed, none of Ripley's murders are planned in any great detail, even if they are contemplated in advance as possible outcomes. Instead, his genius lies in his singular ability to react quickly and effectively cover up his crimes under the scrutiny of the police and the advocates of his victims.

But does Ripley *lack any realistic long-term goals*? Interview a real psychopath and they might regale you with their grandiose plans for accomplishment, fame or fortune. Not so with Ripley. He just gets on with it, saving the money he embezzles and investing in fine art and architecture. Yet he will never achieve his ambition of acceptance into high society. Indeed, his long-term plan to survive on the proceeds of murder, theft and forgery could hardly be termed realistic, especially as his reputation becomes increasingly tarnished.

Ripley's *need for excitement and stimulation* is a little doubtful in the first novel. In Minghella's adaptation, he is portrayed by Matt Damon as a rather frightened and naïve young man at times, whose behaviour is sometimes driven out of necessity. Early in the film, we hear a couple arguing loudly next door to Ripley's New York apartment and sense our anti-hero's desperation to escape from a life in which he feels threatened and miserable. Still, as his character matures, Ripley acquires a keen nose for the scent of blood. In the second and subsequent novels, his wealth does not prevent him from dabbling in a variety of crimes largely, we suspect, out of boredom. As such, Ripley develops a need for excitement as his character evolves.

Of course, there are some psychopathic characteristics that Ripley does not display at all. There is no evidence of *promiscuous sexual behaviour*, for example. Although he is often portrayed as homosexual or bisexual, he does not appear especially active in this regard. As far as we know he only marries once, so we cannot reasonably accuse him of having *many short-term marital relationships*.

Score for lifestyle traits = 8/14

Finally, we come to the antisocial traits and here we run a little short of evidence. For example, we have no idea if Ripley had *early behavioural problems*; all we are really told is that he was orphaned at a very young age and harshly treated by his aunt Dottie. He ran away when he was sixteen, but there is no evidence of *juvenile delinquency* that we know of. Ripley does have *poor behavioural controls*, however. Apart from the fact that he tends to murder people when arguments get out of hand, he cannot help himself when it comes to stealing (Dickie's rings, for example) or impulsively impersonating others on a whim. Indeed, Ripley shows obvious *criminal versatility*, with a repertoire that includes art forgery, fraud, deception, perversion of the course of justice and, most importantly, murder. But *revocation of conditional release* does not apply, as Ripley is never actually caught (unless we count the ending in *Plein Soleil*, when Alain Delon's Ripley seems on the verge of getting his comeuppance).

Score for antisocial traits = 4/8 (one item not applicable)

Ripley scores 28 out of 38 overall, placing him firmly in the fictional psychopath category for our purposes. His strong scores in the interpersonal and affective domains, coupled with his moderate scores in the lifestyle and antisocial domains, suggest a leaning towards *manipulative* psychopathy, although his ability to score at least moderately in all four domains equally suggests he could be a *classic* psychopath. Either way, any decent individual really ought to find it difficult to sympathise with him. Even the rapacious onomatopoeia of his name suggests violence. Instead, we find ourselves ambivalent and even sympathetic to Ripley and his plight. Stranger still, as the plot thickens and the pages turn, our anti-hero dexterously charms us into openly rooting for him to evade capture. So, why should this be the case?

Perhaps Ripley is not a pure psychopath. Indeed, it might reasonably be argued that his character traits just as easily amount to what is termed an emotionally unstable (or *borderline*) personality disorder. In psychiatry, as discussed in Chapter 1, mental illness and its allied disorders are categorised in the *Diagnostic and Statistical Manual of Mental Disorders* (DSM-5). In the DSM-5, personality disorders are grouped together in three clusters. Cluster B contains both antisocial personality disorder (which, as also outlined, shares some characteristics with psychopathy) and borderline personality disorder. Ripley lacks some of the lifestyle and antisocial traits of psychopathy, so what might favour an alternative diagnosis?

It could be said that Ripley experiences instability of mood on a day-to-day basis and is prone to feelings of emptiness that he projects onto others around him. This might be regarded as the *emotional dysregulation* inherent in a borderline personality rather than the emotional shallowness of psychopathy. Similarly, the manner in which he turns close friends and relatives against each other might in fact be an unconscious borderline mechanism termed *splitting*, rather than psychopathic impression management.[8] Also consistent with a borderline personality in Ripley is his relationship with Dickie: intense and unstable due partly to our anti-hero's chronic uncertainties about self-image and sexual preference. He is frequently impulsive (often the case with a borderline personality) and has a tendency to act out his emotional distress. Finally, he goes to considerable lengths to avoid being abandoned by Dickie. People with a borderline personality have a profound fear of abandonment.

Still, I know a lot of very nice people with borderline personality disorder; it certainly never explains murder and, as such with Ripley, it seems far more reasonable to err on the side of psychopathy. So, why is he so incorrigibly likeable?

His talent for secrecy is certainly a source of fascination, while it is hard not to admire his obvious courage in the face of danger. And yet, some of the traits that lead us to consider a borderline personality would also support the supposition that he is exquisitely vulnerable. When we first meet him, he has nothing: no qualifications, no social status, no wealthy trust fund and no prospects. As a young man, he seems easily bullied by wealthy and well-connected characters such as Freddie Miles and Dickie Greenleaf. Indeed, so isolated is Ripley that even his later marriage to Heloise exudes an aura of estrangement; he does not confide in his wife and she equally turns a blind eye to his shady dealings. Occasionally he forges a connection with some other character, such as Peter Smith-Kingsley or Frank Pierson, but Ripley always ends up alone and out in the cold. Who could be unsympathetic to all this?

Moving to other items on our *Psychopath Likeability Scale*, the next question is whether or not Ripley takes us into his confidence. Highsmith writes about her anti-hero in the third person and retains the omniscience inherent in this approach. But, in literary terms, Ripley remains the *viewpoint*, with virtually no scene taking place in book or film alike in which he is not present. Highsmith consistently describes what her anti-hero thinks and feels (or doesn't feel). In the films, we see Ripley's reaction to every event that happens. Ultimately, we feel privileged, as though he were telling the tale himself. In this sense, he garners our sympathy with ease.

Superficial as it is, we are consistently seduced by Ripley's charm. As we have already noted, his ability to beguile those around him is almost boundless and extends to the reader and viewer as much as to the characters in the plot. And, of course, Ripley is not referred to as *talented* for nothing. He is an accomplished pianist with a knowledge and appreciation of music, fine art, architecture and history. In Minghella's adaptation, note how quickly Ripley picks up a passable knowledge of jazz. He is a brilliant mimic and impersonator, and an expert at forgery, penning Dickie's suicide note with ease before modifying his passport. Ripley is intelligent, single-minded and diligent. All in all, he has a plethora of talents and skills any reasonable person might admire. What a pity he puts them to such dishonest use.

So, is Ripley ever boring? Returning to Minghella's adaptation, Dickie's final excursion is a boating expedition with Ripley off the coast of San Remo. As already described, events suddenly escalate when Dickie responds with contempt to his companion's suggestion that he return to Italy the following year so that they might become housemates. Dickie tells his soon-to-be murderer rather candidly, 'Tom, you can be quite boring' and remarks that he will be glad to see the back of him.[9] We know what happens next, as Ripley's narcissistic rage takes over. The irony is, of course, that Ripley is anything but boring. He keeps us constantly entertained, while also appealing to that part within us all that longs for his evident freedom to act as he likes with such impunity. Ripley is not constrained by guilt or fear of consequence. Perhaps there is something perversely admirable about this.

Furthermore, many of Ripley's victims make him look good. Dickie, as we know, is shallow, selfish, capricious and unfaithful.

Among Ripley's other victims are a cruel and bourgeois bully (Freddie Miles), an arrogant tycoon (Thomas Murchison), an obnoxious busybody (David Pritchard) and several members of the Italian Mafia. Even the more sympathetic victims (Bernard Tufts and Jonathan Trevanny) seem rather pathetic next to our courageous anti-hero. While Ripley has a number of notable redeeming features, those who succumb to his homicidal tendencies are by and large nasty, self-centred, histrionic, materialistic and of weak character, notwithstanding their social advantage over our anti-hero. And so, as Ripley rises up against the bullies and claims the spoils and status for which he has always yearned, we are sufficiently sympathetic to overlook the occasional murder.

Finally, in a sense, Ripley's backdrop makes him look good. At least this is the case in the novels and many of the film adaptations (with *The American Friend* being a notable exception). Ripley starts out as an impecunious young man amidst the glamour of the 1950s Mediterranean, but this glitz soon rubs off on him. He eventually outshines it, as he evolves into a cultured connoisseur of opera and a patron of fine art against an era of loud jazz and brash postmodern iconography.

So, in terms of our *Psychopath Likeability Scale*, Tom Ripley scores highly. A vulnerable anti-hero who takes us (to a degree) into his confidence, he is charming, talented and never boring. His victims and backdrop alike make him look good and he even appeals to the inherent devilment and secrecy in the voyeur. It is little wonder we want him to succeed.

In the end, we should really celebrate the talented Ms Highsmith. In creating Tom Ripley, she has served us up the perfect anti-hero: a psychopathic killer disguised as a charming rogue. Few fictional psychopaths are quite as complex or as likeable.

7

THE MINOR PSYCHOPATH

'Is that where Kevin got it? In prison, that marionette smile, as if pulled up by strings.'

– *Eva Khatchadourian*[1]

It is difficult not to empathise with a child in any novel, even if they seem to tick most of the boxes for psychopathy. Twelve-year-old Josephine Leonides murders her grandfather and her nanny in Agatha Christie's novel *The Crooked House* (1949), yet most readers would feel at least a pang of sorrow for her in the end. Alas, the same cannot be said for Kevin Khatchadourian, the protagonist in Lionel Shriver's dramatic thriller *We Need to Talk About Kevin*. Many readers will be familiar with this book; it sold over a million copies and garnered its author the prestigious Orange Prize for Fiction in 2005. It was subsequently adapted for film by director Lynne Ramsay and starred Tilda Swinton and Ezra Miller. It premiered at the 2011 Cannes Film Festival and was screened in September of the same year at the Toronto International Film Festival to much critical acclaim.

The novel is written in the epistolary style, namely a series of letters by Kevin's long-suffering mother, Eva, to her presumably estranged husband, Franklin. The story charts their life together before Kevin was conceived, a difficult pregnancy culminating in an excruciatingly protracted labour, behavioural disturbance throughout Kevin's childhood, the eventual arrival of his timid and unfortunate younger sister, Celia, and finally Kevin's perpetration of a brutal crossbow massacre at his local high school. Film and book alike are powerful and certainly not for the faint-hearted. They raise important questions about psychopathy and society, and the theme of 'nature versus nurture' as the primary reason for a deplorably evil individual. They also explore the danger of indulging in denial when faced with an evolving harsh reality.

From the outset, Eva is ambivalent about having children. She is already a successful travel writer with a happy marriage; despite her thirty-seven years and a growing sense of obligation to procreate, she doesn't really have the emotional desire for a child. The opening chapters are filled with her rumination and a sense of foreboding. Franklin feels differently, however. He is temperamentally softer, perhaps more obsessional and certainly more paternal. In the end, Eva's decision to become pregnant is almost on impulse and, in this context, Shriver poses the question of whether her protagonist's mixed feelings towards Kevin ultimately seal his fate. Nevertheless, although we see Eva's misgivings gradually evolve into fatigue, desperation and even revulsion, she consistently puts these feelings aside as she goes to considerable lengths to treat her son well. She is steadfastly loyal to him to the end of the story and beyond.

Eva's perseverance throughout Kevin's childhood is in the face of marked behavioural disturbance on his part, from constant screaming in his crib to the way he bites her nipple when breastfeeding, to his refusal to toilet train until the age of six, to his deliberately hurtful comments to vulnerable strangers, to his enticement of a naïve schoolgirl to inflame her eczema by scratching, to his sabotage of a young neighbour's bicycle causing a serious accident, to the constant cruelty meted out to his much younger sister, Celia, that ultimately culminates in her losing an eye, to a spurious accusation of sexual assault against an innocent drama teacher and finally to the intricately planned massacre of eleven people. Throughout all this, the person who suffers most at Kevin's cruel hands is Eva. The fact that his attitudes and behaviour exist from birth casts considerable doubt on her culpability.

So, does all this amount to psychopathy? As per usual, we should try to be scientific, even if we are limited by Kevin being a fictional character whom we can never interview. Much of his biography exists only in the imagination of the author. Still, permitting a little artistic licence to account for the gaps, we can be guided by the *Youth Psychopathy Checklist* (PCL-YV) to discern whether or not a (fictional) psychologist might have reasonably marked Kevin down as an emerging psychopath.[2] The *Youth Psychopathy Checklist* differs slightly from the adult version in terms of specific content, but still contains twenty items scored in the same way (with a score of 0, 1 or 2) and categorised into *interpersonal, affective, lifestyle* and *antisocial* domains:

Interpersonal Traits

1. Impression management
2. Grandiose sense of self-worth
3. Pathological lying
4. Manipulation for personal gain

Affective Traits

5. Shallow affect
6. Callousness or lack of empathy
7. Lack of remorse or guilt
8. Failure to accept responsibility

Lifestyle Traits

9. Parasitic orientation
10. Impulsivity
11. Lack of goals
12. Stimulation seeking
13. Irresponsibility
14. Impersonal sexual behaviour[3]
15. Unstable interpersonal relationships

Antisocial Traits

16. Poor anger control
17. Early behavioural problems
18. Criminal behaviour
19. Criminal versatility
20. Serious violation of conditional release

Beginning with the interpersonal traits, perhaps the first item to consider is *impression management*. This is a deliberate attempt to influence how others perceive you by controlling the information they receive. Of course, we could all be accused of this from time to time. Think of the last job interview you did.

But with psychopaths it is slightly different. They make sure they appear attractive to specific people who have something they want, be it power, influence or money. Kevin is mostly frighteningly honest throughout the story. Eva is often the recipient of the brutal truth; so too are peers, neighbours and even perfect strangers. He makes no effort to manipulate the psychological tests he is given. When his mother brings him to a doctor, wondering if perhaps he might have autism, it transpires that 'apparently he did not display the tell-tale rocking and repetitive behaviour of such unfortunates trapped in their own world'.[4] But crucially, Kevin goes to considerable lengths to appear utterly normal to those people whose influence he needs. His father is a case in point. Kevin is always careful to appear kind and trustworthy to Franklin, whom he deems an essential ally. As Eva puts it, 'even in his crib, Kevin was learning to divide and conquer'.[5]

In a similar manner, the novel is comprised almost entirely of specific episodes in which Kevin engages in *manipulation for personal gain*. Sometimes this gain is to exact revenge on those who have scorned him; at other times, it is simply for his own amusement. Eva spots this early, observing that 'he was a singular, unusually cunning individual who had arrived to stay with us and just happened to be very small'.[6] Undoubtedly, Kevin has a *grandiose sense of self-worth*. When Eva visits him in prison, he boasts about his mass murder and the infamy he has achieved and tells her that he is worshipped by his fellow inmates. Eva observes in her letters that 'he thinks very well of himself, especially since becoming such a celebrity'.[7]

The final interpersonal trait is *pathological lying*. Recall that this is not the usual type of lying – the kind we all do to spare the feelings of others or cover up minor peccadilloes. Instead, the pathological liar falsifies constantly out of habit, sometimes without even realising they are doing it. If found out, the psychopath will simply shrug it off without any sense of embarrassment or they will rework the facts to iron out any inconsistencies. In Kevin, notwithstanding his other interpersonal traits, pathological lying is not overtly evident. On one occasion, at the age of six, he lies to his father about his mother assaulting him in a fit of anger and frustration. Kevin covers up for Eva despite the fractured arm he has sustained, but this is not pathological lying. It is manipulation for personal gain. Kevin knows it gives him the moral high ground, a currency he can (and does) use to good effect in the months that follow in order to get what he wants.

Score for interpersonal traits = 6/8

So, what about Kevin's affective traits? Certainly, he is capable of mimicking the emotions of others when called upon to do so. Aside from those whom he targets, many of his peers and acquaintances do not seem to notice anything wrong with him until the day he commits his signature crime. He is capable of great charm when needed, but we get little sense that he understands human emotions such as anxiety, sadness, despair, love or humour. In short, he has a *shallow affect*, although it is only really Eva who notices this as she remarks on 'that marionette smile, as if pulled up by strings'.[8]

Guilt is one of the many emotions that Kevin does not routinely experience. He has no conscience. We are told by Eva that his therapists have diagnosed him with 'empathic deficiency', which we can easily translate as *callousness or lack of empathy*. A distinct *lack of remorse* is clearly evident. He denies damaging his sister's eye but equally taunts his mother with the likelihood that he did it. He gives little thought to his other misdemeanours. He feels no connection with his murder victims, as he talks about his heinous crime in chillingly matter-of-fact terms. He even describes the pride he feels in prison over the massacre, and tells his mother he was largely motivated by the infamy he would achieve. In Eva's words, 'Kevin regards a refusal to stand by one's own handiwork as not only undignified but as a betrayal of the tribe.'[9]

At the end of the story, Kevin admits that he does not really understand his true motive for killing, but this is not expressed in any emotive sense. And although he ultimately admits to some of his crimes, there is a clear *failure to accept responsibility* in that he doesn't seem to comprehend that (or, at the very least, why) what he did was wrong.

Score for affective traits = 8/8

Kevin's lifestyle equally lends itself to the label of psychopathy. He displays *impulsivity* consistently throughout the story. That is not to say that he is incapable of planning (clearly he is meticulous when he wants to be), but he seizes any opportunity to inflict hurt or pain on others. An example is when Eva decides to decorate her new study with maps and paraphernalia from her worldly travels and Kevin barely waits until she has left the room before he vandalises it to utter destruction. At no point does he weigh up the pros and cons.

Parasitic orientation refers to the psychopath's tendency to leech off others instead of engaging in productive activity themselves. Kevin's productive activity is very limited (he is almost entirely destructive from the outset); however, it is important to bear in mind that he is only a child. In many respects, he is independent of his parents, partly because he seems to require so little of the emotional nurturing that most children need. Still, he is fed and sheltered by his family and gives back nothing but sorrow in return. He is therefore parasitic to a degree.

Kevin *lacks goals* and this is part of the problem. According to Eva, 'You can only punish people who have hopes to frustrate.'[10] Ask any young boy what he wants to be when he grows up and he might cite a career as an airline pilot, an astronaut or a doctor. Kevin has no real plan in life and thus it is very difficult for Eva to guide his behaviour. On the other hand, he does not harbour any unrealistic goals either.

Kevin gets easily caught up in *stimulation seeking* and has an unquestionable taste for the macabre. Although he appears initially disinterested in everything, it soon becomes evident that he simply does not want his mother to derive any pleasure from his learning, in that he seems to keep any school accomplishments hidden from her. Meanwhile, he constantly challenges boundaries, finding new and inventive ways to destroy everything around him, from his mother's study to passing cars (with water bombs from a highway overpass). All of this – and more – illustrates his *irresponsibility*.

Impersonal sexual behaviour is not so evident in Kevin during much of the story, although he does deliberately and repeatedly masturbate in front of his mother as a teenager. She later observes that he is probably a virgin. In terms of *unstable interpersonal relationships*, Kevin – like any psychopath – represents the main destabilising factor in his own family. His well-adjusted and affluent parents were very happily married before he was born; by the time Kevin is finished they are planning a divorce. As for Kevin, it seems unlikely he will ever enjoy an enduring and stable relationship (other than with his mother and, even then, entirely due to her efforts rather than his).

Score for lifestyle traits = 11/14

Finally, we come to Kevin's antisocial traits. Kevin is perhaps one of the angriest characters in fiction; from the moment he is born he is positively seething as he channels his rage in the most destructive ways he can. While he may not lose his temper in the classic sense, he frequently acts out impulsively and with considerable malice. Ultimately, he allows much of his anger to build up before channelling it towards the story's bloody climax. As such, Kevin has *poor anger control*. This is present from an early age. Kevin's *early behavioural problems* include pulling his mother's hair, screaming loudly in his cot, throwing his toys out of the playpen, hurling food on the floor and a refusal to toilet train that seems quite deliberate. These behaviours may seem normal for any child, but it is the sheer relentlessness of them that Eva, and a string of never-to-return babysitters, find so hard to deal with.

In time, Kevin becomes embroiled in serious *criminal behaviour*. His *criminal versatility* – over and above his signature atrocity – ranges from slander to assault to infecting a large and successful business with a catastrophic computer virus. Indeed, the only antisocial trait Kevin does not yet display is a *serious violation of conditional release* and only because it is not yet applicable. He is still in prison at the end of the story. We cannot help but wonder what will happen in the future.

Score for antisocial traits = 8/8 (one item not applicable)

Kevin scores a total of 33 out of 38 in the *Youth Psychopathy*

Checklist, which places him firmly in the range of psychopathy. In many ways he is the perfect fictional psychopath; he is certainly a *classic* psychopath in that he scores highly in all four domains, and the purity of his psychopathy is a good reason to include him in this book. Indeed, he serves as a contrast to the more likeable fictional psychopaths that appear in other chapters. Kevin garners very little of our sympathy, even though Eva, Franklin and Celia are all sympathetic characters in their own right. If anything, they highlight the degree to which Kevin is utterly horrifying to any decent individual with a conscience. So, why is this?

Firstly, although Kevin is a child, he is calm and fearless in the face of danger and does not seem remotely vulnerable. Recall Eva's observation of him as a 'singular, unusually cunning individual'.[11] When he falls ill on one occasion, he seeks his mother's comfort, albeit briefly; this is quite out of character and we cannot help but think that he is simply being manipulative. When his mother assaults him just once out of sheer frustration (and immediately feels ashamed of what she did), he quickly seizes the opportunity to turn it to his advantage. Even at the end of the story, when he faces five harsh years in an adult prison, any sense of vulnerability in Kevin is quickly eclipsed by our presumption that he will always be capable of fending for himself.

Although readers (and, indeed, society) are fascinated by secrecy, this sentiment does not really extend to Kevin. Perhaps this is partly because he never takes us into his confidence. Most of his actions are difficult for the average reader to fathom, while even his own mother (as narrator) tends to objectify him like a strange specimen under her scrutiny. And despite Kevin's ability to charm some of the other characters, we readers are certainly not fooled by his rare pretensions of warmth. Indeed – perhaps unlike many psychopaths in real life – Kevin is devoid of charisma. Were we to meet him in real life we would probably tire of him just as quickly as he would of us. From the moment he is born, Eva gets very little in return for her efforts to engage him. Kevin is a creature of extremes – when he doesn't shock us, he simply bores us. He is not a loveable rogue.

Similarly, unless you count an instinct for archery, Kevin has few talents or skills to admire. He is a skilled manipulator but, as he doesn't channel this to any good use, we cannot really applaud it. And far from appealing to any part deep within us that longs to be bad, he commits deeds so abhorrent that we are inclined to identify far better with his long-suffering mother. We also identify with his victims – seven school children, an English teacher who reached out to him, a caterer going about his daily work, his own younger sister and a father who was consistently kind to him throughout his life. All of Kevin's victims are kind and vulnerable people for whom we feel truly sorry. Finally, the story's backdrop is so ordinary that it does nothing to excuse Kevin's behaviour.

In short, notwithstanding Kevin's youth and calmness under fire, he has almost no redeeming features. It is his mother, Eva, who commands our sympathy as a tired and ageing parent driven to hell and back by her innately horrible son. She is the character with true courage. Symbolically, the opening scene of the film shows her stained in crimson at the *La Tomatina* festival in the Valencian town of Buñol, Spain. So vivid is the bloody imagery that we are initially uncertain whether or not we are witnessing first-hand Kevin's signature atrocity. Similarly striking is Eva's prolonged attempt to wash away the red enamel paint with which her house has been vandalised. Like the blood she sees on her own hands, this stain becomes ever more stubborn the harder she scrubs. She will never escape the stigma; she has visited every dark corner of the world and knows there is nowhere to hide.

Eva is not the only fictional mother to feel guilty in such circumstances. Some fifty years before Lionel Shriver's masterpiece was published, a similar novel was penned by the American writer William March. First appearing in 1954, *The Bad Seed* is the story of a mother's realisation that her eight-year-old daughter, Rhoda, is an evolving psychopath quite capable of committing murder. Rhoda presents a charming, intelligent and obedient façade that belies her true self and her nefarious deeds. As her mother – Christine Penmark – gradually learns the truth, she increasingly worries that Rhoda may have inherited her psychopathy from a wayward grandparent. Vivid and terrifying, the novel was nominated for the (US) National Book Award for Fiction. It was then adapted for the stage by Maxwell Anderson and enjoyed a long and successful run on Broadway. In 1956, it was further adapted into an Academy Award-nominated film directed by Mervyn LeRoy.[12]

***

If Kevin Khatchadourian and Rhoda Penmark do not pull at our heartstrings, the same is not necessarily true of all fictional psychopaths who happen to be children. Doris Lessing's novel *The Fifth Child* (1988) is the moving tale of how a happy family can be utterly fragmented by one troubled and troublesome individual. The tale begins with Harriet and David first meeting at an office party in the mid-1960s. It is plainly love at first sight; they are perfect for each other. Both are old-fashioned, middle-class, rather naïve individuals who want little more from life than a large family. They announce without ceremony that they plan to have as many as eight children, much to the disapproval of their respective families who cite economic constraints and other reasons to curtail their number of offspring. Still, the Lovatts settle down to their domestic bliss and quickly grow used to entertaining even the most distant of relatives *en masse* each Easter, summer and Christmas.

The couple have a spacious eight-bedroom Victorian house outside London in which to rear their first four children, each as attractive, clever and conscientious as the next. Harriet and David are earnest and smug in equal measure. When Harriet's sister, Sarah, gives birth to a child (Amy) with Down syndrome, the extended family are quick to patronise (their attitude perhaps not inconsistent with the zeitgeist of the early 1970s) and even Harriet and David have the temerity to act vaguely superior. It all adds to a strong sense of foreboding as Lessing skilfully and subtly hints at the calm before the storm.

From the outset of her fifth pregnancy, Harriet detects a difference from the others preceding it. Even *in utero*, the baby is hyperactive, constantly kicking and moving, invoking an insatiable restlessness in his mother. Harriet expresses her concerns but nobody sympathises, not even her physician Dr Brett. Opinions range from the view that she should simply put up with her discomfort, to admonishment for carelessly allowing herself to become pregnant with a fifth child that she and David will clearly be unable to manage. This will prove to be an understatement.

Ben is finally born, a month early and yet – at eleven pounds – still very large indeed. His appearance does not help to ingratiate him with the family:

> *He was not a pretty baby. He did not look like a baby at all. He had a heavy-shouldered hunched look, as if he were crouching there as he lay. His forehead sloped from his eyes to his crown. His hair grew in an unusual pattern from the double crown where started a wedge or triangle that came low on the forehead, the hair lying forward in a thick yellowish stubble, while the side and back hair grew downwards. His hands were thick and heavy ...*[13]

At this point, the overture draws to a close and we are left with a vacuum quickly filled by the antics of a troubled child.

We have observed already the argument that psychopathy is partly innate – possibly even genetic. In this context it is worth noting that from the moment of birth everybody takes such an ardent dislike to Ben that their attitudes could not reasonably have anything but a negative impact on his likely outcome. For example, Harriet's sister Sarah remarks: 'That Ben gives me the creeps. He's like a goblin or dwarf or something. I'd rather have poor Amy any day.'[14] Ben is constantly described in the language befitting a beast, 'like an angry, hostile little troll'.[15] His bedroom window has bars to prevent him from escaping. His mother refers to him as a 'Neanderthal baby' and later concedes (as though she doth protest too much) that 'after all, I don't want to kill the nasty little brute'.[16] In truth, she toys with the idea of infanticide quite a lot.

And young Ben is certainly a challenging child to live with. He cries incessantly, bites his mother's nipples when breastfeeding, hisses and spits, assaults his older brother at every opportunity, breaks toys and kills visiting pets. Despite some early milestones, he is clearly different from the other children; for example, he walks at an early age but his stature (having been large at birth) soon diminishes relative to his age. His emotional intelligence seems limited. We do not see him psychometrically tested by a psychologist or psychiatrist, but it is noteworthy that any time Harriet brings him to see a doctor she is told that there is nothing wrong with him or that whatever may be happening is probably her fault. Indeed, the story makes no reference to any mental illness, genetic issue, specific disability or developmental disorder (such as autism), but Ben's siblings and babysitters – even his father – treat him with a mixture of disgust, horror and fear. Seasonal visitors to the household, once so copious and enthusiastic, start to dwindle, arrive late and depart early. After a while they make their excuses and stop coming at all. Eventually they stop making excuses. Now at breaking point, the family implore Harriet to send the child to an institution. She knows the prospect will break her heart.

So, is Ben an evolving psychopath? This is debatable, and while I will put forward a strong argument that he is, based on the text and the plot, there is at least one other plausible diagnosis that I shall come to shortly. Indeed, in a purely abstract sense, he is not a character at all, but rather a symbol of any major upheaval that might befall a normal, heretofore-happy family. But in terms of characterised psychopathy, if we refer to the interpersonal traits of the *Youth Psychopathy Checklist*, the first item we might seek is *impression management*. Even as a teenager, Ben makes virtually no effort to influence how others perceive him. He utterly lacks charm – one of the essential tools for deceiving others. If there is any *manipulation for personal gain* on the part of Ben, his attempts to trick others are at a very basic level indeed. He is far more likely to resort to violence to achieve his aims.

Similarly, Ben does not engage in the type of *pathological lying* often seen in psychopaths. Admittedly, as a teenager he hangs out with a group of delinquents and is somewhat covert about whatever antisocial behaviours he is involved in (even if he is not remotely embarrassed at being captured on television at a violent demonstration). But he doesn't lie in the way a psychopath does – for the sheer hell of it and without any sense of self-consciousness. His dishonesty is usually by omission. Finally, there is little in the story to suggest that Ben has a *grandiose sense of self-worth*. A well-developed ego on some level perhaps, but not pomposity.

Score for interpersonal traits = 0/8

So, what about the affective traits? Ben displays a *shallow affect* throughout the novel. Psychopaths, as we have said, do not 'feel' the way the rest of us do; they know that emotions exist in most people (their 'cold' empathy allows this), but they do not experience the normal range of emotion themselves. The psychologists J. H. Johns and H. C. Quay describe this phenomenon well when they observe that the psychopath 'knows the words but not the music'.[17] Ben as a young child studies his siblings and mimics their emotional responses to what they see on television. He laughs when they laugh; he expresses dismay when they do. It is easy to infer that, because he doesn't experience normal emotions himself, he must look to others in order to know how to react. It is a trick many psychopaths learn.

Perhaps this stunted repertoire of emotion is the reason he also seems *callous and lacking in empathy*. Again, by this we mean 'hot' empathy. He is often cruel to other children and family pets without any appreciation of how these actions might affect his victims on an emotional level. He cannot even empathise with his mother; on the occasion Harriet realises Ben may have to go to an institution, he observes tears in her eyes at the prospect. With little or no understanding, he simply remarks that 'She is crying', before helping himself to some bread and then leaving the room.[18]

Similarly, when Ben is a toddler, Harriet suddenly hears screaming from the direction of his bedroom. She 'ran upstairs to find that Paul [Ben's slightly older brother] had put his hand in to Ben through the cot bars, and Ben had grabbed the hand and pulled Paul hard against the bars, bending the arm deliberately backwards'.[19] Ben shows a distinct *lack of remorse* over what he has done and is observed by his mother to be 'crowing with pleasure and achievement'. In a third example, Ben attacks an older girl at his school and the teacher observes that he 'doesn't seem to be remorseful in any way'.[20] Indeed, the book is replete with Ben's absence of remorse over the havoc he wreaks in his family and beyond. And for all of this, there is a consistent *failure to accept responsibility*. He simply doesn't care.

Score for affective traits = 8/8

In terms of lifestyle traits, Ben has virtually no control over his *impulsivity*. Like any psychopath, he simply doesn't do delayed gratification. When he doesn't get what he wants immediately, he screams or acts out in some other way. In one example when he must have been hungry, his mother arrives down to the kitchen to find him 'squatting on the big table, with an uncooked chicken he had taken from the refrigerator, which stood open, its contents spilled all over the floor. Ben had raided it in some savage fit he could not control.'[21]

Ben also displays *parasitic orientation*. At no point in the story does he engage in any kind of productive endeavour whatsoever. Of course, to live off parents is entirely appropriate for any child, but he or she usually returns the gesture by affording the parents joy in their every milestone. Not so with Ben. He is utterly *lacking in goals*. He is also *irresponsible*, displaying no sense of obligation to others. He plays truant from an early age as he adopts an inertia we assume will be lifelong. By the time he is nine, his mother has abandoned any attempt to compel him to attend school. His parasitic inclination becomes especially evident as he becomes a teenager. After Harriet's family have long since left, her only regular visitors are Ben and his gang of friends. They descend upon her house like a plague of locusts, taking what they need and giving nothing but grief in return. One of them even remarks to Harriet, with reference to the house, that 'One day we'll take it away from you.'[22]

Notwithstanding this, Ben does not like boredom. He displays a *need for stimulation* that may partly explain his reluctance to subscribe to the daily humdrum of school. Instead he hangs out with a young biker named John. So, does this need for novelty lead him to *impersonal sexual behaviour*? David makes reference to this as Ben approaches his teenage years.

'The thought of Ben sexual scares me,' he remarks. Later, when Harriet sees news items relating to serious crime on the increase in the area, she assumes Ben is involved.[23] 'There were rapes, too, among those news items …' she observes.[24] Still, we have no concrete evidence of any illicit sexual activity – or any sexual activity at all, for that matter. Ben has *unstable interpersonal relationships* but there are some notable exceptions. John the biker has a stabilising influence on him, while Ben also has consistent friends as a teenager. He forms an attachment to his mother, albeit only because of her supreme effort. Everyone else in Ben's life is driven away, including his siblings and his father.

Score for lifestyle traits = 11/14

Finally, we come to Ben's antisocial traits. *Poor anger control* is evident throughout the story and acknowledged by all characters who have the misfortune to come into contact with him. For example, when Harriet witnesses him repeatedly banging a stone against a metal tray, she is very reluctant to intervene, observing that 'interrupted, he would have raged and hissed and spat'.[25] His *early behavioural problems* have been listed already, and include the assault of other children and the killing of family pets. More serious *criminal behaviour* is strongly implied (but unconfirmed) towards the end of the story, consisting mostly of 'muggings, hold ups, break ins' and so forth, with sexual assaults also alluded to by Harriet. This suggests *criminal versatility,* but again we can never be sure.

We might reasonably award 1 out of 2 for both of these last two items. The final item on the checklist is *serious violation of conditional release*, but this is not applicable as Ben has never been in prison.

Score for antisocial traits = 6/8 (one item not applicable)

Ben's overall score is 25 out of 38, which gives us the sense that, were he to be assessed by some fictional forensic psychologist as part of the plot, he would score just enough points to earn the psychopathy label. More specifically, he scores poorly in the interpersonal domain, but highly in the affective, lifestyle and antisocial domains, indicating a leaning towards *macho* psychopathy. Essentially, he would be more likely to assault you than to relieve you of your life savings. But there is a major fly in the ointment that we cannot ignore, in the form of another plausible diagnosis that the book appears to discount.

Ben displays many of the features of autism, a neuro-developmental disorder affecting social development, communication skills and behaviour. Children with autism tend to be socially impaired and often show a lack of empathy and have difficulty forming relationships with others. They have poor 'theory of mind', meaning they are less well able to predict the actions of others by understanding a given situation from another's perspective. Language development is usually delayed and poorer in quality, with such children having a tendency to talk 'at' rather than 'with' others. Sometimes, they will simply repeat the words they hear without grasping the meaning. Indeed, up to half of children with autism never develop language. They can be hyperactive and may engage in time-consuming, compulsive behaviours or repetitive movements such as body rocking or hand flapping. They usually like a stringent routine and thus tend to resist change. Often, they are preoccupied with restricted areas of interest and display few signs of creativity or fantasy.

Autism at the milder end of the spectrum is sometimes termed *Asperger's syndrome*. Autistic spectrum disorders are three times more common in boys and their onset is usually before the age of three; thus, this represents a competing diagnosis for Ben that some readers may find more fitting. If so, he is an unusual example. Of course, we can only base an opinion on the evidence available and it is doubtful Doris Lessing had either psychopathy or autism specifically in mind when she described her protagonist. Regardless, while there is nothing likeable about Kevin Khatchadourian, the same cannot be said about Ben Lovatt. So, why might this be?

Some reasons do not stand up to scrutiny. Firstly, Ben does not appeal to any fascination we may have with secrecy, while he has no opportunity to win us over by taking us into his confidence. The novel is written in the third person and mostly from the viewpoint of his mother. Any insight we gain into Ben's psyche is through Harriet's eyes and thus it is she who garners much of the reader's sympathy. Indeed, Ben is objectified throughout the story like an animal or beast. In this regard, there is nothing remotely charming about him, and while he may not be boring per se, this is for all the wrong reasons. Ben is neither calm nor fearless under fire and does not beguile us with cleverness or humour; instead it is the constant threat of his bad behaviour that lends tension to the story. As readers, we find ourselves feeling scared both *of* him and *for* him.

Ben has no looks, talents or skills we admire, nor does he appeal to any part deep within us that longs to be bad. Possibly we project onto him a little of our own goodness, especially as his mother clearly does the same. Otherwise, there is little to find appealing about Ben. His victims are primarily comprised of his siblings, his parents, family pets and innocent members of society. They certainly do not serve to make him look good. Moreover, with a family primed to care for him in any other set of circumstances, and with no other adverse social or political undercurrents, Ben's backdrop does not cast him in any better a light. So, the question remains as to why we want him to prevail.

The answer lies in his vulnerability. Minutes after his birth, Ben 'opened his eyes and looked straight up at his mother's face'. Harriet's 'heart contracted with pity for him: poor little beast, his mother disliking him so much …'[26] Harriet's ambivalence evolves into devoted loyalty to her son. Alas, her sentiments are not matched by those of his father and siblings. The odds seem stacked against poor Ben from the start. Like some fierce but endangered animal, Ben is eventually shipped off to a dismal and neglected institution in the north of England. Everyone is relieved by Ben's absence but Harriet is plagued by guilt. Refusing to sit back and abandon her young child, she tracks him down and rescues him from a filthy padded cell:

> ... *the door opened on a square room whose walls were of white shiny plastic that was buttoned here and there and looked like fake expensive leather upholstery. On the floor, on a green foam-rubber mattress, lay Ben. He was unconscious. He was naked, inside a strait-jacket. His pale yellow tongue protruded from his mouth. His flesh was dead white, greenish. Everything – walls, the floor, and Ben – was smeared with excrement. A pool of dark yellow urine oozed from the pallet, which was soaked.*[27]

Harriet takes her frightened, wounded young boy home as the reader silently cheers her on. Like any hero, she may live to regret her bravery, but she is resolved at that moment to endure the consequences of her decision. And like both Eva Khatchadourian and Christine Penmark, Harriet is the front-line recipient of her offspring's antisocial behaviour, while also bearing the stigma of a society that assumes it is all her fault. Readers can see the odds stacked heavily against both her and her child, so it is little wonder that the two protagonists garner our sympathy.

Such is the brilliance of Doris Lessing. Although born in Persia in 1919, she was British by nationality and celebrated as a novelist, poet, playwright and biographer. Her most notable works are *The Grass is Singing* (1950), *The Golden Notebook* (1962) and *The Good Terrorist* (1985), and she was the recipient of numerous awards including the Somerset Maugham Award (1954), the James Tait Black Memorial Prize (1995) and – most notably – the Nobel Prize for Literature (2007). She died in London in 2013. *The Fifth Child* stands among her best work, powerfully illustrating that society's most vulnerable people need kindness, however troublesome they may be.

8

THE PSYCHIATRIC PSYCHOPATH

'I'm having an old friend for dinner.'

– Hannibal Lecter[1]

Perhaps the most obvious fictional psychopath examined in this book is the psychiatrist Dr Hannibal Lecter. When he first meets trainee FBI agent Clarice Starling in *The Silence of the Lambs*, he wastes little time in shocking her with what must be one of the most singular of culinary claims in literary history. Lecter reminisces on a meeting with a census taker who once tried to test him, recalling that he 'ate his liver with some fava beans and a nice Chianti'. Lecter's subsequent staccato inhalation leaves us in little doubt that we are in the presence of a very dangerous psychopath indeed. Such a spine-tingling portrayal of 'Hannibal the Cannibal' earned Sir Anthony Hopkins an Academy Award in 1991, while the American Film Institute later cited Lecter as its Number One Movie Villain.

In many ways, Lecter is a difficult character to diagnose. All that seems certain is that he does not have a 'conventional' mental illness such as psychosis or depression. No mention is ever made of him taking any form of psychiatric medication; it seems likely he is on *something* but, in recalling his most famous dish, we can at least be sure that he has not been prescribed a monoamine oxidase inhibitor (MAOI). This is one of the older varieties of antidepressant, highly effective but noteworthy for a number of rather harsh side effects. Among these is the risk of sudden and potentially fatal high blood pressure when the patient consumes certain types of food such as cheese, beans, pulses, liver, well-hung game and varieties of alcohol that include Chianti wine. As such, if Lecter were prescribed an MAOI, his diet of liver, fava beans and Chianti would almost certainly have brought about the so-called 'cheese reaction'.

So, if Lecter does not have a mental illness, are we sure he is a psychopath? To answer this, we should go back to his inception. Our anti-hero first appeared in 1981 with the publication of Thomas Harris' novel *Red Dragon*. Lecter plays a supporting role in the book, existing mostly to assist FBI criminal profiler Will Graham in arresting an entirely different (and far less likeable) serial killer nicknamed the 'Tooth Fairy'. To anyone with expertise, it is obvious that the Tooth Fairy is psychotic, displaying systematised delusions that lead him to murder entire families and capture the events on camera for his later perusal. During the course of the book, we learn from the backstory that Lecter was originally caught by Graham, who was almost killed in the process.

Lecter enjoys a greater share of the limelight in Harris' 1988 sequel, *The Silence of the Lambs*. The plot is similar to that of the first novel, in that our anti-hero comes to the aid of trainee

FBI agent Clarice Starling in profiling another (again far less likeable) serial killer who has been nicknamed 'Buffalo Bill'. As he did with the Tooth Fairy, Lecter offers a forensic opinion of Buffalo Bill's *modus operandi*, providing psychological analysis in return for details of Clarice's unhappy childhood. Clearly Lecter is a bored inmate who craves excitement or (better still, given the opportunity) sheer entertainment. Clarice (played by Jodie Foster in the film) provides him with some semblance of a *raison d'être* in the form of her own case study that interests him far more than yet another boring old serial killer.

It is only in *Hannibal* (1999) and *Hannibal Rising* (2006) that Lecter takes centre stage.[2] Both novels are far more biographical of Lecter, allowing us to see the evolution of an intelligent and highly cultured individual who appreciates music and art, pretends to form somewhat caring relationships and displays loyalty to one or two other people. We see that Lecter's fictional childhood was macabre. Born in 1933 to an aristocratic family in Lithuania, he initially led a life of privilege. But these circumstances came to a sudden and violent end in 1944 when the retreating German and advancing Soviet armies both stormed his estate, killing most of his relatives and leaving only Lecter and his younger sister, Mischa, as survivors. We learn that the two children were subsequently captured by Nazi deserters, who proceeded to cannibalise Mischa, leaving our young anti-hero utterly alone.

Lecter was found by Soviet soldiers and spent the next eight years living in an orphanage that was once his family's aristocratic home. Clearly traumatised (as evidenced by his re-peated nightmares), he had almost total amnesia for what had happened. Still, he showed that he was not to be trifled with; one occasion in the *Hannibal Rising* film sees Lecter (played by Gaspard Ulliel) sticking a fork into the hand of a young guard about to hit him. 'Hannibal,' the orphanage master observes, 'you do not honour the pecking order; you are always hurting the bullies.'³

Hannibal eventually ran away to France to live with Lady Murasaki, the exotic wife of his deceased uncle, Count Robert Lecter. Hannibal acquired his first taste for blood when he decapitated a local butcher who insulted Lady Murasaki at the marketplace. Then he lied effortlessly when questioned about it by Inspector Popil of the local police (played in *Hannibal Rising* by Dominic West). Hannibal even passed a polygraph test. 'He reacts to nothing,' Popil exclaims in the film, 'it's monstrous!'⁴

Of course, Lecter is nothing if not tenacious. As the story advances beyond his teenage years, we see a distinguished young man with sufficient intellect to gain entry on a work scholarship to the prestigious Institut de Médicine St Marie in Paris. Indeed, he is the youngest student ever to be admitted to a medical school in France. Later, he attends Johns Hopkins University Hospital in Baltimore, Maryland. But he has not forgotten what happened to his family; determined to exact revenge, he tracks down every last one of his sister's killers and cannibalises them. Yet it is easy to see how a childhood like that might haunt anyone; Lecter tried to protect Mischa and clearly he still cares about her, which is perhaps one of the reasons we find ourselves cheering him on.

Lecter's relationship with Graham forms the basic premise of a more recent NBC television series entitled *Hannibal*, developed by Bryan Fuller. It stars Mads Mikkelsen (an actor perhaps better known for playing Le Chiffre in *Casino Royale*) as Lecter, Hugh Dancy as Graham and Laurence Fishburne as Agent-in-Charge Jack Crawford. Once again, Lecter finds himself aiding the FBI in apprehending the kind of serial killers who have no redeeming features whatsoever. The adaptation is a particularly dark one that requires of the viewer a certain appreciation of the truly macabre.

As Harris rarely gives interviews, the question of whom the author based his anti-hero upon remained a mystery until 2013. Prior to that, plausible speculation involved a claim by a librarian in Cleveland, Mississippi that Lecter was partly modelled on William Coyne, a prison escapee who embarked upon a cannibalistic rampage in the 1930s. According to another story, Lecter was based upon Andrei Chikatilo, a Soviet serial killer convicted of the murder (and the alleged cannibalism) of fifty-three women and children in the 1970s and 1980s.[5] Harris eventually broke his silence to reveal that the inspiration for Lecter lay in a real-life doctor and murderer whom he had visited in Mexico as a young reporter in the 1960s. Harris referred to the killer only by a pseudonym, but investigative reporters subsequently determined the likely inspiration to be Dr Alfredo Ballí Treviño.[6] Harris has otherwise remained silent on the subject.

When Harris first introduces us to Lecter in *Red Dragon*, the psychiatrist's demeanour sends a shiver down the spine. Imprisoned in the Baltimore State Hospital for the Criminally Insane under the supervision of forensic psychiatrist Dr Frederick Chilton, Lecter has murdered at least nine victims and assaulted two others (one survives on a respirator while the other is a psychiatric inpatient in Denver). Or so we are told. Will Graham encounters a 'lithe man' of slight stature with 'small white teeth'.[7] His 'eyes are maroon and they reflect the light redly in tiny points'.[8] He is lying on his bed with a copy of Alexandre Dumas' *Le Grand Dictionnaire de Cuisine* perched open upon his chest, thus implying his penchant for French food. Lecter does not just eat his victims; he lovingly prepares them like a delicacy and then feasts upon them. From his cell, he reads widely and pens 'some brilliant pieces for the *American Journal of Psychiatry* and the *General Archives*. But they're always about problems he doesn't have.'[9] Either way, his incarceration does not seem to bother him much at all.

One of the essential features of psychopathy is that the behaviour is not better explained by a psychiatric illness such as schizophrenia. In this regard, Lecter's sanity is established from the outset. During a conversation, Lecter insists that Graham tell him how he succeeded in apprehending him so easily and the agent admits that it was not his own intelligence that made the difference, but rather Lecter's 'disadvantages', as he puts it. Lecter presses him further on the subject and Graham cites his 'passion' and a view that Lecter is 'insane'. But

Lecter does not suffer from obvious delusions, hallucinations or other symptoms suggestive of psychosis. Moreover, people with schizophrenia who access the right healthcare are not nearly as prone to violence as our rather histrionic tabloid media would have us believe. Lecter may indeed have 'passion' (although this is doubtful, unless you count narcissistic rage), but he is certainly not insane, contrary to the opinion of his custodians. Still, it is easy to see why Lecter (with his intricate knowledge of mental illness) wouldn't quibble; it is observed later in the story that if the authorities were ever to declare him sane, he would stand trial on nine counts of first-degree murder.

Some characters are quite open in regarding Lecter as a psychopath. When Graham seeks the opinion of a local police chief, the latter suggests rather insightfully that Lecter is 'not crazy, in any common way we think of being crazy', but rather that he 'did some hideous things because he enjoyed them' and can 'function perfectly well when he wants to'.[10] The police chief adds that 'they say he's a sociopath because they don't know what else to call him'.[11] He goes on to list some of Lecter's characteristics, namely that he lacks remorse or guilt and was sadistic to animals as a child. It is not entirely clear cut, however. The police chief casts a little doubt over the psychopath theory in asserting that Lecter 'wasn't a drifter, he had no history of trouble with the law', and that he possessed at least some depth of character and sensitivity. He also remarks that Lecter was not 'exploitive in small things, like most sociopaths are'.

But Lecter is undoubtedly a fictional psychopath. If we look at the interpersonal traits of the *Psychopathy Checklist*, we can see that he exudes an abundance of *glibness and superficial charm*. He is quite capable of looking a senator in the eye – a senator whose daughter has recently been kidnapped by Buffalo Bill – and remarking with some sarcasm, '[I] love the suit.'[12] Elsewhere, his skilful deconstruction of Clarice Starling within minutes of meeting her is communicated almost entirely with glib commentary. Prior to his capture, Lecter spends half a lifetime charming colleagues and dignitaries whom he (sometimes literally) has for dinner. Like a spider weaving a beautiful web, Lecter consistently charms his victims sufficiently to lure them into danger.

Lecter also has a *grandiose sense of self-worth*. For example, during his first encounter with Clarice in the film, he asks to see her identification and notes that it expires in just one week. The penny drops and Lecter is instantly offended, remarking sardonically that, 'Jack Crawford sent a trainee to *me*?' In the novel, he insists on Clarice addressing him as Dr Lecter because 'that seems most appropriate to your age and station'.[13] Lecter, after all, was a highly respected psychiatrist throughout a distinguished career, so much so that his eventual exposure as a cannibalistic murderer created quite the scandal. Lecter basks in his own notoriety and considers himself vastly superior to Dr Chilton. So narcissistic is Lecter that he only deigns to interact with those who interest him.

Could we accuse Lecter of *pathological lying*? He certainly deals in riddles a lot, but this is often a well-calculated tactic designed both to amuse and to protect him. Naturally, any murderer will lie to cover up their tracks, but there are few clear examples of Lecter lying simply for the sake of it. Still, he practised as a psychiatrist for some twenty years, presumably lying daily to his patients, colleagues and acquaintances alike. In many ways, his whole life was essentially a well-constructed lie. Either way, he is undoubtedly *manipulative for personal gain*, a champion at impression management. How else could he have gotten away with what he did for so long?

Score for interpersonal traits = 7/8

Moving to affective traits, the term *shallow affect* could reasonably be applied to Lecter. Like so many psychopaths, he seems quite able to mimic the emotions he sees in others, but there is very little evidence he actually feels anything himself other than intermittent rage. He is certainly fearless. Yes, he appreciates fine art and music, but his enjoyment is mostly intellectual rather than emotional. His *callousness* is perhaps less clear cut. Although he is essentially amusing himself in helping Clarice to catch Buffalo Bill, there may be just an ounce of *empathy* thrown in for good measure. More importantly, Lecter practises psychiatry successfully over a career lasting two decades or more. It could be argued that practising psychiatry at all without empathy is impossible. But perhaps 'cold' empathy will suffice. Psychopaths are inherently excellent amateur psychologists who know instinctively what buttons to press in their victims. Why, therefore, should psychopaths not make equally excellent professional psychologists or, indeed, psychiatrists? It is difficult to imagine anyone with 'hot' empathy perpetrating the types of crimes Lecter seems to relish.

Not only does he relish them, but he utterly *lacks any sense of remorse or guilt*. That man who came to interview him (the man whose liver he ate with some fava beans and a nice Chianti) was served his fate for little more than the minor peccadillo of deigning to irritate our anti-hero. Lecter recalls his death like an amusing anecdote with no sense of the devastation the interviewer's demise must have caused to his family. This, like many other examples, also shows us that Lecter *fails to take responsibility for his actions*. His philosophy appears to be that anyone stupid enough to cross his path will have nobody but themselves to blame for their inevitable bloody end.

Score for affective traits = 8/8

From a purely concrete viewpoint, Lecter displays a *parasitic lifestyle*. He literally eats his victims. But in the more abstract sense, can we really say that he perpetually takes what he needs and gives nothing back? Probably not. Instead, he deals in transactions, for example swapping his insight into Buffalo Bill for the intriguing details of Clarice's childhood. As such, Lecter facilitates symbiosis, even if he is motivated mostly by his own need for amusement. And let's not forget that he existed in gainful employment for some twenty years before he was finally arrested by Will Graham.

It could be claimed that Lecter *lacks realistic long-term goals* in thinking that his life will continue as normal while he murders and devours his victims. But then, he also studied hard at university and subsequently forged a solid career for himself as a well-respected psychiatrist. Unlike many psychopaths, Lecter rarely makes any casual claims to achieve things that are far outside his range of capabilities. Like a chess player he contemplates his next move and then executes it smoothly. He is rarely, if ever, *impulsive*. He always considers the consequences as they relate to himself.

But what about his *need for excitement or stimulation*? This is clearly evident throughout his fictional biography, not least in the manner in which he risks being apprehended for murder. His plethora of accomplishments is also a reflection of a constant need to be busy. In his prison cell, Clarice notices immediately his detailed sketches of Florence that are drawn entirely from memory. She compliments him, pandering to his narcissism, and he quietly decides to help her catch a killer. Of course, the easiest thing would be for him simply to tell her what he knows; but that would be no fun. Instead, he teases her with riddles, advising her in the first instance to 'look inside yourself'. (*Your Self* turns out to be the name of a self-storage facility that houses several further clues). Lecter has an enduring need to be entertained.

All in all, Lecter's behaviour is undoubtedly *irresponsible*. He simply does not care about the effect his actions will have on other people. But there is little evidence of *promiscuous sexual behaviour*. Like most people, he has had partners (not least his eventual relationship with Clarice in the novel version of *Hannibal*), but there is little evidence that his sexual behaviour is anything out of the ordinary. Nor does he have *many short-term marital relationships*. If anything, his lifestyle (while at liberty) is a bachelor one.

Score for lifestyle traits = 5/14

So, what about Lecter's antisocial traits? As we have said, he is an excellent planner who rarely acts impulsively. But, as a serial killer who feeds his victims to his acquaintances at dinner parties, he could hardly be regarded as well behaved. On the contrary, our anti-hero has some deep-rooted rage that leads to the *poor behavioural controls* we witness time and again. We have no real evidence of *early behavioural problems*, although cruelty to animals is alluded to once. It is only after the atrocities involving his family that things begin to change. Recall the local police chief remarking that Lecter 'wasn't a drifter, he had no history of trouble with the law'. In this regard, it seems likely that our anti-hero was simply skilled at not being caught, especially given the evolving *juvenile delinquency* (in the form of violence towards fellow orphans and guards) evident in *Hannibal Rising*.

Lecter never actually secures parole and, as such, *revocation of conditional release* should technically not apply. But he is given a new start when he escapes in dramatic fashion during a prison transfer in *The Silence of the Lambs*. And no sooner is he out of incarceration than we see him methodically tracking down Dr Frederick Chilton with a view to 'having an old friend for dinner'. It is reasonable therefore to accuse Lecter of recidivism.[14]

Finally, Lecter displays *criminal versatility*, although murder and cannibalism are the main items on his menu. In *Hannibal*, in the aftermath of his escape, we must assume he breaks the law in many ways in order to survive on the outside. How would he get by without, for example, forgery, deception and perversion of the course of justice? Indeed, his very escape from captivity is a crime.

Score for antisocial traits = 8/10

Lecter's score (28 out of 40) leaves us in little doubt that he is a fictional psychopath (even though such idiosyncratic serial killers are exceptionally rare in real life). It is obvious that he lacks a conscience, as if any of us needed convincing. But what subtype of psychopath is he? This is a little less straightforward because he scores well for interpersonal, affective and antisocial traits, but not for lifestyle traits. This pattern does not fit neatly into any of the three subtypes outlined in Chapter 2. We might have called him a *manipulative* psychopath were it not for his prominent antisocial traits. Equally, we might have called him a *macho* psychopath were it not for his prominent interpersonal traits and relative paucity of lifestyle traits. On balance, he probably most closely resembles a *classic* psychopath, partly because he doesn't fit into either of the other two categories. Lecter is strangely atypical.

And yet, he is also strangely likeable. We cannot help but want him to succeed. So why should this be the case? We can immediately discount a couple of items on our *Psychopath Likeability Scale*. Lecter doesn't take us into his confidence, for example. With his practised poker face, he gives away little detail about himself, concentrating instead on the psychodynamic scrutiny of others. Until *Hannibal Rising* was published, any real information we had about Lecter was derived from a third party, sometimes representing little more than rumour in his police file. There is a sensational scandal in the idea of a doctor abusing the trust placed in him by society, but that does not mean Lecter appeals to any part within us that longs to be bad. He may appeal to our sense of the macabre, but there can be few readers who truly identify with him. Cannibalism is not to most people's taste.

But our fascination with the macabre is nothing new. Our love of all things Gothic is such that Hannibal Lecter is never boring. In some ways, he is a modern version of the vampire – a character that has existed for a long time in popular culture. *Dracula* springs to mind as the archetype, but even Bram Stoker's creation is not the first vampire to appear in literary history. Johann von Goethe mentions them in 'The Bride of Corinth' (1797), while Lord Byron's poem 'The Giaour' (1813) is enough to chill the most sceptical of readers:

> *But first, on earth as vampire sent,*
> *Thy corpse shall from its tomb be rent:*
> *Then ghastly haunt thy native place,*
> *And suck the blood of all thy race.*[15]

The vampire is also described in Samuel Taylor Coleridge's poem 'Christabel' (1816), while even Alexandre Dumas' play *Le Vampire* (1851) precedes *Dracula* by several decades. More recently, various modern films and television series have revitalised the concept, the most impressive being *Bram Stoker's Dracula* (1992) directed by Francis Ford Coppola.

In the novel, Stoker goes to some lengths to describe Dracula's physical appearance in detail, perhaps reflecting the late nineteenth-century popularity of physiognomy (the deducing of someone's character by studying their outward appearance). Stoker ran the Lyceum Theatre in London for many years and his description is perhaps reminiscent of a set of detailed instructions to his wardrobe department. It is unsurprising that his visual portrayal of the vampire has become the established standard. Ask anyone to describe Dracula and you'll hear references to a pale complexion, fangs and the lust for blood. Apart from the fangs (although Harris does make a point of describing Lecter's teeth), both characters seem remarkably similar.

Dracula has several narrators, but much of the story is told from the viewpoint of Dr John Seward, a young psychiatrist. A bit like Dr Watson does for Sherlock Holmes, Seward records the adventures of his old mentor, the dynamic, mysterious and erudite old physician Professor Abraham Van Helsing (coincidentally played by Anthony Hopkins in Francis Ford Coppola's adaptation). Perhaps Hopkins' portrayal of Lecter gave him some insight into Van Helsing, but then Lecter really bears a far closer resemblance to Dracula, with both characters so obviously diabolical, dangerous and aristocratic.

So, are there other potential reasons we root for Lecter to succeed? Like both Dracula and Van Helsing, he is mysterious; it is hard not to be fascinated by the psychopath's ability to hide his true colours from fellow characters until it is too late for them. Equally, Lecter's calmness and audacity is something to behold. Yet, in a small measure, and despite his menace, his likeability is attributable partly to vulnerability. When we first meet him in a prison cell, he is utterly at the mercy of the rather cruel and sleazy Dr Frederick Chilton. When Lecter acts out, his privileges are taken away; he has been emasculated. And even if we feel Lecter deserves to be punished, this does not make him appear any less vulnerable. Meanwhile, his backstory garners some sympathy. In *Hannibal Rising*, we learn that his family were killed *en masse* by soldiers when he was just eleven years old. As such, despite his obvious dangerousness, there are elements of our anti-hero that are inherently vulnerable.

Lecter is seductively charming from the outset, superficial as we know him to be. Yes, we are wary of him but he can be disarmingly perceptive, articulate, observant and witty. He is even polite, apologising to Clarice for the crude behaviour of his fellow inmates and gallantly implying that one of them was murdered on her behalf over a demonstrative insult as she walked past his cell. We know that Lecter entertained colleagues and dignitaries at dinner for years before his apprehension. The success of his soirées may have been due in part to his range of talents and skills. Intelligent, charismatic, well-educated and cultured, Lecter has a love of opera, art, literature and fine dining. And, of course, he is an excellent cook.

Although Lecter's backdrop does not really make him look good (except perhaps the atrocity of his childhood that might help to explain his behaviour), his victims often add to his allure. In *Hannibal Rising*, he bides his time and then picks off his sister's murderers one by one. Those he kills tend to be killers in their own right, while other victims are involved in gangland crime. Likewise, it is hard to muster up any sympathy for the fate of Dr Chilton in the closing scenes of *The Silence of the Lambs*. Moreover, Lecter spends some time assisting Will Graham and Clarice Starling to catch the serial killers we really detest – the types who film themselves murdering entire families or make clothes from the skins of abducted young women. Lecter has some vague semblance of a moral code. He even has the courtesy to contact Clarice after his escape, reassuring her that 'I have no plans to call on you, Clarice, the world being more interesting with you in it.'[16] We know she will never become his prey.

How reassuring.

9

THE GOTHIC PSYCHOPATH

'I was silly enough to pay the full Amontillado price with-out consulting you in the matter.'

– Montressor (to Fortunato)[1]

If we subscribe to popular belief, there should really be a chapter in this book entitled *The Sleuthing Psychopath*. Sherlock Holmes is such a singular character with his eccentric behaviour and sharpness of intellect that at least some commentators have asserted that he might be a psychopath, even if only to a technical degree. Apparently included among these ranks are the scriptwriters of a modern-day BBC adaptation entitled *Sherlock*, starring Benedict Cumberbatch and Martin Freeman. In one episode, Holmes (in response to a policeman who suggests he is a psychopath) declares with some annoyance, 'I'm not a psychopath, Anderson; I'm a high-functioning sociopath; do your research!'[2] Some critics, quite rightly, have cast doubt on whether he is either.

Holmes was, of course, created by the Scottish physician and writer Sir Arthur Conan Doyle. Born on 22 May 1859, Doyle was educated by the Jesuits, first at the Stonyhurst College in

Lancashire and later at the Stella Matutina School in Feldkirch, Austria. He studied medicine at the University of Edinburgh and was subsequently employed as a ship's surgeon, first on the Arctic whaler *Hope* and thereafter on a steamship off the coast of Africa. He eventually returned home to become a general practitioner in Plymouth and Southsea, although he quickly grew tired of this. He resolved his boredom by travelling to Paris and Vienna to train as an eye specialist. Upon his return, he established an ophthalmology practice near Wimpole Street in London. In the 1890s, he wrote articles on Africa for the *Westminster Gazette* and, in 1900, he travelled again as a volunteer field physician in the Boer War. His brave endeavours earned him a knighthood in 1902.

Doyle married Louise Hawkins (the sister of one of his patients) in 1885. She died of tuberculosis in 1906 and Doyle wasted little time in marrying Jean Leckie – fourteen years his junior. He had five children in all, two with Louise and three with Jean. Although he was strong and active for most of his life, Doyle's health eventually waned as he endured several mild heart attacks in later years. He died at the age of seventy-one at his home in Windlesham Manor, Sussex on 7 July 1930 (coincidentally the seventy-eighth birthday of the fictional Dr Watson).

Doyle originally wrote short stories to supplement his income, while also killing time between consultations. His first published work was a short story entitled 'The Mystery of the Sasassa Valley', featured in *Chambers's Journal* in 1878. His writing was clearly influenced by his medical background. A case in point is *The War in South Africa* (1902) based on the time he spent as a volunteer field physician.

Doyle's works of fiction include a historical romance entitled *The White Company* (1891) and a series of novels that featured Professor Challenger, the most notable of which was *The Lost World* (1912). But Sherlock Holmes is undoubtedly his masterpiece. The obsessional sleuth with a penchant for cocaine and opiates was first introduced to readers in *A Study in Scarlet* (1887). As the novella opens, our hero is first acquainted with Watson as narrator, recently wounded in Afghanistan and in search of someone to share rooms with as he convalesces. Through the eyes of Watson, we first witness the singular empirical skills of Holmes as he solves a case that has otherwise confounded the local constabulary. The character of Holmes is thought to be a composite of Professor Joseph Bell (Doyle's former university lecturer), Edgar Allan Poe's Detective Dupin (to whom we will refer later), and a former criminal named Eugène François Vidocq (who became the first chief of the Sûreté in Paris on the principle that it takes a thief to catch one). Of note, Watson is thought to have been based on Doyle's personal secretary, Major Alfred Wood. Indeed, there may well be a bit of Doyle himself in Holmes' sidekick.

The success of *A Study in Scarlet* led to a series of fifty-six short stories in the *Strand Magazine* that appeared between 1891 and 1927. These were subsequently published in book form as *The Adventures of Sherlock Holmes*, *The Memoirs of*

Sherlock Holmes, *The Return of Sherlock Holmes*, *His Last Bow* and *The Case-Book of Sherlock Holmes*. Four additional novels were published, but alas Doyle felt that his literary ambitions were being thwarted by Holmes. He once complained that 'I feel towards him as I do towards *pâté de fois gras*, of which I once ate too much, so that the name of it gives me a sickly feeling to this day.'[3] This subjective sense of tedium led to 'The Final Problem' and that infamous scene at the Reichenbach Falls in which Holmes wrestles with his arch-nemesis Professor James Moriarty ('the Napoleon of crime') and the two men plummet to their supposed deaths. Doyle's broad readership were none too impressed, and showed limited interest in his more literary endeavours. He succumbed to public pressure some ten years later by writing a novella featuring his hero, entitled *The Hound of the Baskervilles* (1902). He would subsequently resurrect the character in *The Return of Sherlock Holmes* (1905).

Since then, Sherlock Holmes has served as the blueprint for virtually every fictional detective, from Agatha Christie's Miss Marple to Colin Dexter's Inspector Morse. Holmes has been portrayed time and again on stage, radio, television and the silver screen; indeed, Guinness World Records lists him as the most portrayed fictional character of all time.[4] By 1916, the actor Harry Arthur Saintsbury had played him over a thousand times on stage. Basil Rathbone was cast as Holmes in fourteen American films – twelve for Universal Pictures and two more for Twentieth Century Fox. And the interest in Holmes has not waned since. In this century, Robert Downey Jr played Holmes in two films directed by Guy Ritchie (with a third directed by Dexter Fletcher in pre-production), while perhaps the most notable television portrayal belongs to Benedict Cumberbatch in the recent BBC series.

The novelty of this latest adaptation is that it is set in modern-day London. The plots are cleverly updated to ensure that Holmes' deductive powers are still as essential as ever, notwithstanding the age of forensic science. Martin Freeman plays a plausible Watson, while Cumberbatch seems made for the role of protagonist. But does this extend to the portrayal of a psychopath? Or indeed a sociopath, given that the scriptwriters appear to be of the view that Holmes fundamentally lacks a conscience?

Despite Holmes' self-diagnosis in the first episode, psychopaths and sociopaths do not diagnose themselves. They are simply not able to. How can a person incapable of empathy decipher their lack of it? Besides, as already stated in Chapter 1, there is considerable overlap in the characteristics of a psychopath and a sociopath. In many ways, they are two different terms arrived at separately to describe a similar phenomenon, even if clinicians and academics continue to argue about the subtle differences. Moreover, Holmes may have a high intellect and a demeanour that is frosty at times, but he clearly does not lack a conscience. So why do people seek to label him a psychopath?

In the manner that some people like to personify a pet snake, others indulge themselves in the idea that a true psychopath can sometimes be good. This is rarely the case; indeed, very few (if any) of the fictional psychopaths in this book could reasonably be regarded as truly 'good' people. Our whole thesis is that we like them nonetheless. But Holmes is 'good' by nature. Yes, he is eccentric, but certainly not a psychopath. To prove this, let us run briefly through the *Psychopathy Checklist*, starting with the affective traits given the apparent accusation of coldness. We must ask, is Holmes really cold or has he simply trained himself to become temporarily dispassionate in order to remove as much bias as possible from his empirical reasoning? Many professionals – doctors, for example – do this in daily practice. So, can we say this of Holmes?

Holmes my pretend to be cold, but there is curious warmth in his wisdom. We can see that he experiences true emotion, showing a consistent affection for his housekeeper Mrs Hudson, his older brother Mycroft, his sidekick Watson and various other characters during the course of his many adventures. He has even been known to let minor criminals off the hook purely out of kindness, when he feels their otherwise inevitable punishment is undeserved. A man who lacks empathy would never do this. Holmes displays a clear sense of guilt and remorse in 'The Adventure of the Three Garridebs' when Watson is wounded. He apologises profusely (which psychopaths never do) when he startles Watson in 'The Adventure of the Empty House'. Holmes is also a man who accepts responsibility for his own actions. In 'A Scandal in Bohemia', he falls in love with Irene Adler, the only villain to ever truly outwit him. Again, such emotion seems implausible in a cold and calculating psychopath.

So, what about the interpersonal traits? Okay, so it could be said of Holmes that he has a somewhat grandiose sense of self-worth. When we meet him for the first time in *A Study in Scarlet*, he is in his laboratory perfecting a scientific test to detect blood, which he refers to as 'the most practical medico-legal discovery for years'.[5] This might give us the initial impression of grandiosity, but hindsight suggests that such a breakthrough would indeed transpire to be revolutionary. Moreover, Holmes is quick to point out his own shortcomings to his prospective new room-mate, namely that he gets 'in the dumps' at times, doesn't open his mouth for days on end and can be sulky. Holmes knows his limitations. In 'The Disappearance of Lady Frances Carfax', he implores Watson (who regularly publishes his dramatic accounts of Holmes' mysteries), 'Should you care to add the case to your annals, my dear Watson, it can only be as an example of that temporary eclipse to which even the best-balanced mind may be exposed.'[6] By this, he presumably means that it took him longer than usual to solve the case. Holmes' charm is not superficial; it is usually heartfelt. He is not glib in his remarks, but rather calculatedly reserved and precise. He does lie, con and manipulate at times (as do we all) but never for personal gain, always in a quest for the truth.

In terms of lifestyle, yes, Holmes has a clear need for excitement. When he runs out of cases to solve, he succumbs to his cocaine addiction and even dabbles in the use of morphine. Perhaps he takes advantage of Watson at times, but the reverse is also the case; their relationship is clearly as symbiotic as it is rich. Moreover, Holmes is not impulsive, irresponsible or unrealistic in his long-term goals. Indeed, he is a man of honour with an ethical code he adheres to. He does not involve himself in *promiscuous sexual behaviour* and he has not had a series of *short-term marital relationships*. If anything, Watson is guiltier of this.

And with antisocial traits, we move even further from the fundamental character of Holmes. Although we know little about his childhood, we are unaware of any early behavioural problems or juvenile delinquency. He is well behaved in general and although prepared to bend the law, he rarely breaks it. As he has never been convicted of a crime and sent to prison, revocation of conditional release does not even apply. So, as we can see, Sherlock Holmes falls far short of the requirements for psychopathy.

Of course, he is likeable, with a hint of vulnerability notwithstanding his intellect. His sleuthing abilities attract the unwanted attentions of numerous villains and arch-nemeses, while he is outwitted by Irene Adler and almost killed by Professor Moriarty. Holmes really should be more careful.

Does Holmes take us into his confidence? Well, yes, Holmes does narrate two of the short stories, namely 'The "Gloria Scott"' and 'The Musgrave Ritual', while two others are told in the third person. The remainder are recounted by Watson and, in this regard, we gain an intimate insight into Holmes' world of intrigue. Our hero is always courageous, often charming, never boring and he clearly has a wealth of deductive skills and talents that we admire. If he does not appeal to a part within us that longs to be bad, it is simply because Holmes himself is not bad. His only 'victims' per se are criminals who deserve their comeuppance and make Holmes look good. Finally, the dark and Bohemian backdrop of Victorian London makes Holmes look all the more noble and true.

But, at first, Watson is not altogether convinced. In *A Study in Scarlet*, he remarks to Holmes that 'You remind me of Edgar Allan Poe's Dupin. I had no idea that such individuals did exist outside of stories.'[7] Holmes is not impressed, and responds by retorting: 'Now, in my opinion, Dupin was a very inferior fellow. That trick of his of breaking in on his friends' thoughts with an apropos remark after a quarter of an hour's silence is really very showy and superficial. He had some analytical genius, no doubt; but he was by no means such a phenomenon as Poe appeared to imagine.' Whether we agree with Holmes' opinion of Detective Dupin (on whom, as previously noted, Doyle partially based his most famous character), Poe was certainly more than capable of describing a psychopath.

***

Edgar Allan Poe did not always enjoy rude health. In addition to epilepsy, he endured alcohol dependence, although, strangely, it was said of him that he could not hold his drink. The *Dictionary of American Biography* observes that 'Less than a little was with him too much.'[8] It also describes him as 'greatly loved by few, hated by many, and memorable to everybody'. A man of robust temperament, it seems, he used opium as well as alcohol and, following the death of his young wife in 1847, he became psychologically very unstable. He attempted suicide by drinking laudanum in November 1848. He died less than a year later, on the morning of 7 October 1849 – just five days after he was found delirious from the combined effects of heart failure, excess alcohol and epilepsy. He was only forty.

He lived in poverty for much of his adult life, partly because he was one of the first American writers to attempt to earn a living primarily from published work. Early nineteenth-century America was a challenging place to do this because a paucity of international copyright law allowed American publishers to print *en masse* the works of contemporary British and French authors rather than pay for original work from their American counterparts. Although magazines were a popular medium in which to publish short stories and poems, competition was stiff. Such magazines came and went with as few as half-a-dozen editions, while contributors were often paid a pittance, paid late and sometimes not paid at all. Poe would go on to become one of the most famous American writers of all time, but daily life for him was frugal.

He was born on 19 January 1809, in Boston, Massachusetts – the second son of David Poe Jr and Elizabeth Arnold, both actors and both of whom died in 1811. Edgar and his two siblings were separated, his older brother William going to live with their grandparents, while Edgar and his younger sister Rosalie were fostered. Edgar was brought up by John and Frances Allan of Richmond, Virginia, who earned their living from the tobacco-export trade. He spent much of his early youth in the United Kingdom on account of his foster-father's occupation and was educated in Scotland and London between the ages of six and eleven. Although never legally adopted, Edgar began signing his name Edgar Allan Poe at the age of fifteen. He studied briefly at the University of Virginia in 1826 but was expelled after only one term because of gambling debts. He later enrolled in West Point Military Academy at the behest of his foster-father but was again expelled (in 1831) for 'gross neglect of duty'. In truth, he allegedly presented himself for parade in his birthday suit, something unlikely to have gone down well with his commanding officer.

Poe's writing career began at the age of eighteen, with *Tamerlane and Other Poems*, self-published in 1827 under the *nom de plume* 'A Bostonian'. By 1835 he was assistant editor with *The Southern Literary Messenger* and by 1839 he was co-editor of *Burton's Gentleman's Magazine*. In 1841, he was appointed editor of the most popular American periodical at the time, *Graham's Lady's and Gentleman's Magazine*. In 1845, he became co-editor and proprietor of *The Broadway Journal*. In January the same year, he found fame with his poem 'The Raven', published in the *Evening Mirror*. This was his stepping stone to widespread fame.

Of course, Poe is most famous for his short stories. In 1840, he published *Tales of the Grotesque and Arabesque*, which included the Gothic short story 'The Fall of the House of

Usher'. Murder is a common theme in many of his stories, including 'The Tell-Tale Heart' (1843), 'The Black Cat' (1843), 'The Cask of Amontillado' (1846) and 'The Murders in the Rue Morgue' (1841). The last of these – which introduced the protagonist Inspector Dupin – is credited as the first empirical detective story in a style that would later influence writers such as Sir Arthur Conan Doyle.

It was once speculated that Poe was himself a murderer. He married his thirteen-year-old cousin Virginia in 1836 (their marriage certificate apparently stated she was twenty-one) and, although they were so in love that Poe wrote very little after her death from tuberculosis in 1847, he was also known to be a womaniser. He allegedly had an affair with Mary Rogers, a twenty-one-year-old cigar merchant who was found strangled in the Hudson river, New Jersey in 1841. A witness recalled seeing Rogers walking with 'a tall dark man, aged about twenty-six' shortly before her death and Poe seemed to fit the description. Although he was never questioned about the murder (which was never solved), suspicion was nonetheless cast upon him. This was not helped by his short story 'The Mystery of Marie Rogêt' (1842), which did not identify any killer but otherwise bore an uncanny resemblance to the forensic detail of the real-life murder.

For a man who died at forty, Poe certainly left his mark. For the purposes of this book, we will examine the protagonists of two of Poe's most famous short stories, 'The Tell-Tale Heart' and 'The Cask of Amontillado'. In comparison with our analysis of other fictional psychopaths so far, we are at something of a disadvantage here because both stories are so short. The *Psychopathy Checklist*, as we have said, is most accurately used when the index event (in other words the reason why the psychopath was caught) is specifically excluded in favour of a frank look back over the subject's life and history to date. Still, it is difficult to do this with most fictional psychopaths because the authors naturally tend to write almost entirely about the index event and Poe is a good case in point. In the name of entertainment, therefore, it is important we allow ourselves a little latitude.

'The Tell-Tale Heart' was first published in 1843 in James Russell Lowell's magazine, *The Pioneer*. Here, an unnamed narrator carefully plans and executes the murder of an old man with whom he lives, before dismembering the victim and hiding him under the floorboards. The relationship is unclear, but a plausible explanation is that the old man is some sort of father figure, landlord or employer and that the narrator is his lodger or manservant. The narrator goes to some lengths to convince us of his sanity, although he admits to being prone to anxiety that results in a sharpening of the senses. We suspect he doth protest too much because when the police eventually arrive, he hears the sound of his deceased victim's heartbeat growing ever louder beneath the floorboards until he can finally stand it no longer and confesses to the murder. It is implied that the sound he hears is an auditory hallucination because the police seem not to notice it. The only other explanation is a supernatural one, which would be consistent with Poe's Gothic leanings.

The motive for the murder is unclear, except that the narrator seems unnerved by one of the old man's eyes: 'One of his eyes resembled that of a vulture – a pale blue eye, with a film over it', suggestive, perhaps, of a cataract.[9] The narrator doesn't harbour any feelings of resentment towards the old man, nor does he feel that his victim has ever wronged him in any way. Indeed, the narrator claims to love the old man and hate only the eye. Perhaps the physical defect is a symbol of excessive parental watchfulness or something more oppressive. It may also suggest mental illness in the form of a persecutory delusion, although the meticulous manner in which the narrator commits the murder suggests not merely good organisation but sanity itself. He denies killing for any sort of financial reason, stating quite clearly that, 'For his gold, I had no desire.'[10] He does not flee the scene with any spoils or money once the murder has been committed, which backs this up.

All this ambiguity is in stark contrast to the forensic detail in which the murder is planned, perpetrated and described. The narrator opens the door of the old man's room in the early hours of seven nights in a row, but each time the victim's vulture-like eye is closed, which the narrator interprets as a reason to defer the deed. Finally, on the eighth night, the old man opens his eye and, as he senses an interloper in the room, his heart grows 'quicker and quicker, and louder and louder every instant'.[11] The narrator jumps out 'with a loud yell' and the old man shrieks just once before he is quickly but noisily smothered to death. Once the body has been cleanly disposed of, it is this noise that causes a suspicious neighbour to summon three policemen the next day. The narrator tells the police that he simply had a nightmare and woke up screaming, while he smugly shows them the old man's room left tidy and intact. There are clearly no signs of any struggle. All goes according to plan until the narrator begins to notice the thump of the old man's beating heart beneath the floorboards.

We know that Poe likes to inject an element of the supernatural into his fiction, but can we truly call the narrator a psychopath? This is difficult to judge, given the subjective nature of the narrative. From an interpersonal perspective, there is little evidence of *glibness*, although we sense some *charm* might have been necessary for the narrator to ingratiate himself with the old man in the first place. But is this charm superficial? Perhaps so, as the narrator tells us chillingly, 'I was never kinder to the old man than during the whole week before I killed him.'[12] Conversely, it is difficult to detect any *grandiose sense of self-worth* in the narrator. He spends much of the story trying to convince us of his sanity rather than his brilliance or innocence. By his own admission, he is 'very, very dreadfully nervous', suggesting a man with relatively low self-esteem rather than overt narcissism.

So, what about *pathological lying*? Interestingly, the first word of the story is 'True!' implying a narrator who may have grown used to not being believed. Naturally, there is a distinct lack of honesty in his dealings with the old man in the week leading up to the murder. In this regard, the narrator appears *manipulative* but, as the motive remains unclear throughout, we cannot say for certain whether or not it is for personal gain. And by the time the narrator confesses to the reader, he has already done so to the police and we can surmise that he has little left to lose.

Score for interpersonal traits = 4/8

In terms of affective traits, there is a strong sense of anxiety followed by smugness and then outright fear in the narrator. *Shallow affect* is therefore debatable. Equally so are the narrator's *callousness and lack of empathy*. On one occasion, he remarks that, 'The old man's terror must have been extreme!'[13] although such a statement may represent 'cold' morbid fascination as much as it does 'hot' empathy. More obvious is the narrator's *lack of remorse or guilt*. Describing the murder, he tells us, 'In an instant I dragged him to the floor, and pulled the heavy bed over him. I then smiled gaily, to find the deed so far done.'[14] Later, when the police arrive, he describes how he 'brought chairs into the room, and desired them here to rest from their fatigues, while I myself, in the wild audacity of my perfect triumph, placed my own seat upon the very spot beneath which reposed the corpse of the victim'.[15] Of course, the narrator eventually confesses to the police, but this is likely out of fear rather than guilt. Still, in the end he *takes responsibility for his own actions*.

Score for affective traits = 2/8

The narrator might well lead a *parasitic lifestyle*, if we assume that he lives with the old man and takes advantage of his hospitality. We cannot say for certain, but there is little or no evidence that the narrator gives anything in return for the old man's trust. In terms of other lifestyle traits, the planning and patience involved in his crime are impressive; he waits a full eight nights before finding the perfect time to strike. It is reasonable to say therefore that the murder is not *impulsive*. We might have conjectured that he has a *need for excitement* based on the idea that he commits a murder at all, but it soon becomes evident that he cannot cope with the anxiety inherent in trying to evade the police. Beyond the index event, it is difficult to determine any *lack of realistic long-term goals* or pervasive *irresponsibility*. Moreover, we cannot comment on *promiscuous sexual behaviour* or *many short-term marital relationships*, although neither seems likely in the narrator.

Score for lifestyle traits = 2/14 (with limited information available)

Finally, in terms of antisocial traits, we do not have any information on *early behavioural problems* or *juvenile delinquency*. The haste with which the neighbours call the police in response to a couple of shrieks in the dead of night could lead us to infer previous transgressions of the law; however, there is little evidence overall to suggest pervasively *poor behavioural controls* or *criminal versatility* beyond the index event. *Revocation of conditional release* does not apply if we assume the narrator has never been to prison. Again, we have no information.

Score for antisocial traits = 1/8
(with limited information available
and one item not applicable)

Overall, the narrator scores a meagre 9 out of 38, which tells us that he is not a fictional psychopath, even if we consider the dearth of relevant information about his backstory. In clinical terms, this shows the value of a good history. But more importantly, it is strongly implied that the narrator experiences both auditory hallucinations and persecutory delusions in relation to the old man. He is most likely suffering from psychosis, a phenomenon (as established in Chapter 1) that is utterly different from psychopathy despite sharing a first syllable that sometimes leads to confusion.

The same cannot be said of all of Poe's protagonists. A case in point is the narrator in another of his most famous short stories, 'The Cask of Amontillado', published in November 1846 in *Godey's Lady's Book*. The tale is set during a carnival in Italy and involves one of Poe's favourite Gothic themes: victims being buried alive. The anti-hero is the aristocratic Montressor, who recounts an incident in which he takes revenge against a fellow nobleman ironically named Fortunato. The latter, it seems, has insulted Montressor profoundly, leaving the narrator's ego so badly wounded that he plots to murder his adversary during the aforementioned carnival when he knows the victim will be drunk.

Montressor lures the unsuspecting Fortunato to his private cellar under the ruse of an exclusive sherry-sampling opportunity. He claims to have acquired a 'pipe' of what he thinks may be a rare vintage of Amontillado.[16] Montressor informs Fortunato that he is on his way to seek the opinion of a fellow wine connoisseur named Luchesi, secretly knowing that the narcissistic Fortunato will insist on stepping in. As predicted, Fortunato remarks sardonically that Luchesi 'cannot tell Amontillado from Sherry' and proceeds to accompany Montressor to his private catacombs entirely according to plan.[17]

The two men wander from cavern to cavern in vaults that seem to run endlessly from the basement of Montressor's palazzo. On the way, Fortunato is plied first with Medoc, then with De Grâve as the narrator endeavours to keep his adversary inebriated. Fortunato happens to have a bad cough and Montressor suggests several times that they abandon their excursion on account of vaults being 'insufferably damp' and 'encrusted with nitre'.[18] His companion counters that he 'shall not die of a cough' and demands that they proceed.[19] As they walk, Montressor points out his family's coat of arms on the wall, 'A huge human foot d'or, in a field azure; the foot crushes a serpent rampant whose fangs are imbedded in the heel.'[20] The motto on the coat of arms is *Nemo me impune lacessit* ('no one provokes me with impunity') and hints strongly that Montressor views himself as the foot, about to tread upon the serpent who has dared to bite him. The narrator then makes a clumsily failed attempt to pretend he is a member of the Freemasons.

They arrive at their destination and Montressor informs his companion that the Amontillado is kept within a small interior crypt. Fortunato, still drunk, enters unsuspectingly and is slow to react when the narrator suddenly and dexterously binds him in chains. Montressor, using bricks and mortar he has stored in advance, begins to construct a wall aimed at entombing his unfortunate companion alive in the crypt. By now the latter is sobering up and, as he struggles against the chains in an effort to escape, he emits a 'low moaning cry' for help.[21] Montressor simply responds by mocking him, whereupon Fortunato begins laughing as though it is all some kind of elaborate joke. His mention of Lady Fortunato waiting at home for him does nothing to give Montressor pause. And as the wall nears completion, Fortunato implores his murderer to desist 'For the love of God, Montressor!'[22] The latter replies with sarcasm, 'Yes, for the love of God!' before dropping a burning torch through the remaining gap and pushing the last stone into place. Montressor describes feeling sick, but then attributes this to the dampness of the catacombs.

At the end of the tale, we realise it is being narrated some fifty years after the events originally unfolded. Montressor, it seems, was never caught and tried for his crime. As for Fortunato, the narrator adds one final injunction: *In pace requiescat!* ('May he rest in peace').[23] Such *glibness* is chilling to say the least, but is not the only reason to consider Montressor a psychopath. From an interpersonal perspective, he is certainly *charming*, superficial as he is. He manages with some skill to entice a rich, albeit inebriated, acquaintance deep into the catacombs under the ruse of a vintage sherry. Effortlessly sycophantic, he adds that 'I was silly enough to pay the full Amontillado price without consulting you in the matter.' We are left in no doubt that Montressor is a smooth operator.

Montressor's *grandiose sense of self-worth* is evident throughout the tale. The reason he gives for his heinous crime is some unnamed insult by his victim. In some ways, Fortunato's very existence seems to offend the narrator; while the latter conveys a sense of decaying aristocracy, it is implied that the victim is 'new money' who may have gleaned much of his status from his membership of the Freemasons. The victim seems less well educated, arguing that 'Luchesi cannot tell Amontillado from Sherry' and in doing so revealing his own ignorance of the fact that one is actually a subset of the other. Indeed, rather than being a connoisseur of fine wines, Fortunato bears closer resemblance to a simple alcoholic. This is in contrast to the knowledgeable Montressor, who grandly asserts that, 'I was skilful in the Italian vintages myself, and bought largely whenever I could.'[24] All in all, the murderer's disdain for his victim seems born largely of snobbery.

Strictly speaking, we should not utilise the index event when describing a psychopath, but with a short story such as this we have little else to go on. Notwithstanding this, Montressor shows evidence of *pathological lying*. For example, he has no reason to pretend to be a member of the Freemasons; it provides no additional advantage in his plan to commit murder. But he lies impulsively anyway. Add to this the fact that the entire ruse is a well-constructed lie from start to finish. Mostly, Montressor's impression management is seamless, and amply demonstrates his skill at *manipulation for personal gain*. He knows instinctively his victim's weaknesses and how to exploit them, appealing to Fortunato's lust for social status as well as his thirst for yet another drink. By the time Montressor has finished, Fortunato is determined to taste that damned Amontillado, even if it kills him.

Score for interpersonal traits = 8/8

So, how does Montressor score in terms of affective traits? Certainly, a *shallow affect* appears to be one of his characteristics. As he coolly recounts his nefarious deeds, we get very little sense of any emotion in him other than jealousy and rage. Similarly, he *lacks empathy* and is callous to such a degree that he makes a point of prolonging the murder when he notices that his victim is sobering up. He tells us:

> *I laid the second tier, and the third, and the fourth; and then
> I heard the furious vibrations of the chain. The noise lasted
> for several minutes, during which, that I might hearken to*

> *it with the more satisfaction, I ceased my labours and sat*
> *down upon the bones. When at last the clanking subsided,*
> *I resumed the trowel, and finished without interruption*
> *the fifth, the sixth, and the seventh tier.*[25]

Even fifty years after the murder, Montressor expresses *no sense of remorse or guilt*. Although he admits his crime to the reader, it is obvious he has told nobody else, and certainly not the police. He *takes no responsibility for his actions*; his anger with Fortunato seems to have endured for half a century, the clear implication being that the murderer still believes the victim deserved everything that happened to him. In Montressor's eyes, Fortunato had only himself to blame for his death.

Score for affective traits = 8/8

Montressor's lifestyle traits include a *need for excitement and stimulation*. It is obvious that he has spent some time elaborately planning the perfect murder. He must have inspected the catacombs at length to find the ideal 'interior recess, in depth about four feet, in width three, in height six or seven'.[26] We know he stowed bricks and mortar behind a pile of bones in advance of the operation, and brought a trowel with him beneath the folds of his *roquelaire*. He even gave the servants 'explicit orders not to stir from the house'.[27] Is this detailed planning born partly of boredom? Possibly so, but more importantly we sense a rush of adrenaline as he commits the murder itself, presumably knowing full well that failure to complete the task properly might result in his trial, imprisonment or even death. Or maybe his heart rate slows, as happens to some psychopaths during ordeals that others might find stressful. Either way, his behaviour is undoubtedly *reckless and irresponsible*; the profound implications for Lady Fortunato, for example, are of little concern to him. But he is not *impulsive*. If anything, the sheer patience implicit in his planning is remarkable, as is his ability to keep the whole crime secret for fifty years. There is nothing in the story to suggest that Montressor *lacks realistic, long-term goals* either. At no point does he boast of achievements that will never be his. Indeed, he judges his own abilities quite well insofar as the perfect revenge killing is concerned.

Does he lead a parasitic lifestyle? It is difficult to say this for certain, given the brevity of the story and its natural focus on the index event. Still, an aristocratic background is strongly implied by his snobbery, the size of his property and the existence of a family coat of arms. As he lives for at least another fifty years, we can assume he is a relatively young man at the time of the murder and it is easy to imagine him benefiting from an allowance afforded by some wealthy relative or benefactor while he awaits his inheritance. It seems unlikely he has ever done an honest day's work in his life. Still, does he routinely take advantage of the kindness and vulnerability of others? Dotty aunts with piles of cash under the mattress? Possibly so. On balance, we might reasonably score Montressor positively when it comes to a parasitic lifestyle, acknowledging our limited information. But we cannot comment on the presence or otherwise of *promiscuous sexual behaviour* or *many short-term marital relationships*.

Score for lifestyle traits = 6/14

Finally, we come to antisocial traits. The fact that Montressor will commit murder in revenge for an insult strongly suggests *poor behavioural controls*. But there is little in the story to imply he might have had any *early behavioural problems* or *juvenile delinquency*. As murder is the only crime described in the story, he cannot be said to be guilty of *criminal versatility*, while *revocation of conditional release* does not apply as we assume Montressor has never been to prison.

Score for antisocial traits = 2/8
(with limited information available and
one item not applicable)

Overall, it seems likely that Montressor is a fictional psychopath. Even though he scores only 24 out of 38, we are entitled to a modicum of poetic licence given the brevity of the tale. No doubt, our anti-hero would have scored higher had Poe written a longer story with more background detail. In terms of subtype, Montressor scores better across the interpersonal and affective domains than the lifestyle and antisocial domains, suggesting he is a *manipulative* psychopath. So, why do we find ourselves rooting for him to succeed? Again, as with most psychopaths, it is easy to be fascinated by Montressor's demeanour of secrecy. His sheer audacity and nerve is also something to behold. But he is not the least bit vulnerable. Indeed, he is ruthless in the extreme and any person who dares to insult him had better watch out. Does he appeal to the devil within us? This also seems unlikely, but it is important to note that we are interpreting a Gothic tale of the macabre that is penned to appeal more to our sense of horror than any inherent need to identify with the protagonist.

But equally we do not identify with Montressor's victim, the rather pathetic Fortunato. Except perhaps for a brief moment at the end when he mentions Lady Fortunato, who will likely be waiting at home wondering what has become of her husband. We know she will never find out, which makes her as much a victim of the whole episode as Fortunato himself. As such, Montressor's victims do not make him look good. Instead, they garner the reader's sympathy. And the backdrop affords little opportunity to make him look good either because we get very little sense of it. Of course, we know the story is set in an Italian city during the time of a carnival, but beyond that we can say very little. Was it set in the nineteenth century, the Renaissance or earlier still? Was it acceptable for a man at the time to demand satisfaction when insulted? We do not know, so ultimately it has little influence on Montressor's likeability.

He does take us into his confidence, however. The story is narrated in the first person and thus we are permitted to see the entire episode from his viewpoint. He explains his reasons for committing the murder and has the last word on the victim's shortcomings. Montressor is also charming, or at least more charismatic than the inebriated Fortunato. So expert is Montressor at impression management that he has no trouble luring a fellow nobleman down to the catacombs under a ruse. He probably fools *us* too. He is clearly a talented planner and knowledgeable about wine and sherry, despite the premise of his invitation to Fortunato. It is difficult not to admire Montressor's audacity. He is anything but boring.

But the real talent lies with Edgar Allan Poe, Gothic writer and poet, aficionado of early murder mysteries, pioneer of early science fiction and ghost stories, and creator of likeable psychopathic characters. He even invented the 'whodunit' detective story – a style that has been emulated time and time again until this day. *The Murders in the Rue Morgue* is the obvious case in point, which leads us nicely back to where we started: the strange and singular fictional detective with whom we always side (but who, alas, is not a psychopath), Mr Sherlock Holmes.

10

THE SINISTER PSYCHOPATH

'Yes, I want to play, I really, really do!'

– Dexter Morgan[1]

Some characters are clearly showcased as psychopaths. An obvious case in point is Dexter Morgan, the protagonist of a Showtime television series that ran from 2006 to 2013. Based on the novel *Darkly Dreaming Dexter* (2004) and its sequels by Jeff Lindsay, the concept was adapted for television by James Manos Jr and was nominated for numerous awards. The Season Eight premiere attracted over three million viewers when it aired. It seems the public has an unquenchable thirst for blood.

But not nearly as much as the eponymous protagonist himself, as portrayed by Michael C. Hall. Dexter is a vigilante serial killer who tracks down murderers, rapists, mobsters and various other hardened criminals who have evaded the justice system, and then kills them cleanly before carving them up and disposing of their corpses in the sea. Although top of his class at medical school, Dexter never qualified and has, instead, chosen the career of blood-spatter-pattern analyst for the Forensics Department of the fictional Miami Metro Police.

Thus, he has acquired the necessary esoteric knowledge to murder clinically without leaving any traceable evidence. He is a master manipulator whose true identity is rarely discovered until it is too late.

Each season involves Dexter taking on a different major antagonist, usually in the guise of another serial killer. In Season One, it is the 'Ice Truck Killer' (played by Christian Camargo); in Season Three, it is Assistant District Attorney (and rookie serial killer) Miguel Prado (played by Jimmy Smits); in Season Four, it is the 'Trinity Killer' (played by John Lithgow); and so forth. Season Two differs slightly, in that an FBI manhunt is triggered when Dexter's heretofore disposed-of corpses are found by a group of deep-sea divers. The presumed killer is nicknamed the 'Bay Harbour Butcher' by the press, as Dexter tries desperately to avoid discovery. Ultimately, he frames his colleague and nemesis, Sergeant James Doakes (played by Erik King).

The reasons for Dexter's singular behaviours are evident in his backstory. Essentially, he was orphaned at the age of three by the brutal murder of his mother – an event he witnessed in all its gruesome detail. I say 'essentially' because, in a plot twist, it transpires that his biological father is alive and well until halfway through Season One.[2] Still, Dexter has sealed over the trauma of his mother's grisly demise, largely thanks to his adoptive father Harry (played by James Remar). In Dexter's past, Harry would vaguely refer to a time 'before we took you in', while remaining suitably elusive about Dexter's biological parents. Harry even destroyed the police files related to the crime, along with any evidence that he had had an affair with Dexter's mother, and any reference to Dexter's older biological brother, Brian Moser (the major antagonist of Season One who transpires to be the Ice Truck Killer). Harry nevertheless recognised latent homicidal tendencies in Dexter at an early developmental stage and, in response, trained him to channel these urges elsewhere for the benefit of society to a degree, but mostly for his own survival. Thus, a 'code' was imposed on Dexter's psychopathic self, his 'Dark Passenger' as he calls it.

Throughout eight seasons, Harry's 'ghost' appears intermittently before Dexter, offering the same advice and coaching as he did when he was alive. Should we interpret this as the auditory and visual hallucinations suggestive of a mental illness such as psychosis? Alas, probably not. Simultaneous hallucinations in two different modalities (for example, seeing someone who isn't really there and hearing them talk to you at the same time) are exceedingly rare. Harry's presence is better interpreted as a cinematic representation of our anti-hero's inner monologue and we are probably not meant to take it too literally.

Thanks to Harry, Dexter is an insightful psychopath. He seems to understand himself. Although he is clearly the worst type of vigilante, his code is such that he kills only nasty people – the types of individuals society can easily do without. He makes it clear in the narrative that his primary motivation is not to save lives; instead he experiences the constant compulsion to kill and his code (as guided by Harry) deems hardened criminals to be the victims least likely to be mourned or avenged. He is meticulous in his execution. Unlike many real serial killers, he does not possess any *paraphilia* (an extreme or violent sexual fetish). This, combined with his level of insight, makes his psychopathy appear somewhat 'painted by numbers' at times, as he almost seems to recite items from the *Psychopathy Checklist* during key moments in the narrative.

Similarly, Dexter appears to care about key characters – or, at the very least, is loyal to them. These include his sister and colleague, Debra (Jennifer Carpenter), his wife, Rita (Julie Benz), Rita's two children and especially his own son, Harrison. On one occasion, Dexter and Rita split up and Dexter claims to feel bad about abandoning the children. Such an ethical code seems somewhat at odds with the concept of Dexter lacking a conscience. So too is his apparent utter devastation at Rita's eventual murder by the Trinity Killer. In later seasons, Dexter forms loving attachments to other female characters such as Lumen Pierce (a homicidal sexual-assault victim played by Julia Styles) and Hannah McKay (a serial poisoner with a considerable backstory in her own right, played by Yvonne Strahovski). Or is Dexter just manipulating the viewer?

As a serial killer, Dexter collaborates with both Pierce and McKay, but mostly he is a lone operator. Indeed, Sergeant Doakes makes it clear in Season Two that Dexter is a member of no organisations or alumni groups, keeps all of his assets in cash, works as a forensic technician despite being top of his class in medical school, and keeps secret his advanced skills in jujutsu.[3]

Such an isolated existence makes impression management easier, as friends are given little opportunity to cross reference his activities and detect inconsistencies. Aside from Doakes, only dogs seem to recognise the alleged psychopathy in Dexter. So, from the outset, we are told to believe he is a psychopath, but is he really?

Interpersonal traits are evident in our anti-hero. He is certainly *charming on a superficial level*, seemingly well liked while antagonising almost none of the major recurrent characters. He cheerfully lavishes doughnuts on grateful colleagues and cons illicit case files out of the woman in the records department who tells him he is 'charming like your father'. He is *glib* at almost every opportunity. Rather than shocking him as they do others, gruesome crime scenes merely offer opportunities for pithy one-liners. In one such example, an emotive colleague surveys a harrowing crime scene and asks Dexter imploringly, 'Going after a cop's family; who would do such a thing?' Dexter seems unmoved and answers with a cheerful smile: 'That's why we're here!'[4]

Although ostensibly modest in demeanour, Dexter displays considerable *narcissism and grandiosity*. He is undoubtedly the centre of his own universe. In an episode entitled 'The Dark Defender', he identifies with Marvel superheroes who are vigilantes just like him, remarking that, 'Lately it seems like we have a lot in common: tragic beginnings, secret identities, part-human part-mutant, arch enemies'.[5] Dexter revels in the connection, certainly far more so than in any association he might have with the fake but headline-grabbing Bay Harbour Butcher. As Miami is gripped by the concept of a vigilante serial killer, copycats naturally emerge, but Dexter views their techniques as amateur. And, like any narcissist, he is capable of intense rage, as he demonstrates, for example, when he tracks down his mother's murderer and violently assaults him.[6]

Harry acts as Dexter's wise mind throughout the seasons, teaching him to lie effectively from a young age. When Dexter was a child, a psychologist enquired whether he tended to become angry when teachers told him what to do, whether he often found himself bored or whether he had ever killed an animal.[7] Dexter confirmed (in a roundabout way) that all three were the case and was promptly advised by Harry to up-skill in impression management for the sake of his own survival. Dexter now has little trouble following this advice. See how easily he contrives a fake backstory in Season Two at a Narcotics Anonymous meeting, for example.[8] (Although he initially attends as a cover for his surreptitious behaviour, he ironically learns to characterise his thirst for blood as a kind of addiction – his 'Dark Passenger'.) Dexter has evolved into a brilliant liar over the years, although he never seems to lie without good reason. As such, the *pathological' nature of his lying* is questionable. Still, he is proficient at impression management.

Dexter's manipulation of victims onto his dissecting table is usually flawless. His *modus operandi* is to inject them with heavy sedatives acquired under the prescribing pseudonym of Patrick

Bateman MD, coincidentally (or otherwise) the name of the psychopathic serial killer from *American Psycho*, whom we discuss in our next chapter. Even Doakes, strongly suspicious of Dexter from the outset, is outwitted at every turn. Dexter skilfully pushes his buttons, provoking him into assaulting him at the police station in front of all their colleagues.[9] And in a final *coup d'état*, Dexter frames Doakes for all the atrocities of the so-called Bay Harbour Butcher. Alas, Dexter certainly has a talent for *manipulation with personal gain* in mind.

Score for interpersonal traits = 7/8

There can be little doubt that Dexter would like to experience emotion. He certainly tries when it comes to Rita, the kids, Debra, Harry and a few select others. He is loyal to these people as per his code, but his ability to truly feel is limited at best. He says himself (as have others before him) that he knows the words but not the music. Meanwhile, he observes curiously – even enviously – the fear, joy, sadness, love and despair of family and friends. Occasionally he borders on vaguely feeling guilt, for example when he accidentally murders Oscar Prado – an 'innocent' who also happens to be the brother of Assistant District Attorney Miguel Prado. But, as Dexter muses, 'I see their pain; at some level I understand their pain; I just can't feel their pain.'[10] Instead, when he watches a stricken woman identifying her fiancé's body, he remarks, 'That must be what love looks like; the inability to feel has its advantages.'[11]

Elsewhere, the incarcerated Doakes tries to dissuade Dexter from murder with tales of how his own family will miss him, but Dexter counters with the observation that Doakes never visits his mother or his sisters. 'It puts a pit in my stomach,' he says, 'that I can only interpret as sadness.'[12] Dexter has a *shallow affect*; although a brilliant amateur psychologist like many psychopaths, he is essentially empty.

Similarly, he displays very *limited empathy to the point of callousness*, albeit politely so. Observe how bored he is at his Narcotics Anonymous meeting as a fellow attendee pours his heart out from the podium.[13] Any vague sense of *remorse or guilt*, as we have said, is limited to when someone innocent is inadvertently caught up in the drama. These thoughts are easily rationalised; in his own words, 'I've never felt a moment of remorse, doubt, regret.'[14] To be fair, Dexter seems troubled at having to kill his biological brother, Brian Moser – a serial killer in his own right.[15] Indeed, Dexter narrowly avoids being caught in the act of other murders shortly after because of his clumsiness in the face of traumatic flashbacks. But Dexter's overall sense of remorse for countless murders is very limited indeed.

Equally, he *takes little responsibility for his own actions*. He believes that he was simply made to do what he does and that his compulsions are outside his control, like an addiction. He almost congratulates himself for having a strict code, as though this offers vindication. He takes solace in the knowledge that he is meticulous in his practice and that his victims have only themselves to blame for their own demise. But there are important exceptions. In Season Three, for example, he remarks about his one-time friend and fellow murderer Miguel Prado that, 'He taught me how to golf, I taught him how to kill; I'm responsible if Miguel takes another innocent life.'[16]

Score for affective traits = 7/8

Dexter's lifestyle traits are a little more variable. The opening credits (and numerous other scenes besides) show him ravenously devouring food like the predator he is. He even refers to himself as a predator and tells us this is part of the reason he is able to spot other predators so easily. But truly, is his *lifestyle parasitic*? Does he really take advantage of the kindness and vulnerability of others? It could be said that he does this to Rita by using her family as a cover, but equally he has a good job, supports and protects three young children (two of whom are not even his own) and has an inherent sense of obligation that extends to ridding society of serial killers other than himself. On balance, perhaps Dexter should score 1 for parasitic lifestyle.

Equally, Dexter does not *lack realistic long-term goals*. Indeed, he himself supposes he will eventually be caught. As such, his ambitions are almost all grounded in reality, while he has an insightful grasp of his own limitations. Dexter does not indulge in *multiple short-term marital relationships*; on the contrary, he displays some difficulty negotiating the marriage he has. In his own words, sex 'always just seemed so undignified'.[17] Elsewhere, it is pointed out to him that, 'In ten years you've never rented a single porn title.'[18] But his behaviour could be regarded as *promiscuous* at times. During Season Two, he breaks up with Rita and engages in a sexual relationship with Lila Tournay (Jaime Murray), his Narcotics Anonymous sponsor. Or is this just a healthy sex drive?

Dexter scores strongly in some other traits. His *behaviour* is obviously highly *irresponsible* by any standards. He jeopardises the reputation, sanctity and security of all those around him, mostly to indulge his own compulsion. Rita's murder is a direct consequence of Dexter's decision to trifle with the Trinity Killer. Despite his ability to plan meticulously, Dexter often behaves *impulsively*. Witness his angry assault of Rita's ex-husband Paul Bennett (played by Mark Pellegrino) using a frying pan in her kitchen.[19] His hasty removal of the unconscious body almost sees him caught. There are numerous other examples.

But Dexter's strongest trait in this domain is his *need for stimulation and excitement*. Despite his sometimes farcical evasion of the law, serial killing is his *raison d'être*. In Episode One, when a thus-far unidentified serial killer begins toying with him by leaving a dismembered doll in his refrigerator, Dexter is thrilled by the prospect of a worthy adversary. 'Yes, I want to play, I really, really do!' he exclaims. On another occasion, he stands atop a tall building clearly contemplating what it would be like to jump, and later tells Harry, 'I don't want to die! I'm just trying to figure out some way to feel alive.'[20] This need for excitement is met only by the thrill of near apprehension by the law.

Score for lifestyle traits = 8/14

Finally, we come to Dexter's antisocial traits. He certainly displays *poor behavioural controls* exemplified by his complete inability to quash his compulsion to kill. Perhaps he over-compensates by becoming highly obsessional in other domains of his life. 'I'm a very neat monster,' he tells us, while his crime scenes are clean and clinical to prevent capture. In Season One, he sits in court as a witness and recounts to the jury the precise number of cases he has participated in to date (exactly 2,103, as it happens).[21] In Season Three, it is revealed that he fills his grocery list alphabetically. Dexter's obsessional nature is of course one of his implausible characteristics; true psychopaths, as we have said, do not worry about things they might have forgotten to do. They simply don't care. Still, during the course of eight seasons, we are treated to innumerable flashbacks, all highly suggestive of *early behavioural problems* and *juvenile delinquency*. But there is limited *versatility in his criminal behaviour*, while *revocation of conditional release* does not apply as he has never been incarcerated.

Score for antisocial behaviour = 6/8
(one item not applicable)

In total, therefore, Dexter scores 28 out of 38, which puts him firmly in the territory of fictional psychopathy. He scores reasonably highly across all four domains (making him a *classic* psychopath), although a slight emphasis on interpersonal and affective traits gives him a leaning towards *manipulative* psychopathy.

But what if there are other plausible explanations for his singular presentation? As with Ben Lovatt, might a reasonable case be made for the autistic spectrum, for example? Recall that autism is a neurodevelopmental disorder affecting social development, communication skills and behaviour. People with autism tend to be socially impaired, often show a lack of empathy and have difficulty forming relationships. They have poor 'theory of mind', meaning they are less well able to predict the actions of others by understanding a given situation from their perspective. Language development is usually delayed and poorer in quality, with such individuals having a tendency to talk 'at' rather than 'with' others, especially when they are children. People with autism usually like a stringent routine and therefore tend to resist change strongly. They may engage in time-consuming, compulsive behaviours, and are characteristically preoccupied with restricted areas of interest, with few signs of creativity or fantasy. They can also be hyperactive. Does this all sound a little like Dexter?

Alas, it gets even more complicated because there may instead be a personality disorder in Dexter other than psychopathy. Recall our explanation of personality disorders in

Chapter 1. One such example is a potential match for Dexter, namely the *schizoid* variety. Such individuals display emotional coldness and often have a blank facial expression, with a limited ability to express warmth or tender feelings towards others. They like to be alone, have few (if any) enduring friendships, and show a marked (and unintentional) disregard for social norms or conventions. They are largely indifferent to praise or criticism, and are preoccupied with fantasy and introspection, while deriving little pleasure from any normal daily activities.

So, there we have it: Dexter might easily have mild autism or a schizoid personality disorder. The trouble is that neither diagnosis is ever an explanation for serial killing. In neither group will you find the level of narcissism, irresponsibility, antisocial behaviour or remorseless cruelty seen in psychopathy. And so, we are left with our original (and more convincing) reason for Dexter's enduring pattern of behaviour – he is a psychopath. Let's face it – his biological father and brother were both psychopaths, so his genes were almost certainly stacked against him. Yet audiences have sided with Dexter over eight full seasons, actively rooting for him to succeed. So, why should this be the case?

As it turns out, Dexter scores highly on our *Psychopath Likeability Scale*. He seems constantly on the verge of being caught, while his frequent flashbacks to a traumatic early childhood convey a real sense of vulnerability. These experiences probably explain why he is a serial killer and not a stockbroker or a surgeon. His obvious affinity for his sister, wife, children and a few select others is a further Achilles' heel, especially when his misdeeds result in their becoming a target. Although Dexter works for the police, he holds little legitimate power in law enforcement. Dexter's position is very precarious indeed, but as with all our fictional psychopaths, we admire his calmness and courage under fire.

We are also fascinated by Dexter's singular ability to hide his psychopathy from most of his fellow characters, while still taking the audience into his confidence. He doesn't quite break the Fourth Wall like Francis Urquhart (or Frank Underwood), but he does allow himself the occasional unblinking stare at the camera – enough to remind us that he knows we are there. Dexter's style of narration is more *film noir* perhaps, but this only serves to add to his cloak-and-dagger allure; *film noir* characters are secretive by definition, so we feel all the more privileged that he chooses to confide in us.

Superficial as it is, Dexter's charm works on almost everyone. Doakes and a few other notable exceptions aside, Dexter is careful with most people not to create too many ripples. He goes out of his way to present a 'nice', all-American façade. He is never boring, keeping us intrigued as he does throughout eight seasons. His skills as a forensic investigator are impressive, but more impressive still is his talent for not getting caught. He is also highly skilled at unarmed combat, although we do not get to witness it too often. This is the point at which his 'superhero' status begins to impress us, as his true identity remains concealed amid constant discussion (sometimes positive) about his vigilantism.

Conversely, the subtropical Miami backdrop doesn't really add to Dexter's redeeming features. It's not like he's operating in the Cold War, after all. Whether or not he appeals to a part deep within us that longs to be bad is also questionable. The whole 'clinical murder and dissection' thing is a little too graphic for most of us to identify with. But Dexter's victims certainly make him look good. Fetishist serial killers, paedophiles and mobsters will usually make anyone look good. So, too, do many of the ordinary characters, such as Rita's nasty neighbour in Season One, whose whining dog distresses Rita's children to such a degree that Dexter is sorely tempted to dispose of the animal.[22]

In the end, Dexter Morgan is a well-described psychopath, even if a few inconsistencies here and there make him seem a little unrealistic. Perhaps he is sometimes less sinister than he ought to be, but on the other hand that might be the whole point. His likeability stems from his vulnerability, *film-noir*-style narration, charm, talent and skill, and the fact that his victims make him look good. Moreover, unlike the serial killer in our next chapter, Dexter is not a fetishist. He is just a vigilante who goes a step or two further than most.

11

THE WALL STREET PSYCHOPATH

'... there is an idea of a Patrick Bateman, some kind of abstraction, but there is no real me, only an entity, something illusory, and though I can hide my cold gaze and you can shake my hand and feel flesh gripping yours and maybe you can even sense our lifestyles are probably comparable: I simply am not there.'

– Patrick Bateman[1]

Beyond Dexter and Lecter, many of the obvious fictional psychopaths are not classic serial killers. Of course, the likes of Kevin Khatchadourian and Tom Ripley have the blood of numerous victims on their hands, but they lack the integration of psychopathy and sexual perversion (or *paraphilia*) we might see in a serial killer in real life. So does Dexter, indeed. Our fictional psychopaths are generally far more likeable and tend to have impressive occupations; they include a writer, a politician, a spy, an aristocratic wine connoisseur and a doctor. So, what line of work might we turn to when seeking the more archetypal serial killer outlined above? The answer, it appears, is the Wall Street investment banker.

More specifically, the best decade to find a fictional psychopath in the New York money markets seems to be the 1980s. Think of Michael Douglas' character Gordon Gekko in Oliver Stone's 1987 film *Wall Street*. Brazenly declaring that 'greed is good', Gekko ruthlessly takes what he wants, regardless of the consequences and without any semblance of a conscience. So vivid was Douglas' portrayal of a psychopath that he won an Academy Award for his efforts.

But a more compelling Wall Street psychopath is Patrick Bateman. An investment banker who leads a double life as a serial killer, Bateman is the narrator of the novel *American Psycho* (1991) by Bret Easton Ellis. The film was adapted for the silver screen in 2000 by director Mary Harron and starred Christian Bale in the leading role. Coincidentally, Oliver Stone was originally chosen to direct the film.

Bret Easton Ellis was born in 1964 and raised in Los Angeles. He made his debut as a bestselling author in 1985 (aged just twenty-one) with *Less Than Zero*, a novel about wealthy and amoral young individuals, the types of characters that have subsequently become the frequent protagonists of his satirical works.

Upon its initial publication, *American Psycho* was vituperated by the literary establishment for being gratuitously violent and misogynistic. The critics may have had a point; either way, Ellis ultimately parted with his then publisher Simon & Schuster. Alfred A. Knopf published *American Psycho* in paperback a year later and the book has since claimed cult status among an entire generation of readers. In his later work, Ellis' satirical style has become more metafictional, similar perhaps to the work of Paul Auster.

Patrick Bateman first appears as a peripheral character in one of Ellis' earlier novels, *The Rules of Attraction* (1987). Here, he is introduced as the brother of Sean, one of the novel's main characters. Bateman also surfaces in novels published subsequent to *American Psycho*, as if to remind us that he is still out there, doing what he does. In *Glamorama* (1998), for example, he makes a cameo appearance with a stain on the lapel of his Armani suit, while in *Lunar Park* (2005) he haunts Ellis and is finally killed off, meeting his demise in a fire at the end of a pier.[2]

Our anti-hero works for the mergers and acquisitions department of the fictional firm Pierce & Pierce (coincidentally the name of Sherman McCoy's firm in Tom Wolfe's *The Bonfire of the Vanities*). He hails from a wealthy family that owns property in Long Island and Newport, although his parents are long since divorced. His mother resides in a sanatorium, while his father (who was 'already noticeably dying' in *The Rules of Attraction*) is presumably dead by now.[3] Bateman, meanwhile, lives in the Upper West Side. He attended prep school at Phillips Exeter Academy and subsequently graduated from Harvard Business School. He is the archetypal 'yuppie', being wealthy, brash and shallow, and an ostentatious consumer of illicit substances and branded goods. He indulges in detailed monologues on anything from his grooming and workout regimes, to the advantages of consumer choices like certain stereo systems or styles of business card, to the biographies of mainstream musicians like Whitney Houston, Genesis and Huey Lewis and the News.

Bateman's social conscience is skin deep. In a scene in the film, he sits in a restaurant, brow furrowed, asserting that:

> *Well, we have to end apartheid for one. And slow down the nuclear arms race, stop terrorism and world hunger … We have to provide food and shelter for the homeless and oppose racial discrimination and promote civil rights while promoting equal rights for women … We have to encourage a return to traditional moral values … Most importantly we have to promote general social concern and less materialism in young people.*[4]

His monologue, utterly rehearsed as though narrating a commercial video, is greeted with sarcastic amusement, but Bateman doesn't seem to notice. At first, it is hard to know if he is just winding us up.

But then, Bateman's peers are shallow too. So unmemorable are they to each other that they seem confused about who is who. His fiancée is similarly superficial, while his mistress is engaged to a gay man whom Bateman really does not like. Our anti-hero habitually pays for the services of prostitutes, while also taking home various women from the nightclubs he frequents. The only woman in his life with any depth, it seems, is his secretary, Jean. His respect for her is something he probably doesn't understand; nevertheless, it marks her down as someone he would never dare to harm. At one point, he surmises that he will most likely end up marrying her. But even Jean is oblivious to the truth that, underneath his preppy demeanour, Bateman is a ruthless serial killer. We witness him murdering a homeless person and his dog, a colleague (Paul Allen), numerous prostitutes and even (on one occasion in the book) a child. He indulges in torture, rape, necrophilia and cannibalism, all of which are graphically described in the novel. He is probably not Jean's 'Mr Right'.

Indeed, Bateman is disliked by most of the people he encounters. His colleagues mock him for his affluent background and his shallowness, while his attorney refers to him as a 'bloody ass-kisser' and a 'brown nosing goody-goody'. These sentiments are mirrored by Bateman's own intense self-loathing, thinly masked by his narcissism. Perhaps this is partly what leads him to kill; many of his victims have deliberately or inadvertently insulted him: the homeless man who asks for money; Paul Allen who can get a Friday-night reservation in the exclusive Dorsia restaurant when Bateman cannot; various insufficiently deferential women. Sometimes he murders for sadistic pleasure during or shortly after sex, while, at other times, he appears to kill simply out of boredom or curiosity.

It might be suggested that these murders do not take place at all, but rather reflect a psychosis in Bateman. He uses a lot of cocaine, after all, which can produce paranoid delusions and vivid (often visual) hallucinations as part of intoxication or a drug-induced psychosis. A more chronic psychotic illness such as schizophrenia is not really plausible in Bateman, however; were this the case, it is unlikely he would take such good care of himself and hold down his job in mergers and acquisitions without medication and other treatment. Although he occasionally takes benzodiazepines, there is no mention of anti-psychotic medication and, as far as we know, he has never attended a psychiatrist. Moreover, as we have already said in relation to Dexter, simultaneous hallucinations in more than one modality (for example, seeing people who are not there while also hearing them talk to you) are exceptionally rare.

Still, towards the end of the film we witness a chase through the streets of downtown New York culminating in the murder of an elderly lady, a cat, several policemen, a security guard and a janitor. Other than a hovering helicopter (which could be there for any reason), there are no obvious repercussions for his apparent behaviour. He returns to Paul Allen's apartment (where he has supposedly stashed several corpses) but finds it has been redecorated and is now being re-let. No explanation is given for the whereabouts of the bodies. There is no police investigation and no media coverage. As such we are left guessing whether or not the events we have witnessed are a figment of Bateman's imagination.

To compound our uncertainty, Jean stumbles across Bateman's office diary and peruses increasingly violent drawings scrawled across the more recent pages. These images seem to reflect the exact events Bateman has been experiencing as his feelings of desperation escalate. Are they simply the violent fantasies of an immature, insecure and narcissistic young man prone to anger and maladaptive coping strategies and with limited access to any meaningful support?[5] Why else would he write them down, given that he also spends much of his time trying to avoid the enquiries of a private detective (played by Willem Dafoe) investigating the disappearance of Paul Allen? At other times, Bateman boasts of his crimes to colleagues, friends or even strangers, but they seem to barely notice. On one occasion, he phones his attorney and leaves a detailed account of his homicides, but the latter assumes Bateman is joking. Indeed, his attorney claims to have met Paul Allen in London subsequent to the time he was supposedly murdered. As Bateman puts it, 'this confession has meant nothing'.

But, for our purposes, let's assume that Bateman is not psychotic and that he actually commits the murders he purports to. In terms of interpersonal traits, he certainly possesses *glibness and superficial charm*. He is always ready with well-rehearsed observations designed to beguile his social circle. With his expensive shoes, tailored suits and designer watches, he appears virtually photo-shopped as he gently sips scotch at his gentleman's club. There, he spends hours discussing the stock market, the newest exclusive restaurants and whatever shade of off-white hue decorates his latest batch of business cards. His opinions are carefully scripted, as if he has borrowed them from a magazine, always delivered like he is narrating a documentary.

In some ways, Bateman has a *grandiose sense of self-worth*. With his affluent roots, his college education and his well-paid job, he feels entitled. And like any narcissist, he is utterly enraged when scorned, such as when he fails to acquire a reservation at his chosen restaurant or when a colleague (Paul Allen) mistakes him for someone else. But then, he also possesses the insecurity and self-loathing of a troubled adolescent. He is in a relentless state of fury at the person he is doomed to be. Such is the paradox of his self-esteem.

Bateman lies constantly, even when he doesn't need to. He is a *pathological liar*. He lies to Jean when he phones the exclusive Dorsia restaurant (as alluded to above) to make a reservation. The concierge laughs rudely and informs him there is no table available, but Bateman simply hangs up and assures Jean that he has secured the booking. She points out that he has not given his name over the phone, but he simply shrugs this off as though the inconsistencies are irrelevant. Meanwhile, he impulsively impersonates a colleague for whom he is mistaken by Paul Allen; he later murders Allen, commandeers his apartment and then masquerades as his victim in front of various prostitutes and escorts. Indeed, Bateman habitually lies to lure his victims to their deaths. And then he lies to the private detective investigating Allen's disappearance. Ironically, when Bateman eventually tries in sheer frustration to be truthful about his crimes (by phoning his attorney, for example), nobody believes him. He is just too brilliant at impression management, too skilled at *manipulation for personal gain*.

Score for interpersonal traits = 7/8

So, what about Bateman's affective traits? His *shallow affect* is obvious, notwithstanding (or more likely exemplified by) his glossy monologues on social justice. Indeed, he admits to chronic feelings of emptiness as he tells us, 'though I can hide my cold gaze and you can shake my hand and feel flesh gripping yours and maybe you can even sense our lifestyles are probably comparable: I simply am not there'. Elsewhere, he describes himself as devoid of any clear, identifiable emotion other than 'greed or disgust' (although, to be fair, there are also plentiful examples of rage). At best, he is incapable of describing his own emotion. After committing murder he usually seems relieved, as though some pent-up anger has been purged. Beyond this, he makes vain attempts to fill the void with obsessional attention to detail in the fashionable and expensive clothes he wears, his time-consuming personal-grooming 'routine', the descriptive *à la carte* menus from which he orders unique dishes typically preceded by the word 'the', his tastefully decorated apartment (although he sees Paul Allen's is better) and the manufactured biographies of 1980s pop bands and artists.[6]

Bateman certainly displays no sense of *remorse* for his actions, nor is there any convincing *empathy* for his victims. No 'hot' empathy, anyway. His telephone confession to his attorney seems born of frustration rather than guilt; so absorbed is he in his own suffering (or the extreme, self-indulgent disappointment of a narcissist who fails to be noticed) that he is largely oblivious to that of others. Admittedly, he changes his mind about killing Jean during their ill-fated date together and beckons her to leave his apartment immediately because, as he puts it, 'I think if you stay, something bad will happen; I think I might hurt you'; but he is not normally in the habit of taking any *responsibility for his own actions*. His passive demeanour in this scene is chilling; he seems to view himself as some sort of conduit for suffering that is universal and simply channelled through him towards his victims. As he says himself, 'I simply am not there', and he later elaborates:

> ... *the vicious and the evil, all the mayhem I have caused and my utter indifference toward it, I have now surpassed. I still, though, hold on to one single bleak truth: no one is safe, nothing is redeemed. Yet I am blameless. Each model of human behaviour must be assumed to have some validity. Is evil something you are? Or is it something you do? My pain is constant and sharp and I do not hope for a better world for anyone. In fact I want my pain to be inflicted on others. I want no one to escape. But even after admitting this – and I have, countless times, in just about every act I've committed – and coming face-to-face with these truths, there is no catharsis. I gain no deeper knowledge about myself, no new understanding can be extracted from my telling. There has been no reason for me to tell you any of this. This confession has meant nothing ...*[7]

Score for affective traits = 8/8

Moving to the lifestyle traits, is Bateman *parasitic*? In a sense, he takes and takes while giving little back. He hails from a wealthy family who probably fund, in part, his stylish abode in the Upper West Side, having already paid for his expensive college education before positioning him advantageously for the post of vice-president with Pierce & Pierce. His job has a title but there is little evidence of long hours with hard labour to justify his presumably exorbitant salary. Many of his colleagues do not even seem to know who he is. But perhaps a lot of wealthy-but-otherwise-ordinary people fall into this category. The real question is whether Bateman takes advantage of the kindness and vulnerability of others in the way a psychopath would. At this point we cannot ignore the fact that he is a serial killer. Bateman feeds off the lives of others – some of whom have shown him kindness – before ruthlessly murdering them for his own purposes. Like Hannibal Lecter, he occasionally resorts to cannibalism, which makes him literally parasitic.

Although superficially ambitious, Bateman shows little evidence of possessing any *long-term goals*, realistic or otherwise. At one point he contemplates marrying Jean, a grounded and emotionally intelligent woman who might well be considered out of his league, but this ambition is not unrealistic; indeed it is implied years later by Ellis that he eventually does so. He is certainly *irresponsible*. Throughout the story, he does whatever he wants with little regard for the consequences. He also has a strong *need for excitement* such is his boredom with the life he has inherited. He drinks copious amounts of alcohol, snorts cocaine and has a thirst for blood that must be quenched constantly. The risk of getting caught seems to thrill him, while the variety in his victims suggests he has even tired of killing the same type of person.

However, it is difficult to determine whether or not Bateman is truly prone to *impulsivity*. In many ways, he is quite a measured individual, meticulously planning his acts of homicide down to the last detail. For example, he tapes newspaper to the floor and wears a pre-purchased raincoat before he kills Paul Allen with an axe. Such preparation is presumably the reason he never gets caught. Equally there is no evidence of *many short-term marital relationships*. As far as we ever know, he marries only once. But he is habitually involved in *promiscuous sexual behaviour*. Aside from the constant television pornography in the background as he does stomach crunches and press-ups in his apartment, he hires escorts and prostitutes with whom he engages in sadistic sexual behaviour. He is engaged to be married, but nevertheless routinely picks up women in nightclubs and brings them home with him. His contemplation of an affair with his secretary is a deliberate cliché for our amusement.

Score for lifestyle traits = 8/14

Last, we have the antisocial traits of psychopathy, with *poor behavioural controls* notable in Bateman. He seems incapable of tolerating those who irritate him; instead, he lets the pressure build up until he eventually lashes out violently. But we know little about any *early behavioural problems* or *juvenile delinquency*. Indeed, we are given little detail about his childhood at all. But he gains full marks for *criminal versatility*. Examples of his varied transgressions include perversion of the course of justice, deception, murder, rape, torture, necrophilia and cannibalism. Finally, we cannot comment on *revocation of conditional release* because, as far as we know, he has never actually been in prison.

Score for antisocial traits = 4/8 (one item not applicable)

In total, Bateman scores 27 out of 38 on the *Psychopathy Check-list*, which puts him in the bracket of a fictional psychopath. This score might have been higher had we had more information on his life outside the film and the novel. In terms of sub-type, he scores well across all four domains, which likely makes him a *classic* psychopath. He is clearly both a 'talker' and a 'doer'. But is he likeable?

There are many reasons why he should not be so. There is really nothing in him that appeals to the devil within us. If anything, his worst actions are not just immoral but amoral. They are utterly heinous. His victims do not lend him any redeeming features. Although Paul Allen is irritating (he is a blander version of Bateman himself), the remaining victims are far more deserving of our sympathy, and include among them a homeless man and his dog, various women driven to prostitution, lost young ladies frequenting the New York nightclub scene and, worst of all, a defenceless child. Most of these people would presumably have families haunted by their relatives' disappearance.

Bateman's victims do not make him look good but perhaps his backdrop does to some degree. The story is often so surreal that we feel a little detached from it, like the whole scenario is simply an allegory from the start. It makes the circumstances a little more forgiving. And there are at least seven other reasons why we warm to Bateman, notwithstanding his despicable deeds.

Bateman's whole existence is enveloped in secrecy; much as he would like to be noticed, he simply is not. He can be courageous, and is certainly audacious, while he has obvious admirable talents and skills. He is well organised, for a start, planning such 'perfect murders'. He has an encyclopaedic knowledge of various banal topics that paradoxically seem to entertain. And then, of course, he has wealth, good looks and good taste, all of which anyone might envy. It is hard not to admire aspects of his lifestyle just a little.

Still, Bateman seems strangely vulnerable. From the outset, he appears emotionally lost and rather pathetic as he recites his morning beauty regimen and his derivative opinions. As the story evolves, we realise his behaviour is born partly of inadequacy. Witness his sense of helplessness when he gains brief insight and asks Jean (whom he is about to murder) to leave his apartment or 'something bad will happen'. See his desperation as he confesses tearfully to his attorney over the phone while the searchlights of a police helicopter penetrate his office window. And we still haven't ruled out the possibility that he may actually have a psychotic illness that torments him daily.

As such, Bateman is an unreliable narrator, but he nevertheless takes us into his confidence. As we have observed already, confidence is the classic trick of any charming scoundrel, a crucial ingredient of their impression management. Tell the reader what you think and you will garner their loyalty. In Bateman's case (as with the other such examples we have seen) we feel oddly privileged to be a part of his inner circle. We also feel protected from him; not only do we gain an insight into his motivation, but we also assume (perhaps erroneously) that he would never turn on us, were we a character in his fictional world. This is what happens with Jean, in whom he also partially confides. Bateman confides in other characters too, not least his attorney. Alas, they are not listening.

Bateman can be very charming, albeit superficially. How else would he lure his unsuspecting prey to their deaths? Moreover, the glossy verbosity of his prefabricated opinions and the fact that he takes himself so seriously are such that it is difficult not to see the humour in him. For these reasons we never find him boring, even if his colleagues seem to think he is pretty mundane. On the contrary, his secret life as a serial killer makes him fascinating to the reader and viewer alike. It could be psychosis or it could be mere vivid imagination. More likely, he is a psychopath whom we cannot help but side with just a little. Call Patrick Bateman what you like, but he is certainly not ordinary.

12

THE GANGSTER SOCIOPATH

'You got any idea what my life would be worth if certain people found out I checked into a laughing academy?'

— *Tony Soprano*[1]

In this book we have examined some high-profile television series that have achieved a second wind of success in 'box-set' format. We have devoted entire chapters to *House of Cards* and *Dexter*, yet perhaps the two most celebrated box sets of them all are *The Wire* and *The Sopranos*. But are the protagonists in both these series more likely sociopaths than psychopaths? Recall from Chapter 1 that sociopathy is a more informal term that describes an individual with a persistent pattern of behaviours and attitudes that are at odds with what society considers acceptable and lawful. Furthermore, sociopathic behaviours are usually appropriate within the sociopath's social milieu (such as in a criminal gang, for example).

Some might regard a sociopath as having a more defined moral code with a greater capacity for guilt, empathy, loyalty and caring relationships. The sociopath may even have a conscience, albeit in a narrower context than is normal. Moreover, a sociopath may go to greater lengths to hide their distress and unacceptable behaviour from certain people, where a psychopath may not bother. Finally, some researchers suggest that sociopaths are essentially the result of adverse or neglectful childhood environments. Of course, as we have observed, this is often true of psychopaths, but (unlike sociopaths) they also tend to be temperamentally abnormal from birth. It could be said therefore that psychopaths are partly 'born' of genetics and biology, while sociopaths are exclusively 'made' by adverse early experiences.[2]

We might take the character Stringer Bell from *The Wire* as a good example of a sociopath. Although he displays many of the features listed on the *Psychopathy Checklist*, he is largely a product of his environment. His pattern of antisocial behaviour is a function of his necessity to survive on the mean streets of Baltimore. Indeed, the HBO series was created by David Simon as a 'warts 'n' all' look at the drug-infested streets of that city, with its gangs, its politics and its corruption. Each series deals with a social institution (the illegal drugs trade, the seaport unions, the city government, the school system and the print news media) and its relationship with law enforcement. The added twist is the use of various forms of surveillance by the police to apprehend criminals.

The Wire ran for five full seasons between 2002 and 2008 and garnered a cult following that transcended its original television viewership. It employed mostly character actors thus far unknown who went on to become household names, not least several British and Irish actors such as Dominic West, Aidan Gillen and Idris Elba. Elba is well known in the UK for playing the maverick-but-likeable Detective Chief Inspector John Luther in the award-winning BBC television series of the same surname. He won an award at the sixty-ninth Golden Globes for his performance in the second series. Like Stringer Bell, however, Luther likely falls short of qualifying for this book on the grounds of psychopathy. Both could reasonably be labelled sociopaths but not psychopaths. They may behave badly but they have feelings.

But what about Tony Soprano? *The Sopranos* was an enormously successful HBO crime drama series that ran from 1999 to 2007, spanning a total of eighty-six episodes over six seasons. It was created by David Chase (the Emmy Award-winning producer of numerous prior television series such as *The Rockford Files* and *Northern Exposure*) and brilliantly cast with James Gandolfini as the eponymous mob boss. The role won Gandolfini three Emmy Awards in his own right, along with a Golden Globe and several other accolades. The series co-starred Lorraine Bracco as Tony's psychiatrist, Dr Jennifer Melfi. Bracco was also known for her Academy Award-nominated portrayal of Karen Friedman Hill in Martin Scorsese's 1990 film *Goodfellas*. A final layer of gritty credibility is lent to *The Sopranos* by its theme tune, the techno-bluesy 'Woke Up This Morning' by Alabama 3.

The basic premise of *The Sopranos* is that its principal character leads a kind of double life. He is the heir apparent to an Italian-American crime syndicate (loosely based on the real-life DeCavalcante crime family) in New Jersey. Tony is a family man, reasonably content in a traditional and loving marriage to Carmela (played in the series by Edie Falco). He has two teenage children – a daughter named Meadow and a son named Anthony Jr (or A. J.). Tony dotes on his mother Livia, years after his two sisters (Janice and Barbara) have tired of her manipulation and emotional blackmail. And although Tony's relationship with his uncle Corrado Soprano Jr – referred to as 'Junior' – is frosty at times, he retains a certain affection for the old man who used to play baseball with him as a child. As such, we often see a kind side to Tony Soprano.

Ostensibly, he works as a waste-management consultant for Barone Sanitation. He is also co-owner of Satriale's Meat Market and a strip club called Bada Bing. In reality, he is less a legitimate businessman and more a ruthless predator. As the *de facto* street boss, he is routinely involved in extortion, protection rackets, fraud, dealing in stolen goods, assault and, from time to time, murder. He occupies a senior position within the Mafia and, given the queue of capos waiting to take his place at the first sign of weakness, he needs to retain his ruthless demeanour.[3] So, when he begins to feel depressed and have regular panic attacks, he takes the bold step of booking himself an appointment with a psychiatrist.

Tony is initially very uncomfortable attending sessions with Dr Melfi. To begin with, his trade and culture alike might be regarded as somewhat misogynistic and the fact his psychiatrist is a woman pleases nobody who learns about it. This is especially true of Carmela, who is well aware that Tony keeps mistresses, but cares far more about the emotional disloyalty she deems inherent in confiding in a psychiatrist of the opposite sex. Tony is worried for a slightly different reason; were his comrades to discover his weekly visits they might view him as weak, thus endangering his senior position and possibly even his life. But Dr Melfi soon shows herself to be insightful and courageous, especially given the obvious risks she takes in allowing a crime boss to confide in her his dangerous secrets.

It is mostly through his visits to Dr Melfi that we witness Tony's backstory. During a series of flashbacks played out in several episodes as Tony sits in his psychiatrist's consultation room, we learn that our anti-hero was born in 1959 (possibly 1960) and is the son of 'Johnny Boy' Soprano, a capo in the DiMeo crime family. Tony's paternal grandfather, Corrado Soprano Sr, was apparently a master stonemason who arrived by ship from Avellino, Italy in 1910. In one episode, Tony informs his son A. J. that Corrado Sr was one of the construction workers involved in building the local church where Tony grew up in Newark, New Jersey. The teenage A. J. is less than impressed.

In Season One, A. J. gets into a series of fistfights at school and Tony is reminded of his own troubled childhood.[4] The young Tony came to the realisation that his father was involved with the Mafia when he witnessed Johnny Boy and Junior assaulting a local businessman. His curiosity aroused, Tony stowed away in the boot of his father's car during one of the latter's many business sojourns, only to find his father bringing his older sister Janice to a local amusement park. Later, it transpired that Johnny Boy was in fact using Janice as a cover while he attended an organised crime rendezvous. On another occasion, we witness Livia threatening to stick a fork in her young son's eye. In therapy, Tony is asked by Dr Melfi to recall some happy childhood memories of his mother. He finds it hard to remember any, but then recalls one incident when his father fell down the stairs and the whole family collapsed with laughter. Ultimately, Tony voices his view that his mother was a dour and cruel woman who wore her husband down to 'a little nub'.

At the dinner table, Livia and Junior make reference to Tony's childhood antics. Livia tells A. J. and Meadow that she 'practically lived in the principal's office' when Tony was at school. We learn that Tony stole a car at the age of ten and that he also made a habit of stealing lobsters to sell to the highest bidder. Still, he remained in school and went on to attend (what we presume to be) West Orange High School, where he played baseball and football and met Carmela for the first time. Thereafter, he spent a semester at Seton Hall University before dropping out to pursue his career with the DiMeo crime family. He gained early notoriety by robbing a card game operated by Michele 'Feech' La Manna. Our anti-hero then claimed his first murder victim (a small-time bookie named Willie Overall) at the tender age of twenty-two.[5] Early on, Johnny Boy guided Tony's career until his death from emphysema in

1986, whereupon Junior took on a paternal role. The same year, Tony became the youngest capo in the family, aged just twenty-six. In 1995, the boss – Ercole 'Eckley' DiMeo – was sent to prison and Tony's old friend and fellow capo Jackie Aprile took over the role of street boss. Alas, within four years, Aprile was dead from cancer, leaving an awkward vacancy. Tony cleverly set up Junior as the official street boss of the family, secretly knowing that his uncle would act as a decoy for the FBI, while Tony himself would still have sufficient gravitas to act as *de facto* boss behind the scenes.

Thus we have the fictional biography of Tony Soprano. Although he uses his authority to have numerous people killed, we only witness him committing eight murders in person. These are:

1. Willie Overall (1982 – to establish Tony's place as a member of the Mafia)
2. Fabian 'Febby' Petrulio (1999 – for informing on members of the Mafia and then joining the witness protection programme)[6]
3. Chucky Signore (1999 – shot point blank for conspiring with Junior to kill one of Tony's men)[7]
4. Matthew Bevilaqua (2000 – shot point blank for attempting to murder Tony's protégé and cousin-in-law Christopher Moltisanti)[8]
5. Salvatore 'Big Pussy' Bonpensiero (2000 – executed on a boat by Tony and his cronies Silvio (played by E Street Band guitarist Steven Van Zandt) and Paulie after they discover that he is an FBI informant)[9]

6.   Ralph Cifaretto (2002 – choked and bludgeoned to death over a disagreement involving a prize-winning racehorse)[10]

7.   Tony Blundetto (2004 – shot for committing unauthorised killings and jeopardising the safety of Tony's crew)[11]

8.   Christopher Moltisanti (2007 – suffocated following a major car accident)[12]

Tony's conscience varies in relation to these murders. Those of Febby Petrulio and Chucky Signore are born purely of retribution and Tony does not dwell upon them for long. Matthew Bevilaqua's murder is also out of revenge, but Tony shows a hint of conscience because his victim is so young. It is Big Pussy's murder that causes Tony the most distress. As an old friend, he is initially in denial about Big Pussy's involvement with the FBI until he finally realises that the boss must be ruthless for the sake of the family. Conversely, the demise of Ralph Cifaretto is unplanned, but Tony's loss of temper ensures it is also thorough. The murder of Tony's cousin, Tony Blundetto (played by Steve Buscemi), is partially out of kindness, in that it spares him a far worse ending at the hands of rival mobsters. Still, it is also Tony's way of ensuring he retains respect.

Tony's final murder (of his wife's cousin Christopher Moltisanti) is less traumatic for him than we might expect. Christopher has long been a liability to the family, with his cocaine, heroin and alcohol addictions and his consequently capricious behaviour. Tony has little apparent difficulty convincing himself that Christopher's murder is utterly necessary. Although the killing is impulsive in the end (by suffocation after a road traffic accident in which both men are badly injured), Christopher's days would likely have been numbered anyway. Tony loses little sleep over it, notwithstanding the evident pain and distress caused to the family and the fact that Tony was once the closest thing to a father that Christopher ever had.

The real paradox is that throughout all this Tony remains a dedicated and loving husband and father. Yes, he is unfaithful to his wife; indeed, they separate for a while during Season Five. And yes, his relationship with his children can be fraught at times. But Tony is visibly moved by Meadow when she sings a solo with her high-school choir. He criss-crosses New England with her, looking for a suitable college until they finally decide on Columbia University. He boasts to his friends about her college achievements and her ambitions. And he cares sufficiently about her to disapprove of most of her boyfriends.

Tony has the same paternal instinct when it comes to A. J., cheering him on regularly at football games, sitting down with him from time to time to play video games, and putting real thought into his education and discipline. He worries about A. J. more than he does about Meadow, knowing his son to be more vulnerable and less academic than his daughter. On one occasion, he confides in Dr Melfi that he fears his son would never survive in the Mafia. Ultimately, A. J. drops out of college without graduating and tries his hand at various occupations until his father eventually gets him a job in construction. He also shows susceptibility to depression, something for which Tony blames himself – or rather what he terms the 'rotten putrid Soprano gene'. Above all, Tony yearns for both his children to grow up to be upstanding citizens and escape the life of crime he himself has led.

So, it seems Tony Soprano has a conscience, but there are a number of other reasons he is likeable as a villain. First and foremost is his vulnerability. He is a family man and we are constantly reminded that Tony has something important to lose. Moreover, the very premise of *The Sopranos* is the idea that a tough mobster can succumb to mental illnesses such as panic disorder or depression and be prescribed lithium and Prozac with recovery in mind. Tony attends a psychiatrist every week and in doing so discloses his innermost secrets, fears and desires. In a sense, therefore, he takes us into his confidence. Not directly – unlike Frank Underwood, for example – but we are still privileged witnesses to his psychotherapy.

Tony can be somewhat charming, although never seductively so. He is intelligent and streetwise, but not especially well bred or well educated. His blue-collar roots hold him back when he makes any efforts at social mobility, such as when he tries to befriend his neighbours, all of whom are doctors, lawyers or stockbrokers. Ironically, some of these individuals might be somewhat psychopathic in their own right, but they are also more conventionally charming. Tony is not as polished in his demeanour, nor is he necessarily even polite, but he has plenty of friends who like and respect him on account of his direct-ness. Of course, his street-boss status undoubtedly influences his popularity. Alas, Tony can be charming but only to a degree.

Still, we cannot dispute his obvious talent and skill at what he does. And we are not talking about waste-management con-sultancy. Tony has a nose for untapped 'business' opportunities, for crime without the risk of punishment. His negotiating skills are second to none, as is evident in his serpent-like placement of Junior on a pedestal ready for toppling by the FBI. Tony then skilfully carves out a niche for himself as *de facto* street boss and is the legitimate boss by the final season. He is a courageous and natural leader. What a pity he could not have applied these talents and skills to something else.

Either way, Tony is anything but boring. Perhaps he appeals to that part within us that longs to be bad. Many a thirty-something male will claim that Francis Ford Coppola's *The Godfather* (or possibly *The Godfather II*) was the greatest film ever made. For years, *The Sopranos* afforded such fanatics a weekly dose of devilment. Similarly, Tony's victims usually make him look good. In keeping with the Mafia code, those he kills are themselves criminal thugs that the world can easily do without. And Tony's backdrop has the same effect. His strong Mafia pedigree and lack of formal education have left him with little choice but to follow his chosen path. In New Jersey only two options are depicted: (a) join the Mafia or (b) open a legitimate business and be exploited by them. If this is simply the way the world works, how can Tony be at fault?

So, it seems we like Tony Soprano. He appears to have a conscience, but how does he score on the *Psychopathy Checklist*? It might be argued that, as with *Breaking Bad*, the major theme of *The Sopranos* is that a non-psychopath finds himself in a role traditionally reserved for psychopaths. In *Breaking Bad*, it is obvious that Walter White is not a psychopath but rather a man driven to extreme behaviour by his intolerable circumstances. Indeed, his desperation arises from his conscience, his primary motivation being to use his unique skills to provide for his family after his death. But then Walter White is not a sociopath either. He has no lifelong pattern of antisocial behaviour. At the outset of Season One, he has spent most of his adult life as a chemistry teacher. Can the same type of excuse be made for Tony Soprano?

Applying the *Psychopathy Checklist* to what we know about his life, let's begin with the interpersonal traits. We have already questioned Tony's *charm*. It is neither seductive nor superficial; indeed, he can be honest and direct, sometimes to the point of rudeness. *Glibness* is not his style. He has a big ego, but no more than we might expect from a high-ranking member of an organised crime family. His sense of self-worth is not *grandiose*. Indeed, there are plenty of scenes in which Tony shows due deference to senior members of his organisation. Certainly he lies, but not relentlessly for the sake of it, and only when to do otherwise might place his position in jeopardy. He is not a *pathological liar*. So, does he *con and manipulate*? Yes, without a doubt, but this is presumably standard behaviour for any member of the Mafia. By the same token, there is very little impression management evident; with Tony, what we see is what we get. Add to this the strong ethical code he consistently cites in relation to his fellow Mafia 'soldiers', and we can see that any manipulation is often for the good of the syndicate rather than specifically for personal gain.

Score for interpersonal traits = 1/8

Moving to the affective traits, it would be difficult to accuse Tony of having a *shallow affect*. Anger and jealousy feature prominently in his emotional repertoire, but so too do joy, sadness, anxiety and a host of other emotions. Indeed, his need to attend Dr Melfi is born of overwhelming emotion that he is able to recognise but unable to process. In the same light, Tony is also capable of *empathy*. He clearly cares about his wife, children and various other family members. He worries about Meadow being hurt in a relationship and A. J.'s unlikelihood of surviving were he ever to become involved in organised crime. He worries about his cousin-in-law Christopher, his mother, Livia, and his dying friend, Jackie Aprile. He sometimes worries about Dr Melfi. He cares so much for an injured racehorse that he is prepared to bludgeon Ralph Cifaretto to death out of revenge. Such murders sometimes involve a profound sense of *guilt* in Tony.

But then, other murders do not bother him so much. He does not always accept responsibility for his actions and has a tendency to blame others for bringing about their own misfortune. In the episode 'From Where to Eternity', in which Christopher lies in a hospital bed having been shot (and claims to have seen hell in the brief moment he was technically dead), Tony is asked by Dr Melfi if Christopher deserves to go to hell. Tony is incensed and lists all the other types of people in society he thinks deserve such an outcome ahead of Christopher. The list interestingly does not include himself. He goes on to cite his Italian ancestry, how they were the workers who built America and how mob rule was the only way to make any money without an education. Referring to himself as a 'soldier', he speaks of codes, orders, honour, family and loyalty. He takes responsibility for his duty, as he sees it, but not for the suffering he may cause the innocent victims of his life of crime.

Score for affective traits = 2/8

So, what about lifestyle traits? Is Tony *parasitic*? Does he feed off others relentlessly while giving nothing back? Surely, this is the essence of what the Mafia do. They threaten local business owners with the prospect of physical harm and then offer to protect them from such harm for a cut of the profits. Tony buys into this practice without question. Although he presents the façade of a legitimate businessman, his money is mostly a function of extortion, protection rackets, gambling and theft. He has never done an honest days' work in his life.

Tony is often *impulsive*, acting as he does (often violently) without thinking. He is quite prepared to smash up the kitchen telephone when enraged. He throws his chair across Dr Melfi's office when uncomfortable with her line of questioning. His murder of Ralph Cifaretto is completely unplanned. But this does not necessarily mean Tony is *irresponsible*. He shows a consistent regard for the welfare of his organisation, as would be expected of any street boss. He would not last long in the role otherwise. He harbours no *long-term goals* that might be deemed unrealistic. He has no plans to run for public office or write a bestselling novel, for example. His *need for excitement* is also questionable; given his proneness to panic attacks, it is evident that he longs for nothing more than a quiet life. Provided, of course, he remains solvent and well fed.

Tony runs a strip club and engages in dangerous liaisons with a mistress in almost every season. Carmela seems to accept his infidelity to a degree. She even asks him on one occasion to have a vasectomy, lest one of his extramarital adventures leads to an illegitimate child, thus bringing shame upon the family. So, he displays frequent *promiscuous sexual behaviour* but he does not have *many short-term marital relationships*. Despite his behaviour, his ultimate loyalty lies very much with his family.

Score for lifestyle traits = 6/14

And finally, we have the antisocial traits associated with psychopathy. This is the part in which Tony's score begins to increase. We are already aware of his *early behavioural problems* and *juvenile delinquency*. Recall the tales of the ten-year-old boy stealing cars and dealing in illicit lobsters. Tony also displays *poor behavioural controls* from the outset. All of this is consistent with his role in organised crime. His *criminal versatility* is unequalled. To sample but a few items, he has his psychiatrist's partner assaulted, he burns down a friend's restaurant in an insurance scam (and also to prevent Junior having an associate assassinated there), he assaults the father of Meadow's school friend over a gambling debt, and he has his gang steal a car from a young family (with children in the back seat). Indeed, Tony commits robbery, fraud, extortion, assault and murder with impunity. But as he is never apprehended by the FBI, *revocation of conditional release* does not apply.

Score for antisocial traits = 8/8 (one item not applicable)

In all, Tony Soprano scores a mere 17 out of 38 but with an emphasis on antisocial traits that marks him out as a potential sociopath rather than a psychopath. Certainly, his persistent pattern of behaviours and attitudes is at odds with what society would normally consider acceptable and lawful, but it is nevertheless appropriate within his criminal subculture. Tony has a more defined moral code with a greater capacity for guilt, empathy and loyalty than we might expect in a psychopath. Indeed, he has a conscience, with the ability to engage in caring relationships, albeit in a narrower context. Tony goes to some lengths to hide his distress and unacceptable behaviours, while his nature is more likely the product of his upbringing than his birth.

Still, I wouldn't like to be in Dr Melfi's shoes as his treating psychiatrist. Would you?

III

CONCLUSION

13

THE LIKEABLE MR PSYCHOPATH

'Forging signatures, telling lies, impersonating practically anybody.'

– Tom Ripley[1]

United States' presidential candidates do not necessarily have to win to make history. In 1964, Senator Barry Goldwater lost by a landslide to Lyndon B. Johnson and partly blamed unfair media coverage for his misfortune. Specifically, he referred to an article in the magazine *Fact*, entitled 'The Unconscious of a Conservative: A Special Issue on the Mind of Barry Goldwater', in which 12,356 American psychiatrists were polled on the candidate's suitability for presidency.[2] In total, more than 1,800 doctors responded of whom 1,189 concurred that Goldwater was psychologically unfit to hold the office. Many of the remainder asserted that he was likely to be negligent in the role.

After the election, Goldwater unsurprisingly sued the publisher Ralph Ginzburg over the damage to his reputation, which he claimed likely contributed to his campaign loss. Goldwater won the case and was awarded $75,000. The upshot to this day is that psychiatrists are very careful not to comment in public about living people without first assessing them and gaining their permission to speak out. In 1973, the so-called 'Goldwater Rule' was formalised in the American Psychiatric Association's Code of Ethics, which still states that in certain circumstances, 'a psychiatrist may share with the public his or her expertise about psychiatric issues in general. However, it is unethical for a psychiatrist to offer a professional opinion unless he or she has conducted an examination and has been granted proper authorisation for such a statement'.[3]

Like many psychiatrists, I am occasionally asked to comment on whether certain public figures might have specific psychiatric diagnoses. I am careful never to answer. So, it should be of little surprise that there are no real people featured in this book. Much as psychopathic traits seem evident in certain public figures, the truth is we have no access to the kind of biographical detail that is necessary to make any kind of reliable personality assessment. The only ethical approach is to comment on anonymised case vignettes or fictional characters. The latter seems like much more fun, while authors and screenwriters often provide much of the backstory needed in lieu of several days' worth of careful history taking. Of course, more purist researchers and commentators will inevitably bemoan my misuse of a widely respected psychological inventory for such a trivial exercise. Others may not concur with my assertions on the difference between psychopathy, sociopathy and antisocial personality disorder. Still more might disagree with my views on which fictional characters are psychopaths and which are not.

And perhaps the deeper issue is whether it is ever ethical to admire a psychopath, be they fictional or not, likeable or not. Are we not condoning, even glamorising, bad behaviour on a societal level? Highly respected forensic psychologists such as Robert D. Hare have observed that (and expressed puzzlement at how) society increasingly seems to harbour an admiration for some criminals who might score highly on the *Psychopathy Checklist*.[4] People sometimes confuse notoriety with fame. Does this book therefore encourage such a movement?

The simple answer is no – of course it doesn't. The vast majority of us have a conscience; with normal moral compasses we know the difference between reality and fantasy, right and wrong. This book simply pays homage to a wealth of wonderful psychopathic villains and anti-heroes (and the writers who created them) who have captured the public imagination.

And so, we are left with ten characters who, we can determine, are indeed psychopaths, at least insofar as we can tell from the information we are given as readers or viewers. So, how do we decide upon the ultimate likeable fictional psychopath? One approach is simply to list the ten psychopaths and then add their scores from the *Psychopathy Checklist* and our *Psychopath Likeability Scale*. Recall that we scored each item of the latter with 0, 2 or 4 to allow for a potential total score of 40. This gives it equal weight to the psychopathy score when we compare our anti-heroes. A table of the results would look as follows:

Character	*Psychopathy Checklist*					Total	*Psychopath Likeability Scale*										Total	Grand Total
	I	A	L	AS	Type		1	2	3	4	5	6	7	8	9	10		
Amy Elliott Dunne	8	8	8	3	Manip.	27/38	4	2	4	4	4	4	4	4	4	4	38	65
James Bond	4	8	13	0	Macho	25/36	4	2	4	0	4	4	4	4	4	4	34	59
Urquhart/ Underwood	8	7	7	4	Manip.	26/38	4	2	4	4	4	4	4	4	0	0	30	56
Tom Ripley	8	8	8	4	Manip.	28/38	4	4	4	2	4	4	4	4	4	4	38	66
Kevin Khatcha-dourian	6	8	11	8	Class.	33/38	4	0	0	0	0	0	0	0	0	0	4	37
Ben Lovatt	0	8	11	6	Macho	25/38	0	4	0	0	0	2	0	0	0	0	6	31
Hannibal Lecter	7	8	5	8	Class.	28/40	4	2	4	0	4	4	4	0	4	0	26	54
Montressor	8	8	6	2	Manip.	24/38	4	0	4	4	4	4	4	0	0	0	24	48
Dexter Morgan	7	7	8	6	Class.	28/38	4	4	4	4	4	4	4	0	4	0	32	60
Patrick Bateman	7	8	8	4	Class.	27/38	4	4	4	4	4	4	4	0	0	2	30	57

Psychopathy Checklist

I = Interpersonal traits. A = Affective traits. L = Lifestyle (including sexual) traits. AS = Antisocial traits.

Type: Class. = Classic psychopath. Macho = Macho psychopath. Manip. = Manipulative psychopath.

Psychopath Likeability Scale

1   They are calm and courageous in the face of danger.

2   They seem vulnerable.

3   They appeal to our fascination with secrecy.

4   They take us into their confidence.

5   We are seduced by their charm.

6   We never find them boring.

7   They have looks, talents or skills we admire.

8   They appeal to a part deep within us that longs to be bad.

9   Their victims make them look good.

10   The backdrop makes them look good.

As we can see, there is some diversity in the subtypes of fictional psychopathy described by authors, in that two characters are *macho*, four are *manipulative* and four are *classic*. Gaining highest marks for psychopathy is Kevin Khatchadourian (33/38), with Tom Ripley (28/38), Hannibal Lecter (28/40) and Dexter Morgan (28/38) jointly trailing in second position. Most likeable on the list are Tom Ripley and Amy Elliott Dunne in joint-first place (both 38/40), with James Bond (34/40) coming in third. But, in applying equal weight to psychopathy and likeability, the ultimate likeable fictional psychopath is Tom Ripley (66/78), narrowly beating Amy Elliott Dunne (65/78) but some points ahead of Dexter Morgan (60/78).

And so, it transpires that the Talented Mr Ripley is in fact *the* Likeable Psychopath. Manipulative in nature, he scores highly on the interpersonal and affective traits of the *Psychopathy Checklist*. But this does not stop us wishing him to succeed. He seems vulnerable to the core – particularly Matt Damon's rendering of him, existing alone in a state of emptiness, with no friends or family and no role in the social circles of which he so desperately desires to be a part. In literary terms, he remains the *viewpoint* throughout the tales of his endeavours. Superficial as he is, we are consistently seduced by his charm, with his ability to beguile those around him seeming almost boundless. And he is not referred to as talented for no reason; he is an accomplished pianist with a knowledge and appreciation of music, fine art, architecture and history. He is also a brilliant mimic and impersonator, an expert at forgery, and an intelligent reader of the desires of others. Impression management is his greatest talent of all. And he never bores us, whatever Dickie Greenleaf might think.

Furthermore, Ripley's victims make him look good, given that most are shallow, selfish, capricious, adulterous, cruel, bourgeois, arrogant or downright interfering. Even the more sympathetic among them seem rather pathetic next to Ripley. Those who succumb to him are mostly difficult to admire, while their murderer has several important redeeming features. So, in terms of our *Psychopath Likeability Scale*, Tom Ripley scores most highly. He is the perfect anti-hero: the seductive scoundrel who charms us into overlooking his many indiscretions, including his weakness for murder.

ENDNOTES

1. DISSECTING THE PSYCHOPATH

1 McEwan, Ian, *Nutshell* (Jonathan Cape, London, 2016), p. 95.

2 *The Silence of the Lambs,* dir. Jonathan Demme (1991).

3 See http://psychopath.channel4.com/quizzes.html.

4 The clinical psychologist Martha Stout, in her book *The Sociopath Next Door* (Broadway Books, New York, 2006), suggests that four per cent of the population are sociopaths. However, there are thought to be subtle differences between a psychopath and a sociopath, as explained later in this chapter.

5 It is important to point out that most people with paraphilia are not psychopaths.

6 One of the *Characters* of Theophrastus (371–287 BC), he is also translated from the Greek as 'the Shameless Man'.

7 This debate continues to this day, as outlined in Kiehl, K. A. and Sinnott-Armstrong, Walter P. (eds), *Handbook on Psychopathy and Law* (Oxford University Press, Oxford, 2013), pp. vii–x. Foreword by Robert D. Hare.

8 See Lilenfeld, S. O., Watts, A. L., Smith, S. F., Patrick, C. J. and Hare, R. D., 'Hervey Cleckley (1903–1984): Contributions to the Study of Psychopathy', *Personality Disorders: Theories, Research, and Treatment*, Vol. 9, No. 6 (2018), pp. 510–20.

9 Second edition published in 2003. In this book, for the purposes of lite-rary style, we will simply refer to the PCL-R as the *Psychopathy Checklist*.

10 For more detail on the neuroscience of psychopathy, read Kiehl, K. A., *The Psychopath Whisperer* (Oneworld, London, 2014), a distinguished researcher of the psychopathic brain. See also Kiehl, K. A., 'A cognitive neuroscience perspective on psychopathy: Evidence for paralimbic system dysfunction', *Psychiatry Research* Vol. 142, No. 2–3 (2006), pp. 107–28.

2.   THE FICTIONAL PSYCHOPATH

1   From *House M.D.* Gregory House says this on multiple occasions throughout the show's run.

2   Aware that the *Psychopathy Checklist* and its applications are the life's work of Professor Robert D. Hare, PhD, I duly contacted him to ask permission to use his inventory in this book. I could not have received a warmer and more helpful response. A true gentleman.

3   The four domains were first described in the twelve-item *Psychopathy Checklist – Screening Version (PCL-SV)* and are explained in Robert D. Hare's books *Without Conscience: The Disturbing World of the Psychopaths Among Us* (Guildford Press, New York, 1993) and *Snakes in Suits: When Snakes Go to Work* (Harper Collins, New York, 2006), which was co-authored with Paul Babiak.

4   *Impression management* is a deliberate attempt to influence how others perceive you by controlling the information they receive.

5   Strictly speaking, *promiscuous sexual behaviour* and *many short-term* (marital) *relationships* are excluded from the four domains. For the purpose of simplicity, I have taken the liberty of including them with the *lifestyle* traits.

6   Babiak and Hare (2006), p. 185.

7   Hare and colleagues have continued to work on the classification of different types of psychopath in relation to prominent traits. In his paper entitled 'Psychopathy, the PCL-R, and Criminal Justice: Some New Findings and Current Issues', *Canadian Psychology*, Vol. 57, No. 1 (2016), pp. 21–34, Hare outlines factor profiles among offenders, and divides them into 'manipulative psychopaths', 'aggressive psychopaths' and 'sociopaths' (the last being a non-psychopathic subtype of offender).

8   Kevin Dutton explains his thesis in his book *The Wisdom of Psychopaths* (William Heinemann, London, 2012).

9   Convention holds that, in addition to the traditional three walls of the stage set, there is an invisible 'Fourth Wall' between the actor and the audience. The audience can see through this wall to observe the fictional world of the actor but not vice versa. When an actor 'breaks the Fourth Wall', he or she addresses the audience as though they too were on the stage.

10 Psychodynamic psychology is the study of how human emotion and behaviour are influenced by both conscious and unconscious desires and beliefs, particularly in relation to the effect of childhood experiences.

11 This resembles a real psychological behaviour-modification treatment called 'aversion therapy', in which a patient agrees to be exposed to a stimulus (whatever is causing their unwanted behaviour) while simultaneously being subjected to a source of discomfort (nausea, in Alex's case). As the mind is conditioned to associate the stimulus with the discomfort, the stimulus will naturally be avoided, potentially allowing the behaviour to change.

3. THE AMAZING PSYCHOPATH

1 Flynn, Gillian, *Gone Girl* (Weidenfeld and Nicolson, London, 2012), p. 250.

2 *Ibid.*, p. 263.

3 *Ibid.*, p. 365.

4 *Ibid.*, p. 252.

5 *Ibid.*, p. 250.

6 *Ibid.*, p. 81.

7 *Ibid.*, p. 267.

8 *Ibid.*, p. 73.

9 *Ibid.*, p. 298.

10 *Ibid.*, p. 50.

11 *Ibid.*, p. 14.

12 *Ibid.*, p. 117.

4. THE SECRET PSYCHOPATH

1 *Casino Royale*, dir. Martin Campbell (2006).

2 Dutton (2012), pp. 106–8.

3 Jonason, P. K., Li, N. P. and Teicher, E. A., 'Who is James Bond? The Dark Triad as an Agentic Social Style', *Individual Differences Research*, Vol. 8, No. 2 (2010), pp. 111–20.

4 Hare (1993), p. 62.

5 SMERSH was an umbrella organisation for three Russian counter-

intelligence agencies of the Red Army. Formed in 1942, its name was coined by Joseph Stalin. With its motto, 'Death to Spies', it was the main antagonist group in the earlier Bond novels.

6 Fleming, Ian, *You Only Live Twice* (Penguin Classics, London, 2004), pp. 200–1.

7 *Ibid.*

8 SPECTRE was the fictional antagonist group used in the later Bond novels. An acronym for the Special Executive for Counterintelligence, Terrorism, Revenge and Extortion, it differed from SMERSH in that – rather than simply being Russian – it was international and apolitical.

9 'Looking for Mr Bond: 007 at the BBC', *Timeshift*, Season 15, Episode 5. Aired 28 October 2015.

10 *Casino Royale*, dir. Martin Campbell (2006).

11 Fleming, Ian, *Moonraker* (Penguin Classics, London, 2004), p. 130.

12 'James Bond Comes to New York', *The New Yorker*, 21 April 1962.

5. THE POLITICAL PSYCHOPATH

1 Dobbs, Michael, *House of Cards* (Harper Collins, London, 1989), p. 208.

2 *House of Cards*, Season 1, Episode 1 (and other episodes) of the BBC television series *House of Cards* (first aired 18 November to 9 December 1990). Also Dobbs (1989), p. 65.

3 Some of Urquhart's background is reiterated by Andrew Davies (screen-writer of the BBC series) in his article 'Profile: An impeccable player: Francis Urquhart: Is this Prime Minister a Machiavelli or a Macbeth? Andrew Davies ponders his record', *Independent*, 28 November 1993.

4 Dobbs (1989), p. 10.

5 *Ibid.*

6 In the original novel, Urquhart's wife is named Mortima.

7 Dobbs (1989), p. 376.

8 *House of Cards*, Season 1, Episode 2 (BBC).

9 Dobbs (1989), p. 46.

10 *House of Cards*, Season 1, Episode 3 (BBC).

11 *Ibid.*, Season 1, Chapter 9 (Netflix).

12 *Ibid.*, Season 1, Episode 3 (BBC).

13 *Folie à deux* refers to a delusion shared by two people in close association.

6. THE BORDERLINE PSYCHOPATH

1 *The Talented Mr Ripley*, dir. Anthony Minghella (1999).
2 *Ibid.*
3 Highsmith, Patricia, *The Talented Mr Ripley* (Vintage, London, 1999), p. 92.
4 *The Talented Mr Ripley*, dir. Anthony Minghella (1999).
5 Highsmith, Patricia, *Ripley's Game* (Vintage, London, 1999), p. 1.
6 *The Talented Mr Ripley*, dir. Anthony Minghella (1999).
7 *Ibid.*
8 'Splitting' is a psychological defence mechanism that involves 'all or nothing' thinking. People who split tend to view others as 'entirely good' or 'entirely bad' rather than a complex mixture of both.
9 *The Talented Mr Ripley*, dir. Anthony Minghella (1999).

7. THE MINOR PSYCHOPATH

1 Shriver, Lionel, *We Need to Talk About Kevin* (Serpent's Tail, London, 2003), p. 102.
2 Forth, A. E., Kosson, D. S. and Hare, R. D., *The Psychopathy Checklist – Youth Version* (Multi-Health Systems Inc., Toronto, 2003).
3 Strictly speaking, *impersonal sexual behaviour* and *instable interpersonal relationships* are excluded from the four domains. As with the adult version of the PCL, and for the purpose of simplicity, I have taken the liberty of including them with the *lifestyle* traits.
4 Shriver (2003), p. 133.
5 *Ibid.*, p. 105.
6 *Ibid.*, p. 103.
7 *Ibid.*, p. 69.
8 *Ibid.*, p. 102.
9 *Ibid.*, p. 199.
10 *Ibid.*, p. 167.
11 *Ibid.*, p. 103.

12 Academy Award nominations for Best Actress, Best Actress in a Supporting Role, and Best Cinematography (Black and White).

13 Lessing, Doris, *The Fifth Child* (Harper Perennial, London, 2007), p. 60.

14 *Ibid.*, p. 68.

15 *Ibid.*, p. 69.

16 *Ibid.*, p. 67.

17 Johns, J. H. and Quay, H. C., 'The effect of social reward on verbal conditioning in psychopathic and neurotic military offenders', *Journal of Consulting Psychology*, Issue 26 (1962), pp. 217–20.

18 Lessing (2007), p. 89.

19 *Ibid.*, p. 71.

20 *Ibid.*, p. 121.

21 *Ibid.*, p. 117.

22 *Ibid.*, p. 149.

23 *Ibid.*, p. 136.

24 *Ibid.*, p. 147.

25 *Ibid.*, p. 84.

26 *Ibid.*, p. 60.

27 *Ibid.*, p. 99.

8.   THE PSYCHIATRIC PSYCHOPATH

1   *The Silence of the Lambs*, dir. Jonathan Demme (1991).

2   Both of these novels were followed within a year or two by films bearing the same titles.

3   *Hannibal Rising*, dir. Peter Webber (2007).

4   *Ibid.*

5   Grieg, Charlotte, *Evil Serial Killers: In the Minds of Monsters* (Arcturus Publishing, London, 2010), p. 102.

6   Bacchi, Umberto, 'Real Hannibal Lecter was Murderous Gay Mexican Doctor Alfredo Ballí Treviño', *International Business Times*, 31 July 2013.

7   Harris, Thomas, *Red Dragon* (Arrow Books, London, 2009), pp. 75–6.

8   *Ibid.*, p. 74.

9   *Ibid.*, p. 73.

10 *Ibid.*, p. 63.

11   *Ibid.*, p. 64.

12   *The Silence of the Lambs*, dir. Jonathan Demme (1991).

13   Harris, Thomas, *The Silence of the Lambs* (Arrow Books, London, 2009), p. 68.

14   Recidivism is the term used when a criminal reoffends.

15   Byron, Lord, *The Giaour* (CreateSpace Independent Publishing, London, 2016), p. 24.

16   Harris, *The Silence of the Lambs* (2009), p. 420.

9.   THE GOTHIC PSYCHOPATH

1   Poe, Edgar Allan, *Selected Tales* (Oxford University Press, Oxford, 1980), p. 278.

2   *Sherlock*, Season One, Episode 1 (BBC).

3   Bryant, Mark, *Private Lives* (Cassell & Co., London, 2001), pp. 118–19.

4   See www.guinnessworldrecords.com. On 14 May 2012 Guinness World Records News awarded Sherlock Holmes the title for the most portrayed literary human character in film and television. The character had, by then, been depicted on screen 254 times and played by over seventy-five actors.

5   Doyle, Sir Arthur Conan, *The Penguin Complete Sherlock Holmes* (Penguin, London, 2009), p. 18.

6   *Ibid.*, p. 954.

7   *Ibid.*, p. 24.

8   Bryant (1996), pp. 275–7.

9   Poe (1980), p. 186.

10   *Ibid.*

11   *Ibid.*

12   *Ibid.*

13   *Ibid.*, p. 188.

14   *Ibid.*

15   *Ibid.*, p. 189.

16   A 'pipe' is a cask of beverage slightly shy of 500 litres.

17   Poe (1980), p. 279.

18   *Ibid.*

19   *Ibid.*, p. 280.

20   *Ibid.*

21   *Ibid.*, p. 282.

22   *Ibid.*, p. 283.

23   *Ibid.*, p. 284.

24   *Ibid.*, p. 278.

25   *Ibid.*, pp. 282–3.

26   *Ibid.*, p. 282.

27   *Ibid.*, p. 279.

10. THE SINISTER PSYCHOPATH

1   *Dexter*, Season One, Episode 1.

2   *Ibid.*, Season One, Episode 9.

3   *Ibid.*, Season Two, Episode 3.

4   *Ibid.*, Season One, Episode 2.

5   *Ibid.*, Season Two, Episode 5.

6   *Ibid.*

7   *Ibid.*, Season Two, Episode 4.

8   *Ibid.*, Season Two, Episode 3.

9   *Ibid.*, Season Two, Episode 7.

10   *Ibid.*, Season One, Episode 2.

11   *Ibid.*, Season One, Episode 5.

12   *Ibid.*, Season Two, Episode 10.

13   *Ibid.*, Season Two, Episode 4.

14   *Ibid.*, Season One, Episode 6.

15   *Ibid.*, Season One, Episode 12.

16   *Ibid.*, Season Three, Episode 10.

17   *Ibid.*, Season One, Episode 1.

18   *Ibid.*, Season Two, Episode 1.

19   *Ibid.*, Season One, Episode 10.

20   *Ibid.*, Season Two, Episode 1.

21   *Ibid.*, Season One, Episode 2.

22   *Ibid.*, Season One, Episode 4.

11.   THE WALL STREET PSYCHOPATH

1   Ellis, Bret Easton, *American Psycho* (Picador, London, 1991), pp. 376–7.
2   Ellis, Bret Easton, *Lunar Park* (Picador, London, 2011), p. 442. In the novel, Ellis casts himself as the protagonist.
3   Ellis, Bret Easton, *The Rules of Attraction* (Picador, London, 2011), p. 266.
4   Ellis (1991), pp. 15–16. (The monologue is far more extensive in the novel.)
5   Maladaptive coping strategies are methods of dealing with distress that, while providing temporary relief, are at odds with improving one's overall mental and physical health. Examples include substance misuse, excessive alcohol and deliberate self-harm.
6   Admittedly, as we have said, obsessional thinking is often inconsistent with psychopathy.
7   Ellis (1991), p. 377. (The quote is taken from the novel, not the film.)

12.   THE GANGSTER SOCIOPATH

1   *The Sopranos*, Season 1.
2   See 'Psychopathy versus Sociopathy' section in Chapter 1.
3   A *caporegime* (abbreviated to 'capo') is a rank in the Italian-American Mafia. In a crime family, a capo heads a crew of 'soldiers' and reports to the boss. The role of capo brings with it social status and influence.
4   *The Sopranos*, Season One, Episode 7.
5   *Ibid.*, Season Six, Part Two, Episode 3.
6   *Ibid.*, Season One, Episode 5.
7   *Ibid.*, Season One, Episode 13.
8   *Ibid.*, Season Two, Episode 9.
9   *Ibid.*, Season Two, Episode 13.
10   *Ibid.*, Season Four, Episode 9.
11   *Ibid.*, Season Five, Episode 13.
12   *Ibid.*, Season Six, Part Two, Episode 6.

13.   THE LIKEABLE MR PSYCHOPATH

1   *The Talented Mr Ripley*, dir. Anthony Minghella (1999).

2   *Fact*, Vol. 1, No. 5 (1964). The cover headline stated, '1,189 psychiatrists say Goldwater is psychologically unfit to be president', while the entire issue was dedicated to the analysis of the presidential candidate's mental health. This included forty pages of so-called 'psychiatric evaluations', in which Goldwater was described as the product of a 'sadistic childhood', a man with 'chronic psychosis', and a man with an 'obsessive preoccupation with firearms' who 'compulsively must prove his daring and masculinity'. Goldwater is reported to have been very distressed by the coverage, while the ensuing case was an embarrassment to the American Psychiatric Association, whose medical director (Walter Barton) protested in writing to *Fact*. Of note, *Fact* was not normally a heavy-hitting journal; its circulation was relatively limited and its career would span only three years (1964–67).

3   *Ethics Primer of the American Psychiatric Association* (American Psychiatric Association, Washington, 2001), pp. 79–92.

4   Hare (1993), p. 149.

BIBLIOGRAPHY

Amis, Kingsley, *Lucky Jim* (Gollancz, London, 1954)

Amis, Kingsley, *Colonel Sun* (Jonathan Cape, London, 1968)

Babiak, P. and Hare, R. D., *Snakes in Suits: When Psychopaths Go to Work* (Harper Collins, New York, 2006)

Bacchi, Umberto, 'Real Hannibal Lecter was Murderous Gay Mexican Doctor Alfredo Ballí Treviño', *International Business Times*, 31 July 2013.

Bowman, John S., *Dictionary of American Biography* (Cambridge University Press, Cambridge, 1995)

Boyd, William, *Any Human Heart* (Penguin, London, 2002)

Boyd, William, *Restless* (Bloomsbury, London, 2006)

Boyd, William, *Solo* (Jonathan Cape, London, 2013)

Bryant, Mark, *Private Lives* (Cassell & Co., London, 2001)

Burgess, Anthony, *A Clockwork Orange* (William Heinemann, London, 1962)

Byron, Lord, *The Giaour* (CreateSpace Independent Publishing, London, 2016)

Christie, Agatha, *The Crooked House* (Dodd, Mead & Co., London, 1949)

Cleckley, Hervey, *The Mask of Sanity: An Attempt to Clarify Some Issues About the So-Called Psychopathic Personality* (Emily S. Cleckley, London, 1988)

Coleridge, Samuel Taylor, *Christabel* (Leopold Classic Library, Melbourne, 2015)

Crichton, Michael, *Disclosure* (Arrow Books, London, 1994)

Davies, Andrew, 'Profile: An impeccable player: Francis Urquhart: Is this Prime Minister a Machiavelli or a Macbeth? Andrew Davies ponders his record', *Independent*, 28 November 1993

Deaver, Jeffery, *Carte Blanche* (Hodder & Stoughton, London, 2011)

Diagnostic and Statistical Manual of Mental Disorders (DSM-5) (American

Psychiatric Association, Washington, 2013)

Dobbs, Michael, *House of Cards* (Harper Collins, London, 1989)

Dobbs, Michael, *To Play the King* (Harper Collins, London, 1992)

Dobbs, Michael, *The Final Cut* (Harper Collins, London, 1995)

Doyle, Sir Arthur Conan, *A Study in Scarlet* (Penguin, London, 1887)

Doyle, Sir Arthur Conan, *The White Company* (Smith, Elder & Co., London, 1891)

Doyle, Sir Arthur Conan, *The War in South Africa: Its Cause and Conduct* (Cambridge Scholars, Cambridge, 1902)

Doyle, Sir Arthur Conan, *The Lost World* (Hodder & Stoughton, London, 1912)

Doyle, Sir Arthur Conan, *The Penguin Complete Sherlock Homes* (Penguin, London, 2009)

Dumas, Alexandre, 'Le Vampire' in *Théâtre Complet de Alex. Dumas,* Vol. 18 (Forgotten Books, London, 2018)

Dutton, Kevin, *The Wisdom of Psychopaths: Lessons in Life from Saints, Spies and Serial Killers* (William Heinemann, London, 2012)

Ellis, Bret Easton, *American Psycho* (Picador, New York, 1991)

Ellis, Bret Easton, *Glamorama* (Picador, London, 2011)

Ellis, Bret Easton, *Less Than Zero* (Picador, London, 2011)

Ellis, Bret Easton, *Lunar Park* (Picador, London, 2011)

Ellis, Bret Easton, *The Rules of Attraction* (Picador, London, 2011)

Ethics Primer of the American Psychiatric Association (American Psychiatric Association, Washington, 2001)

Faulks, Sebastian, *Birdsong* (Hutchinson, London, 1993)

Faulks, Sebastian, *Human Traces* (Hutchinson, London, 2005)

Faulks, Sebastian, *Devil May Care* (Penguin, London, 2008)

Fleming, Ian, *Casino Royale* (Jonathan Cape, London, 1953)

Fleming, Ian, *Live and Let Die* (Jonathan Cape, London, 1954)

Fleming, Ian, *Moonraker* (Jonathan Cape, London, 1955)

Fleming, Ian, *Diamonds Are Forever* (Jonathan Cape, London, 1956)

Fleming, Ian, *From Russia with Love* (Jonathan Cape, London, 1957)

Fleming, Ian, *The Diamond Smugglers* (Jonathan Cape, London, 1957)

Fleming, Ian, *Dr No* (Jonathan Cape, London, 1958)

Fleming, Ian, *Goldfinger* (Jonathan Cape, London, 1959)

Fleming, Ian, *Thunderball* (Jonathan Cape, London, 1961)

Fleming, Ian, *The Spy Who Loved Me* (Jonathan Cape, London, 1962)

Fleming, Ian, *On Her Majesty's Secret Service* (Jonathan Cape, London, 1963)

Fleming, Ian, *Thrilling Cities* (Jonathan Cape, London, 1963)

Fleming, Ian, *You Only Live Twice* (Jonathan Cape, London, 1964)

Fleming, Ian, *Chitty Chitty Bang Bang: The Magical Car* (Jonathan Cape, London, 1964)

Fleming, Ian, *The Man with the Golden Gun* (Jonathan Cape, London, 1965)

Flynn, Gillian, *Gone Girl* (Weidenfeld and Nicolson, London, 2012)

Forth, A. E., Kosson, D. S. and Hare, R. D., *The Psychopathy Checklist – Youth Version* (Multi-Health Systems Inc., Toronto, 2003)

Gelder, M., Mayou, R. and Cowen, P., *Shorter Oxford Textbook of Psychiatry* (Oxford University Press, Oxford, 2001)

Greene, J. D., Sommerville, B. R., Nystrom, L. E., Darley, J. M. and Cohen, J. D., 'An fMRI investigation of emotional engagement in moral judgement', *Science*, Vol. 293, No. 5537 (2001)

Grieg, Charlotte, *Evil Serial Killers: In the Minds of Monsters* (Arcturus Publishing, London, 2010)

Hare, R. D., Hart, S. D. and Harpur, T. J., 'Psychopathy and the DSM-IV criteria for antisocial personality disorder', *Journal of Abnormal Psychology*, Vol. 100, No. 3 (1991)

Hare, R. D., *The Hare Psychopathy Checklist Revised* (PCL-R) (Multi-Health Systems Inc., Toronto, 1991)

Hare, R. D., *Without Conscience: The Disturbing World of the Psychopaths Among Us* (Guildford Press, New York, 1993)

Hare, R. D., *Manual for the Revised Psychopathy Checklist* (Multi-Health Systems Inc., Toronto, 2003)

Hare, R. D., 'Psychopathy, the PCL-R, and Criminal Justice: Some New Findings and Current Issues', *Canadian Psychology*, Vol. 57, No. 1 (2016)

Harris, Thomas, *Hannibal* (Arrow Books, London, 1999)

Harris, Thomas, *Hannibal Rising* (Arrow Books, London, 2006)

Harris, Thomas, *Red Dragon* (Arrow Books, London, 2009)

Harris, Thomas, *The Silence of the Lambs* (Arrow Books, London, 2009)

Hart, S. D., Cox, D. N., Hare, R. D., *Psychopathy Checklist – Screening Version (PCL-SV)* (Multi-Health Systems Inc., Toronto, 1995)

Hellman, Geoffrey T., 'James Bond Comes to New York', *The New Yorker*, 21 April 1962

Highsmith, Patricia, *Strangers on a Train* (Harper & Brothers, New York, 1950)

Highsmith, Patricia (as Claire Morgan), *The Price of Salt* (Coward-McCann, New York, 1952)

Highsmith, Patricia, *The Blunderer* (Coward-McCann, New York, 1954)

Highsmith, Patricia, *The Two Faces of January* (Doubleday, New York, 1964)

Highsmith, Patricia, *Tales of Natural and Unnatural Catastrophes* (Bloomsbury, New York, 1987)

Highsmith, Patricia, *Small g: a Summer Idyll* (Bloomsbury, New York, 1995)

Highsmith, Patricia, *The Talented Mr Ripley* (Vintage, London, 1999)

Highsmith, Patricia, *Ripley Under Ground* (Vintage, London, 1999)

Highsmith, Patricia, *Ripley's Game* (Vintage, London, 1999)

Highsmith, Patricia, *The Boy Who Followed Ripley* (Vintage, London, 2001)

Highsmith, Patricia, *Ripley Under Water* (Bloomsbury, London, 2003)

Horowitz, Anthony, *House of Silk* (Little, Brown & Co, London, 2011)

Horowitz, Anthony, *Moriarty* (Orion, London, 2014)

Horowitz, Anthony, *Trigger Mortis* (Orion, London, 2015)

Horowitz, Anthony, *Forever and a Day* (Jonathan Cape, London, 2018)

Johns, J. H. and Quay, H. C., 'The effect of social reward on verbal conditioning in psychopathic and neurotic military offenders', *Journal of Consulting Psychology*, No. 26 (1962)

Jonason, P. K., Li, N. P. and Teicher, E. A., 'Who is James Bond? The Dark Triad as an Agentic Social Style', *Individual Differences Research*, Vol. 8, No. 2 (2010)

Kiehl, K. A., 'A Cognitive Neuroscience Perspective on Psychopathy: Evidence for Paralimbic System Dysfunction', *Psychiatry Research*, Vol. 142, No. 2–3 (2006)

Kiehl, K. A., *The Psychopath Whisperer: Inside the Minds of Those Without a Conscience* (Oneworld, London, 2014)

Kiehl, K. A. and Sinnott-Armstrong, W. P. (eds), *Handbook on Psychopathy and Law* (Oxford University Press, 2013)

Lessing, Doris, *The Grass is Singing* (Michael Joseph, London, 1950)

Lessing, Doris, *The Golden Notebook* (Michael Joseph, London, 1962)

Lessing, Doris, *The Good Terrorist* (Jonathan Cape, London, 1985)

Lessing, Doris, *The Fifth Child* (Harper Perennial, London, 2007)

Lilenfeld, S. O., Watts, A. L., Smith, S. F., Patrick, C. J. and Hare, R. D., 'Hervey Cleckley (1903–1984): Contributions to the Study of Psychopathy', *Personality Disorders: Theories, Research, and Treatment*, Vol. 9, No. 6 (2018)

Lindsay, Jeff, *Darkly Dreaming Dexter* (Orion, London, 2004)

Longmore, M., Wilkinson, I. B. and Rajagopalan, S., *Oxford Handbook of Clinical Medicine* (Oxford University Press, Oxford, 2005)

Lycett, Andrew, *Ian Fleming* (Phoenix, London, 1996)

Lykken, D. T., *The Antisocial Personalities* (Lawrence Erlbaum Associates, New Jersey, 1995)

March, William, *The Bad Seed* (Vintage, London, 1954)

Martin-Joy, John, 'Goldwater v. Ginsburg', *American Journal of Psychiatry*, Vol. 172, No. 8 (2015)

McEwan, Ian, *Nutshell* (Jonathan Cape, London, 2016)

Nabokov, Vladimir, *Lolita* (Penguin, London, 1997)

Poe, Edgar Allan, *Selected Tales* (Oxford University Press, 1980)

Poe, Edgar Allan, *Tales of the Grotesque and Arabesque* (CreateSpace Independent Publishing, London, 2016)

Poe, Edgar Allan, *The Raven and Other Selected Poems* (William Collins, London, 2016)

Ramsland, K., *Forensic Psychology of Criminal Minds* (Berkeley, New York, 2010)

Ronson, Jon, *The Psychopath Test: A Journey Through the Madness Industry* (Picador, London, 2011)

Shriver, Lionel, *We Need to Talk About Kevin* (Serpent's Tail, London, 2003)

Stevenson, Robert Louis, *The Strange Case of Dr Jekyll and Mr Hyde* (Penguin, London, 1994)

Stoker, Bram, *Dracula* (Penguin, London, 2003)

Stout, Martha, *The Sociopath Next Door: The Ruthless Versus the Rest of Us* (Broadway Books, New York, 2006)

The Times Book of Quotations (Harper Collins, London, 2000)

Theophrastus, *Characters* (Cambridge University Press, Cambridge, 2009)

Wolfe, Tom, *The Bonfire of the Vanities* (Picador, London, 1988)

World Health Organization, *ICD-10 Classification of Mental and Behavioural Disorders* (1993)

Wright, P., Stern, J. and Phelan, M., *Core Psychiatry* (W. B. Saunders, London, 2000)

ACKNOWLEDGEMENTS

Thank you to Robert D. Hare, PhD, Professor Emeritus of Psychology at the University of British Columbia, Canada, for his generosity in allowing me to use his *Psychopathy Checklist* in this book. Professor Hare is, without a doubt, the father of the modern study of psychopathy. Any misinterpretation of his principles that might appear in this book is entirely my fault.

Thank you to Patrick O'Donoghue, Wendy Logue, Noel O'Regan and their colleagues at Mercier Press for their belief in the idea of *Psychopath?* and for their practical help throughout the process of finishing this book.

Thank you to my late father, Brendan, who taught me from an early age what to read and how to write. Thank you to my mother, Anne, for every sacrifice she has ever made on my behalf (and there were many). Thank you to my four children – Claire, Emma, Isobel and John – for their constant interruptions while I sit in my study, at my computer, trying to concentrate. Most of all, thank you to my wife, Dolores, for her patience and support in everything I attempt to do.

ABOUT THE AUTHOR

Stephen McWilliams is a Consultant Psychiatrist at Saint John of God Hospital, Dublin, and Associate Clinical Professor at the School of Medicine and Medical Sciences, University College Dublin. He is a graduate of the Royal College of Surgeons in Ireland (MB, BCh, BAO, LRCPSI), a member of the College of Psychiatrists of Ireland (MCPsychI) and a fellow of the Royal College of Psychiatrists in London (FRCPsych). Stephen holds a master's degree in medical education (MMEd) and a research doctorate of medicine (MD). In addition to being Medical Editor of *Hospital Doctor of Ireland*, he has authored or co-authored over 250 articles, contributed to three books and authored four more, notably *Fiction and Physicians: Medicine Through the Eyes of Writers*.